MW

W0006394

MW01155981

EASTER

The Rest of the Story

Rick Renner

Easter — The Rest of the Story
ISBN: 978-1-6675-0645-6
Ebook: 978-1-6675-0646-3
Copyright © 2025 by Rick Renner
1814 W. Tacoma St.
Broken Arrow, OK 74012

Published by Harrison House
Shippensburg, PA 17257-2914
www.harrisonhouse.com

1 2 3 4 5 / 29 28 27 26 25
1st printing

Editorial Consultant: Rebecca L. Gilbert and Veronica Bagby
Cover Design: Lisa Moore
Text Design/Layout: Lisa Simpson, SimpsonProductions.net

Illustrations and artwork by Lev Kaplan, www.kaplan-art.de. Copyright © 2020, 2021, 2022 by Rick Renner Ministries, Inc. All rights reserved.

DEDICATION

When I was growing up, I deeply loved Easter, as my parents and church used it as a holiday to teach us about the death, burial, and resurrection of Jesus Christ. I am eternally thankful to my parents, to my pastor, and to the Sunday School teachers who passionately ensured that we understood the real message of Easter. For this reason, I dedicate this book to those who influenced my life when I was young and helped me grow in my understanding of these events that contributed to my salvation.

CONTENTS

Acknowledgments..xi

INTRODUCTION
THE STORY BEHIND THE STORY.............................. 1

CHAPTER ONE
AGONY OF THE SOUL AND DIVINE ASSISTANCE................. 7
A Regular Gathering Place for Jesus and His Disciples..............10
Being in Agony, Jesus Sweat 'Great Drops of Blood'.................12
God Provided Divine Assistance 15

CHAPTER TWO
HOW MANY SOLDIERS DID IT TAKE TO ARREST ONE MAN? 21
Jesus' Power Was Already Legendary 23
What Kind of Soldiers Came To Arrest Jesus? 24
A Great Multitude 27
Bright-Shining Lamps and Long-Burning Torches 29
These Soldiers Were Armed for a Fight............................31
Jesus Neither Hid Nor Fought 32

CHAPTER THREE
THE JUDAS KISS 37
What Kind of Relationship Did Jesus and Judas Have?..............39
A Fatal Flaw From the Beginning..................................42
Paralyzed by His Presence 46
Jesus Is the Great *'I AM!'*.....................................47

CHAPTER FOUR
PETER'S MESS AND THE NAKED BOY IN THE GARDEN OF GETHSEMANE... 53
A Hotheaded Moment Followed by the Lord's Rescue 54
Who Was the Man Peter Assaulted? 57
Jesus Cleaned Up Peter's Mess....................................60

Jesus Could Have Called Upon Twelve Legions of Angels..........63
Who Was the Naked Boy in the Garden of Gethsemane?..........67
The Boy 'Continuously Followed' Jesus....................................68

CHAPTER FIVE
SPITTING IN JESUS' FACE AND PLAYING GAMES WITH JESUS **73**
Who Was Caiaphas?...75
Jesus Entrusted Himself Into the Care of the Father..................78
Spitting in Jesus' Face..79
Spitting on the Anointing 81
Playing Games at Jesus' Expense 82
They Blindfolded Jesus...84
They Blasphemously Spoke to Jesus 85

CHAPTER SIX
PILATE LOOKS FOR A LOOPHOLE **91**
Who Was Pontius Pilate? 93
The Jewish Leaders' Motivation: They Were Jealous
    of Jesus and Despised Pilate for His Cruelty.........................95
Jesus Was Literally Led Like a Lamb to the Slaughter...............97
Jesus' Interrogation Before Pontius Pilate 97
Three Legal Chances To Answer...98
Pilate Looks for a Loophole!..99
The Religious Leaders in Jerusalem
    Devised a Scheme To Get Rid of Either Jesus or Pilate..........101
Hooray! A Way Out of This Dilemma — or So It Seemed 104

CHAPTER SEVEN
HEROD FINALLY MEETS JESUS **109**
Herod Was Jubilant To Meet Jesus 114
The Story of Jesus Was Legendary in the Herod Family............115
Herod Longed To See Jesus Perform a Miracle 116
Herod and the Religious Leaders Accused Jesus
    of Being a Fraud 117
Herod Mocked the King of Kings and Lord of Lords.................119

They Arrayed Jesus in a Royal Robe 121
Jesus Was Returned to Pilate's Court 121
Charged But Not Guilty 122
Pilate Attempts To Release Jesus 123
Who Was Barabbas? 123
'CRUCIFY HIM!' 124
Pilate Publicly Washed His Hands of the Matter..................125
Pilate Changed His Mind To Save Himself 126

CHAPTER EIGHT
THE HORROR OF A ROMAN SCOURGING **131**
The Process of a Roman Scourging....................................133
The Physical Effects History Recorded
   About Roman Scourgings 135
The Differences Between Jewish and Roman Scourgings..........136
Jesus' Appearance After a Brutal Roman Scourging.................137
By His Stripes, We Are Healed...137
Pilate Delivered Jesus to the Roman Soldiers.......................139
They Stripped Jesus Naked 140
They Put a Scarlet Robe on Jesus.......................................141
They Put a Crown of Thorns on Jesus' Head 142
They Put a Reed in Jesus' Hand 143
They Mockingly Bowed Before Jesus..................................144
They Spit on Jesus and Struck Him....................................144
One Day Every Knee Will Bow Before Jesus Christ 146

CHAPTER NINE
GOLGOTHA: 'THE PLACE OF THE SKULL' **151**
The Cross Jesus Carried 155
A Sign in Hebrew, Greek, and Latin To Declare One's Crime.....156
Golgotha — 'a Place of a Skull' 157
Writings by Early Church Leaders About Golgotha 158
What Do We Definitely Know About the
   Place of Jesus' Crucifixion? 159

Jesus Was Crucified...160
What Do We Know About Roman Crucifixion?.....................161
The Grueling Process of Crucifixion.............................162
Why Was a Spear Thrust Into Jesus' Side? 164
The Soldiers Cast Lots for His Garments 165
We Need To Remember What the Cross Was Really Like! 167
Isaiah's Prophetic Words About the Cross.......................168

CHAPTER TEN
'IT IS FINISHED!' **173**
What Happened to That Second Veil
  When Jesus Took His Last Breath on the Cross?....................174
The Sky Turned Dark..180
The Earth Trembled 182
The Way to the Holy of Holies Was Opened 183

CHAPTER ELEVEN
BURIED AND SEALED **187**
Joseph of Arimathea...189
Nicodemus, Who Came to Jesus by Night...........................191
Where Your Treasure Is, There Is Your Heart Also 193
The Tomb Where Jesus Was Buried................................196
Jesus' Dead Body Was Carefully Inspected Again 197
A Great Stone Door Sealed the Tomb 198
The Official Seal of Pilate Was Placed on the Tomb.................199
Four Different Groups of Roman Soldiers
  Guarded the Tomb...200
Multiple Witnesses Verified Jesus Was Dead.....................201

CHAPTER TWELVE
'BEHOLD, HE IS RISEN!' **207**
A Great Earthquake Occurred....................................209
The Stone Was Rolled Away......................................210
The Women Saw Angels at the Site 211
'Why Seek Ye the Living Among the Dead?' 212

Contents

Women Were the First To Preach Christ's Resurrection............213
Peter and John Ran to the Tomb................................215
John Outran Peter to the Tomb 216
Peter Inspected the Interior of the Tomb....................217
John Joined Peter Inside the Tomb..........................218
Concerning the Angels Present at the Tomb of Jesus —
    Which Is the Correct Version of the Story? 219
Who Were the Women at the Tomb That Day?................220
How Many Angels? 221

CHAPTER THIRTEEN
EYEWITNESSES OF JESUS' RESURRECTION **227**
Mary Magdalene Inspected the Interior of the Tomb 228
Mary Magdalene Saw Two Angels in White 229
Mary Recognized Him When He Called Her By Name..........231
Other Eyewitness Accounts That Jesus Rose From the Dead 232
Jesus Appeared to Two Disciples on the Road to Emmaus........233
Jesus Appeared to the Eleven Disciples Behind Closed Doors.....233
The Roman Guards Saw Jesus Resurrected 234
Jesus Told the Disciples To Touch His Resurrected Body..........236
Jesus Appeared to the Disciples Again —
    and Also to Thomas 237
Jesus Appeared to the Disciples at the Sea of Tiberias..............237
Jesus Appeared to the Disciples in Galilee 238
Jesus Appeared to More Than 500 People at One Time............239

CHAPTER FOURTEEN
WHAT HAS JESUS BEEN DOING FOR THE LAST 2,000 YEARS?............ **243**
Where Is Jesus Now and What Is He Doing? 245
Jesus Is Our Great High Priest 246
The Throne of Grace We Can Approach for Help 247
Jesus Has Mercy Waiting for You 248
Grace To Help in Time of Need 249
Divine Help for Anyone in Need 251
So What Has Jesus Been Doing for the Past 2,000 Years?.........252

CHAPTER FIFTEEN
COPY EVERY STROKE OF THE MASTER AND
WALK IN THE FOOTPRINTS OF JESUS! **257**
 Christ's Example in Suffering 259
 We Are Called To Follow Jesus' Steps 264

CHAPTER SIXTEEN
A Final Word 269

Prayer of Salvation 271

Prayer of Forgiveness 272

Prayer for Healing 274

Endnotes 275

About the Author 278

ACKNOWLEDGMENTS

In each of my books, I take time to acknowledge those who contributed in some way to what I have written.

As in my book on Christmas, I feel the need to begin my acknowledgments by thanking my parents, Ronald and Erlita Renner, for rearing me to love Jesus, the Bible, and the local church — and for making Easter a special event in our family when we were children. I am also thankful to my pastor when I was growing up — Rev. Robert Post, who is in Heaven today — and to the Sunday School teachers who in my younger years helped me understand the many facets of Christ's Passion, Jesus' last days and moments on the earth. They instilled a deep love in my young heart for the Easter story, and for all this, I will be eternally grateful.

I wish to also express my thanks to my wife Denise, to our sons Paul, Philip, and Joel and our daughters-in-law Polina, Ella, and Olya, and to our grandchildren William, Anya, Cohen, Abby, Mia, Mika, Daniel, and Mark. In the Renner household as Denise and I raised our family, we joyfully anticipated this precious holiday each year, and it remains an important holiday for us. Just as the Easter story has deeply impacted us, I pray this book will become an instrument you can use to share this marvelous story with members of your own family and with your friends.

When we opted to illustrate my Christmas book with original artwork, I prayed for God to lead me to the right illustrator, and He led me to Lev Kaplan, a Russian-Jew from the former Soviet Union, who has illustrated many books for authors. His work on the Christmas book was so fabulous that I invited him to join me again to create historically accurate illustrations about the various aspects of Christ's Passion. As always, his work is marvelous, and I am sure readers will reap the benefits of his talent as the art captured in this book helps them "see" the story come to life before their eyes.

It requires many minds, eyes, and hands to produce a book of this caliber, and this includes those who edit the manuscript to make it shine. For this reason, I wish to express my appreciation to Becky Gilbert, the chief editor at RENNER Ministries, who reads and edits every word of my books with spiritual sensitivity. I also wish to express my gratitude to Becky's team on this project that included Roni Bagby, Kalea Ellison, Kaitlyn Hong, Pamela Page, and Beth Parker. In addition, Lisa Simpson meticulously laid out the pages in this book to make sure it was produced beautifully for my readers — and Lisa Moore created the beautiful cover for the book. I also wish to express my appreciation to Maxim Myasnikov, my assistant in Moscow, who faithfully assists me in my research of the Greek words that are used in all my books.

But Jesus is the center of this story, and I wish to express my eternal gratitude to Him for giving His life as a ransom for many. If He had not surrendered His life as the Lamb of God who takes away the sin of the world, there would be no Easter story. He changed the course of human history and the hearts of an innumerable company of believers worldwide with His selfless act of coming to the earth and taking His place on the Cross as the Lamb of God.

Not only did Jesus die in our place, but He was gloriously resurrected. With no resurrection, the Gospel would be incomplete — but Jesus indeed rose again "on the third day" and eventually ascended to Heaven to take His seat at the Father's right hand where He ever lives to intercede for us as the Head of the Church. He *was* and *is* our hope for Heaven and our reconciliation with God the Father. And He *is* and *forever will be* exalted as Lord of all!

INTRODUCTION

THE STORY BEHIND THE STORY

When I think of Easter, my mind goes to my childhood, when we woke up every Easter morning to a full basket of special gifts that my parents left next to our bedsides. Then we'd all get into the car and go to church. My sisters were dressed specially for the event, and my parents dressed me — little Ricky — up in black slacks, a white shirt, and a black bow tie. I still have one photo of my sisters and me standing together for a photo all dressed up for Easter day, and that photo is very precious to me. My parents made us understand that Easter, and commemorating the Cross and the Resurrection, was one of the most important events in our lives!

I also vividly remember lying on the floor in front of our black and white television in our home in the days preceding Easter to watch specially aired Easter-themed movies that were broadcast nationally back in those days. I don't intend to sound like I'm writing movie reviews, but I was deeply impacted by several Easter-themed movies that were released to the public. Perhaps you saw those same movies and were as impacted by them as I was at a young age. These blockbuster films and TV dramas were aired at a time in the past when people were honoring of religious holidays and religious-based films.

Among these films was *The Robe*, an epic biblical drama produced in 1953 by *20th Century Fox* that tells the story of a Roman military tribune who commanded the unit responsible for the crucifixion of Jesus and who "won" the robe of Jesus at His crucifixion and became a Christian. I was born in 1958, so by the time I came along this film was already five years old, but it still reigned as the top Easter-related film until 1961 when the movie *King of Kings* was released to the public.

The epic film *King of Kings* was a religious film released by *Metro-Goldwyn-Mayer*, and it was broadcast annually for many years on national television during the days leading up to Easter in commemoration of Christ's birth, death, and resurrection. Even as a four-year-old child, I sat with a frozen gaze at the black-and-white TV screen in our home as I watched every scene of Christ's Passion that was so vividly portrayed in that movie. Although I was so young at the time, that movie dramatically gripped my heart, and as I watched it, I felt profound thankfulness that Jesus died for me as the Lamb of God and that His glorious resurrection followed the horrific event of His death on the Cross.

But also in 1961, another Easter-themed blockbuster film was released that was called *Barabbas*. It was a religious epic film released in the U.S. by *Columbia Pictures* based on the story of Barabbas, the criminal who was released at the time of Christ's crucifixion. The movie included highly acclaimed scenes of a battle of gladiators in a mock-up of the Roman Colosseum and a crucifixion scene that was actually shot during a real total solar eclipse. In the movie, Pontius Pilate offers to release either Jesus of Nazareth or Barabbas, and the crowd chooses Barabbas, while Jesus is condemned to death.

The next big blockbuster Easter film was *Jesus of Nazareth*, which was a 1977 biblical television drama that chronicled the birth, life, ministry, crucifixion, and resurrection of Jesus. That movie featured an all-star ensemble cast of renowned actors, including eight who had either won or would go on to win Academy Awards — *Anne Bancroft, Ernest Borgnine, James Earl Jones, Laurence Olivier, Christopher Plummer, Anthony Quinn, Rod Steiger,* and *Peter Ustinov.* This movie was so outstanding that it mostly replaced *King of Kings* as the drama that aired nationally every year at the time of Easter.

Then came the movie *JESUS* (also known as *The Jesus Film*), which was a 1979 biblical drama primarily based on the Gospel of Luke as the main basis for the story. The movie was shot on location in Israel and was financed primarily by Campus Crusade for Christ. The film was used worldwide for evangelism purposes, and untold thousands of people came to Christ as a result.

Finally came Mel Gibson's magnificent 2004 film called *The Passion of the Christ*, which is an epic biblical drama that depicts the Passion of Jesus largely according to the gospels of Matthew, Mark, Luke, and John. The film is a depiction of the last 12 hours in the life of Jesus. It begins in the Garden of Olives (Gethsemane), where Jesus had gone to pray after what we know as the Last Supper. It portrays His betrayal by Judas Iscariot, His arrest, His abuse by religious leaders, His trial before Pontius Pilate, His appearance before Herod Antipas, His return to Pilate for His final sentencing, and then His scourging and crucifixion. It is unquestionably the most dramatic film ever produced on the Passion of Christ's final hours. This epic film was shown in theaters around the world, and people worldwide were deeply affected by it as they felt as if Christ had really been crucified before them.

All these films affected me deeply along with millions of others who viewed them. Yet as I studied the story of Christ's final hours in-depth, I realized there was much more to the story than I had ever been told. The deeper I dove into the original text of the New Testament and into the story of Christ's final hours — including into historical records of these events — I felt the need to share with my readers "the rest of the story" that they may have never heard so that their appreciation for Christ's death, burial, and resurrection would be even greater.

The illustrations in my book on *Christmas — The Rest of the Story* were warm, beautiful, and almost magical. But as we worked on the illustrations for this book, we were confronted by the fact that there is nothing warm about this dramatic story. Indeed, this story confronts each of us with the agony Christ experienced on our behalf in His final hours. In keeping with the truth of these events, the illustrator and I worked meticulously to ensure both the text and the artwork reflected the ugly but powerful truth about the final hours before the Cross and Christ's resurrection.

When Isaiah wrote of Christ's death, he said, "He is despised and rejected of men; a man of sorrows, and acquainted with grief: and we hid as it were our faces from him; he was despised, and we esteemed him not. Surely he hath borne our griefs, and carried our sorrows: yet we did esteem him stricken, smitten of God, and afflicted. But he *was* wounded for our transgressions, he *was* bruised for our iniquities: the chastisement of our peace *was* upon him; and with his stripes we are healed" (Isaiah 53:3-5. But notice in verse 3, Isaiah said, "…We hid as it were our faces from him."

There is nothing pleasant about looking at the sufferings that Christ endured. At the showing of the film *The Passion of the Christ*, which graphically portrayed Christ's suffering, I couldn't help but notice as people literally hid their faces because they felt it too unbearable to look upon the sufferings of Jesus that were so vividly depicted on the movie screen in front of them, they fulfilled this verse. Each time they hid their faces, they fulfilled Isaiah's words in Isaiah 53:3. When you look at the illustrations that accompany the text in this book, you may also not find it pleasant, but it is vitally important that we understand the price that Jesus paid for our redemption.

When the apostle Paul wrote to the Galatians, he reminded them that when he preached Christ's crucifixion to them, his preaching about the Cross and what Christ endured was so graphic that they actually felt as if before their own eyes *"Jesus Christ hath been evidently set forth and crucified"* among them (*see* Galatians 3:1). In the same way, my prayer is that this book and the illustrations in it will help you to visually see and grasp the price Jesus paid for our redemption. But you will find the images to be bloody, because it was indeed a bloody event when the Son of God was scourged for our healing, pierced for our wholeness, and sacrificed as the Lamb of God for our salvation.

When I was a child, one of the first Bible verses I was taught was John 3:16 and 17, which says, "For God so loved the world, that he gave his only begotten Son, that whosoever believeth in him should not perish, but have everlasting life. For God sent not his Son into the world to condemn the world; but that the world through him might be saved." My prayer is that as you read and view this book, every word and illustration will convey to you how vast is the love of God for you that He would send His Son to die in your place.

But additionally, I want you to fully understand the events that occurred at the resurrection! The apostle Paul wrote, "And if Christ be not risen, then *is* our preaching vain, and your faith *is* also vain that we would be hopeless above all other men" (*see* 1 Corinthians 15:14). But then he continued, "But now is Christ risen from the dead, *and* become the firstfruits of them that slept" (1 Corinthians 15:20). Christ was raised as the firstfruits of Christians who had died, and His resurrection is the guarantee that we will also be raised to life when we die.

You may think this book is too graphic for children, but your children and grandchildren need to appreciate every act of Christ's Passion and to embrace the truth that it was a demonstration of God's love for them. Carefully walk them through each chapter — and carefully look at each illustration with them — and take time to open up a discussion about what Jesus did so they could be free and emancipated from Satan's stronghold upon their spirits, souls, and bodies. Use this book as an opportunity to teach them and lead them into a deeper appreciation for what Jesus has done for each of them.

The Cross is where the price was paid for our redemption, and the resurrection is where death was defeated and Satan was disarmed. I urge you to pay special attention to the chapters and illustrations that focus on Christ's resurrection from the dead, to His exaltation on High, and to His present-day High Priestly ministry that has continued uninterrupted for 2,000 years. Today He is seated alive at the Father's right hand, where He ever lives to make intercession for you and me!

Now...it's time for you to start reading *EASTER — The Rest of the Story!*

Rick Renner

Here Jesus is illustrated praying in the Garden of Gethsemane. The mental and spiritual battle He experienced that night was unfathomably intense. Luke 22:44 says, "And being in an agony he prayed more earnestly: and his sweat was as it were great drops of blood falling down to the ground."

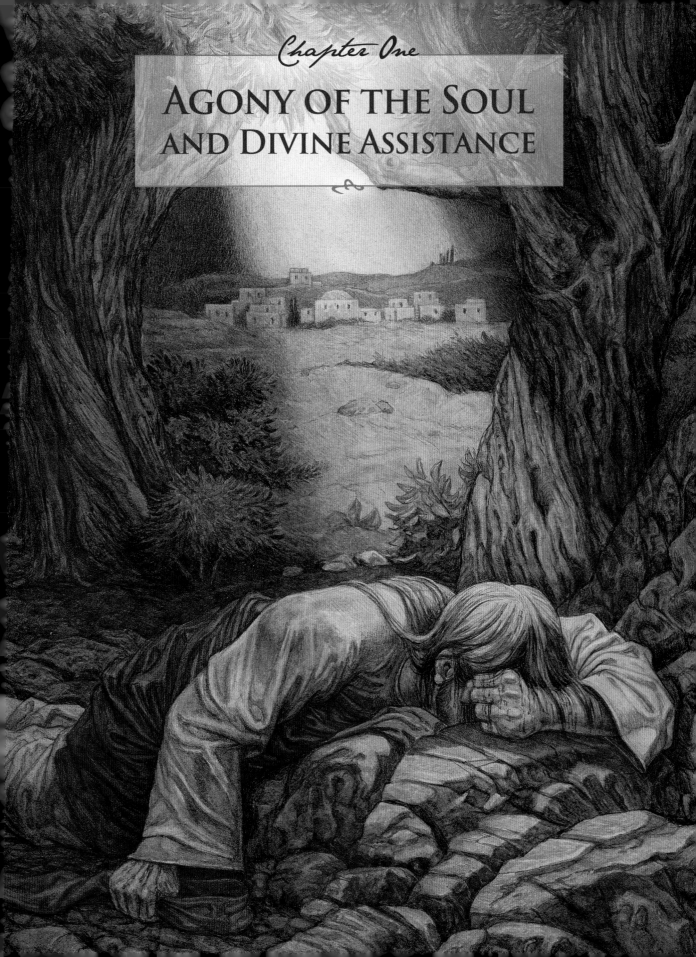

Chapter One

AGONY OF THE SOUL
AND DIVINE ASSISTANCE

On the lower slopes of the Mount of Olives in Jerusalem, there is an ancient garden where olive trees were once grown in large numbers and olives were crushed and pressed to produce abundant amounts of olive oil. A few trees can be seen today, perhaps as a memorial to this site's dramatic past and its critical role in history. Also scattered on these slopes are ancient graves, where wealthier Jews were buried at the time of Jesus. It was in this ancient garden on the Mount of Olives that Jesus spent His last moments with His disciples and notoriously prayed in agony before being arrested and crucified (*see* Luke 22:41-44).

Today, behind an ornamented fence in this ancient olive grove — *the Garden of Gethsemane* — tourists especially notice the timeworn gnarled trunks of eight massive olive trees that some believe date back to New Testament times.

The Jewish historian Josephus recorded that many trees around the city of Jerusalem were cut down by Roman troops, who used the wood to make equipment to assist them as they besieged and plundered Jerusalem in 70 AD.[1]

To determine whether the olive trees in the Garden of Gethsemane dated to the time of Christ, a radiocarbon-dating test was carried out on some of the roots of these ancient trees, and the results indicated that some of the roots sampled could indeed be 2,000 years old.[2]

These massive olive trees could be original to the Garden at the time of Christ — or descended from those ancient trees, having evolved and survived to the present time. But it is at least possible

8

that some of these trees today were there at the time of Jesus' agony and are silent witnesses to the events that occurred in the Garden of Gethsemane before His crucifixion so many years ago.

Many significant events in the life of Jesus took place in the Garden of Gethsemane. It is for this reason that Christians from all over the world have been making pilgrimages to this site for some 2,000 years. Today most visitors enter the Garden of Gethsemane through an ancient stone gate and stroll curiously onto the path encircling the eight ancient olive trees that I just described to you.

Finally, after they explore that fenced-off area, they make their way to the entrance of the Church of All Nations, which was constructed on the ruins of a Byzantine basilica that was originally erected there to commemorate the events that took place in the Garden of Gethsemane in Jesus' last hours.

When archaeologists discovered those Fourth-Century foundations in the 1920s along with fragments of magnificent mosaics, they began to work in conjunction with architects to construct the Church of All Nations, which was officially consecrated in April 1924.[3]

Inside the Church of All Nations is a centerpiece that is an exposed outcropping of rock, which is believed to be the place where Christ agonizingly prayed the night He was arrested in the Garden of Gethsemane — and there is every reason to believe that it really *is* the place where Jesus sweat "great drops of blood" during that time of prayer in His last hours (*see* Luke 22:44).

Today this rock is encircled by a beautiful bronze fence designed to protect the outcropping from visitors, because for centuries, people who visited the site cut small pieces of the rock to take home as a holy relic. Therefore, much of it is now gone.

As one stands in front of that bronze fence and looks upward at the front interior of the church, he can gaze upon a wall that is elaborately covered with marvelous, brilliantly colored mosaics that breathtakingly illustrate Jesus' final hours before He was arrested in the Garden of Gethsemane.

A Regular Gathering Place for Jesus and His Disciples

Just a short distance from the well-known Church of All Nations is another significant site that is pertinent to the story of Jesus, but it's one that many visitors know nothing about.

In fact, they walk right past it, not knowing how significant it is to some of the events we read about in the gospels. I'm talking about an underground grotto, where it is known that Jesus and His disciples regularly met.

Down several flights of worn stone steps, and at the end of a narrow pathway lined with stone walls on either side, is an entrance that leads to an underground grotto. Early Christian writers reported that Jesus regularly used this cave to assemble with His disciples when they visited the Garden of Gethsemane.

Because it was an underground grotto, this cave was an ideal place to gather. It was a quiet, isolated spot that provided shelter from the weather. The grotto can still be visited today, but most people who venture into the area without a guide are oblivious to it because they are so captivated by the massive ancient olive trees that surround this hidden tourist treasure.

Based on early Christian tradition, Jesus regularly gathered in that grotto with His disciples when they were in Jerusalem.[4] It was such a common meeting place for them that when Judas Iscariot led temple police to arrest Jesus, he knew he would find Him and His followers there, because Judas had been to the grotto with Jesus and the others so many times before.

But on the night Jesus was betrayed and arrested, prior to that critical time in His last hours, the Savior felt the deep need to pray, so He left all but three of His disciples alone in the grotto and went a short distance from them to interact with the Father. It is this agonizing period of prayer that we read about in the gospels (*see* Matthew 26:36-46; Mark 14:32-42; Luke 22:39-46; and John 18:1) — and it occurred on the famous outcropping of rock that people still visit today in the Church of All Nations.

According to the New Testament accounts, after Jesus finished serving Communion to His disciples in the well-known Upper Room (*see* Matthew 26:26-29; Mark 14:22-25; and Luke 22:14-20), He led them to the Garden of Gethsemane. Knowing that the Cross and the grave lay before Him, Jesus felt the need to spend time in intercession so He might gain the strength He needed to face what would soon befall Him. Leaving most of the disciples inside the grotto, Jesus took Peter, James, and John with Him to pray (*see* Matthew 26:37; Mark 14:33).

Rarely did Jesus need His friends' assistance — most of the time, they needed *His* help. But in this intense moment, Jesus felt the need to have His three closest disciples near Him to pray with Him. He asked them to pray with Him for just one hour, but instead of faithfully praying at a moment when Jesus desperately needed their support, the three

of them kept falling asleep again and again (*see* Matthew 26:40-45; Mark 14:37-41).

Being in Agony, Jesus Sweat 'Great Drops of Blood'

The mental and spiritual battle Jesus experienced that night in the Garden of Gethsemane was *unfathomably intense*. Luke 22:44 says, "And being in an *agony* he prayed more earnestly: and his sweat was as it were great drops of blood falling down to the ground."

I want you to especially notice the word "agony" in this verse. It comes from a form of the Greek word *agonidzo*, a word that depicts *a struggle, a fight, great exertion*, or *great effort*. This Greek word was used in the New Testament to convey ideas of *anguish, pain, distress*, and *conflict*.

But importantly, the word *agonidzo* comes from the word *agon*, which is the Greek word that depicted the *athletic conflicts and competitions* that were so strenuous in the ancient world.

The Holy Spirit intentionally used this word in these verses to help us understand the battle that Jesus experienced in the Garden of Gethsemane on the night of His betrayal. It tells us that Jesus was thrown into *a great struggle* or *an intense fight* that night. Knowing that the Cross and the grave were before Him, He cried out, "Father, if thou be willing, remove this cup from me…" (Luke 22:42).

The spiritual pressure that bore down upon Jesus' soul was so overwhelming that the Bible says it was *agonidzo*, or *an agonizing event*. In fact, the fight was so strenuous that it involved all of Jesus'

spirit, soul, and body. Indeed, He was in the greatest fight He had ever known up to that moment.

Jesus' intense level of agony is depicted in the phrase "…he prayed more *earnestly*…" (Luke 22:44). The word "earnestly" is from a Greek word that means *to be extended* or *to be stretched out*. A person in this kind of agony might drop to the ground, writhe in pain, and roll around on the ground.

This Greek word presents the picture of a person who is pushed to the limit and can't be stretched much more. Indeed, this individual is on the brink of all he can possibly endure.

In fact, Luke 22 goes on to tell us Jesus' emotional state was so intense that "…his *sweat* was as it were great drops of blood falling down to the ground."

The word "sweat" is from the Greek word *idros*, and the word "drops" is translated from a form of the Greek word *thrombos*, which is a medical word that points to *blood that is unusually thickly clotted*. But when these two words are joined, they depict a medical condition called *hematidrosis* — a real disorder that only occurs in individuals who are in a highly emotional state.[5]

In this condition, the mind, which is under such great mental and emotional pressure, sends signals of stress throughout the human body, and these signals are so strong that the body reacts as if it is under actual physical pressure.

As a result of this perceived pressure, the first and second layer of skin separate, causing a vacuum to form between them, and then thickly clotted blood seeps from this vacuum and oozes through the pores of the skin. Once the blood seeps through the pores, it mingles

with the sufferer's sweat that is pouring from his skin as a result of his intense struggle. In the end, the oozing blood and sweat mingle together in droplets, which flow from the victim's body.

The Holy Spirit included these details about Jesus' sweating blood to alert us that this was the most intense spiritual combat Jesus had ever endured up to that time. And where were His disciples? At this moment, He needed them, but they were *sleeping*.

Jesus had asked His closest disciples to pray with Him — and they couldn't even pray for one hour. But God is faithful, and He provided supernatural strength for Jesus in another way, which we will see in a few pages.

This makes me want to ask you: Have you ever felt the need for help from your friends in a difficult moment and found that your friends couldn't be counted on? Did you find them "sleeping on the job" when you felt a deep need for their help and support? Were you in a situation that caused you such intense agony that you felt you needed someone to stand with you? Are you in that kind of situation right now?

Maybe you've never sweat blood, as Jesus did, but it is likely that you have struggled in your soul at one time or another because of problems with your marriage, your children, your other relationships, your job or ministry, your health, your finances, or your concern for the well-being of others. Have you ever felt like you were constantly living in a "pressure cooker" and it nearly got the best of you?

If so, you know that continuous pressure is hard to deal with — *especially* if you have no one to lean on for strength, encouragement, and help in that moment.

If you are experiencing one of those times now, Jesus understands because He faced the same situation in the Garden of Gethsemane.

God Provided Divine Assistance

As we have seen, on the night of Jesus' betrayal, He beckoned His closest disciples — Peter, James, and John — to come away and pray with Him in those last difficult hours. But every time He went back to check on the three men, He found them sleeping.

Jesus was experiencing a great spiritual battle and extreme pressure, which is why He requested His closest disciples assist Him in prayer. But on that night, they were not found faithful. Instead, He found them sleeping on the job again and again.

When Jesus could not find anyone to faithfully stand with Him in His hour of need, God provided supernatural assistance to help Him. And that supernatural strength made up for any lack of support from Jesus' three closest disciples.

Luke 22:43 tells us that in this moment when Jesus felt a need for help and strength, "…there appeared an angel unto him from heaven, strengthening him."

When Luke wrote that the angel "strengthened" Jesus, he used a form of the Greek word *enischuo*, which is a compound of the words *en* and *ischuo*. The word *en* means *in*, and the word *ischuo* is the word for *might* or *strength*.

Usually in New Testament times, the word *ischuo* was used to denote *men with great muscular abilities*, similar to bodybuilders in today's world. But when these two words *en* and *ischuo* are compounded, the new word means *to impart strength*, *to empower someone*, *to fill a person with heartiness*, or *to give someone renewed vitality*. A person may have been feeling exhausted and depleted, but he suddenly gets a blast of

15

energy so robust that he is *instantly recharged.* Now he's ready to get up, get with it, and get going again!

This means when Jesus' disciples and friends couldn't be depended upon in His hour of need, God stepped in and provided an angel who *empowered, recharged,* and *imparted strength* to Jesus, *renewing His vitality* with the strength He needed to victoriously face the most difficult hour in His life. After being super-charged, Jesus was ready to face the Cross. He soon awakened His disciples and said, "Rise up, let us go; lo, he that betrayeth me is at hand" (Mark 14:42).

Again, let me ask you:

- Have you ever experienced a time in your life when *you* felt trapped and alone?

- Have you ever felt that your friends let you down at a time when you really needed them?

- Can you somewhat relate to Jesus' agonizing prayer over what He was facing — and facing it alone?

Maybe your friends really have fallen asleep on the job, *but God hasn't fallen asleep!* He is absolutely aware of the situation you're facing, and if necessary, He will provide supernatural assistance to recharge you and keep you moving full steam ahead.

Although you may be tempted to feel isolated and alone, if you look with the eyes of your spirit for just a moment, you'll see that you're not alone at all. God is surrounding you with the Holy Spirit's power, with angels, and with anything else you need to recharge you so you can keep going forward in faith and trust in Him.

Regardless of the battle or situation you're facing right now, just as God provided supernatural assistance for Jesus, He will provide it

for *you*. The same divine help He provided for Jesus in the Garden of Gethsemane is what He offers to you. He may send an angel or another unexpected person who understands and wants to help, or He may refill you with the Holy Spirit in a way that super-charges you to face and overcome that difficult moment.

But one thing is sure: When no one else is faithful, you can be certain that God is *always* faithful and that He will see to it that you receive the strength and power you need to triumph in every circumstance.

Supernatural assistance is a part of your inheritance as a child of God in Christ, and you can lay claim to it any time you need it. All you have to do is receive it by faith and walk in obedience to what God tells you to do — and as you do, God will supernaturally empower you to victoriously tackle and overcome whatever is before you.

In the next chapter, you will be surprised to learn the vast number of soldiers that came into the Garden of Gethsemane to arrest Jesus and why they carried such deadly weapons at the moment of His arrest. You'll discover that a small army came to arrest Jesus because they had heard so many reports about His miraculous powers!

QUESTIONS TO PONDER AND DISCUSS

1. Intense emotional stress produces mental and physical distress. Jesus not only suffered on every level, He persevered through pain more difficult than you can conceive. Thus, He not only completely understands everything you could possibly go through, He empathizes with you. *Have you ever thought about that before?*

2. Jesus experienced the full range of human emotion and emotional strain, so He knows exactly what it's like to feel pressure bearing down on Him from every side. Because Jesus understands stress, He can be trusted to understand and help you no matter what you may be facing. What are the areas in your life where you are experiencing stress? *Invite Jesus into that area and trust Him to help you.*

3. Sometimes it's easier to talk with someone who has already been through what you're experiencing. But do you still hurt after talking to your parents, your friends, your spouse, or your pastor? If so, it's time for you to talk to Jesus. Even if you talk to others, *He is the Perfect One to go to about your struggles because He understands them better than anyone else.*

4. At times, circumstances arise and we feel utterly helpless. Can you remember a time when God intervened to strengthen and energize you in a seemingly impossible and difficult situation? Jesus is the same today as He was yesterday and has always been (*see* Hebrews 13:8), so remind yourself of His faithfulness, especially when you are tempted to fear that you won't make it through a challenge.

The Church of All Nations was constructed on the ruins of a Byzantine basilica that was originally erected to commemorate the events that took place in the Garden of Gethsemane in Jesus' last hours. When archaeologists discovered those Fourth-Century foundations along with fragments of magnificent mosaics, they began to work in conjunction with architects to construct the Church of All Nations, which was officially consecrated in April 1924.

In the place where Jesus often met with His disciples, He greeted Judas and the vast number of troops that followed. Here Judas — accompanied by religious leaders, Roman soldiers, and temple police — is illustrated suddenly arriving with a band of men to seize and arrest Jesus.

Chapter Two

HOW MANY SOLDIERS DID IT TAKE TO ARREST ONE MAN?

When Jesus finished praying in the Garden of Gethsemane, He returned with Peter, James, and John to the grotto where the other disciples remained. Jesus knew His hour had come, and He returned to the grotto to spend His last minutes with His disciples before Judas Iscariot would arrive, leading religious leaders, soldiers, and temple police to arrest the Lord.

Because this grotto held an important role in the final hours of Christ's life, it was converted into a chapel in the Fourth Century. This cave was a hallowed space for many centuries and also became a sacred place where a number of Christians buried their dead.

As noted in the previous chapter, this ancient grotto can still be accessed today by a long, narrow passageway lined with stone walls. When visitors enter the cave, they enter the very space where Judas Iscariot betrayed Jesus. Today the interior of the grotto is basically unchanged since the times of Jesus — with the exception that now there is an altar as well as paintings on the walls, including one painting that depicts the treacherous kiss Judas gave Jesus on the night he betrayed Him. There are also wooden chairs in the room for worshipers to use as they stop to pray and worship. And on one of the walls of the grotto, there is an ancient inscription still visible today that states:

Christ, the Savior, frequented this place with His apostles.

On the night Jesus gathered with His disciples after an agonizing time of prayer, Judas Iscariot suddenly entered this space — accompanied by religious leaders, Roman soldiers, and temple police — to help seize and arrest Jesus. Exactly how many Roman soldiers and temple

police do you estimate arrived at the Garden of Gethsemane that night with Judas? You will find out in the next few pages.

Jesus' Power Was Already Legendary

By the time the religious leaders and soldiers came with Judas to arrest Jesus, it was already well-known that Jesus healed the sick, cast out demons, raised the dead, walked on water, changed water into wine, multiplied loaves and fishes, and did so many miracles that they could not all be recorded. In fact, Jesus performed so many miracles that the apostle John said, "…There are also many other things which Jesus did, the which, if they should be written every one, I suppose that even the world itself could not contain the books that should be written" (John 21:25). What a powerful, mind-boggling statement!

People everywhere were aware of Jesus' divine powers, but the religious leaders who didn't follow Him or His ministry were also very aware of the supernatural abilities associated with Jesus. For example, they had tried to capture Him on numerous occasions in the past, but each time, He had miraculously slipped out of their grip and walked away from them.

One instance is recorded in Luke 4:30 (*NLT*), where it says Jesus "…passed right through the crowd and went on his way"! The gospels are filled with examples of Jesus supernaturally *slipping* out of the hands of His aggressors (*see* John 7:30; 8:59; 10:39).

It appears that Jesus' well-known power — and those previous failed attempts to capture Him — was on the minds of His accusers on the night He was arrested.

Because Jesus had supernaturally slipped out of their hands on other occasions, it is likely the religious leaders were worried He might slip away from them this time as well. For this reason, Judas Iscariot led a massive group of Roman soldiers and temple police to arrest Jesus that night. In fact, you will be stunned when you learn how many soldiers came to arrest Him. There were far too many soldiers dispatched to capture just one individual — *unless* that individual was the Son of God!

After serving Communion to His disciples in what we know as the Upper Room, Jesus retreated with them to the Garden of Gethsemane. John 18:2 clearly says it was Jesus' custom to go there to pray with His disciples. And because Jesus and the Twelve went there often, it meant Judas Iscariot had also been there with Him many times in the past, as the Master regularly used that cave to assemble with His disciples in the Garden. That is why Judas knew exactly where to find Jesus when he led the soldiers and temple police to arrest Him.

What Kind of Soldiers Came To Arrest Jesus?

John 18:3 says, "Judas then, having received a band of men and officers from the chief priests and Pharisees, cometh thither with lanterns and torches and weapons."

The verse says that Judas received "…a band of men and officers from the chief priests and Pharisees…." You need to understand exactly who this "band of men" and these "officers from the chief priests and Pharisees" were so you can see the full picture of what happened that night in the grotto inside the Garden of Gethsemane.

You will be flabbergasted when you realize the gigantic number of armed men who came for Jesus!

The soldiers Judas brought with him that night were Roman soldiers who were stationed at the Tower of Antonia — a tower built by the Hasmonean rulers, but was later renamed the Tower of Antonia by Herod the Great in honor of one of his greatest patrons, Marc Antony (the same Marc Antony who fell in love with the Egyptian queen Cleopatra).

The Tower of Antonia was a massive edifice that rose 75 feet into the air, with sides smoothed out flat to make it difficult for enemies to scale its walls. While it had many towers, the highest one was on the southeast corner, and it provided watchmen an uninhibited view of the Temple area as well as of much of Jerusalem.[1]

Inside the massive Tower of Antonia was an inner courtyard large enough to hold a Roman cohort — that is 300 to 600 specially trained soldiers — who were perpetually stationed there. The Temple Mount was a hotspot even in those days, so these troops were poised to act defensively in the event of an insurgency or riot in the vicinity of the Temple. A staircase led from the tower into the Temple that enabled the troops to enter the Temple Mount in a matter of minutes should a disturbance develop.

One writer noted that there was even a secret passageway from the tower to the inner court of the priests to make it possible for these highly weaponized troops to quickly reach even that holy, off-limits location, if necessary.

But John 18:3 specifically states that Judas led "a band of men" to the Garden of Gethsemane to arrest Jesus on the night of Jesus'

betrayal. The words "a band of men" are from the Greek word that describes *a cohort*. So contrary to the images that many people have of only a handful of soldiers showing up to arrest Jesus, in fact, it was somewhere between 300 and 600 soldiers, and these extremely well-trained soldiers were equipped with the finest weaponry of the day.

John 18:3 also says that on the night Jesus was arrested, this cohort of soldiers was also accompanied by "officers" from the chief priests and Pharisees. The word "officers" had several meanings in New Testament times, but in this verse, it describes the *temple police officers* who worked for the chief priests and Pharisees on the Temple grounds.

Once a verdict was issued from the religious court of law, it was the responsibility of these temple police to carry out its judgments. This was a fearsome, religious, armed force that reported to the chief priests, the Pharisees, and the Sanhedrin and worked in conjunction with the Roman cohort stationed at the Tower of Antonia. Hence, when John 18:3 says "officers" also came to arrest Jesus, it is a clear reference to temple police who accompanied the cohort of 300 to 600 Roman soldiers to the Garden of Gethsemane.

Therefore, at a minimum, there were 300 soldiers (and possibly up to 600) in addition to temple police — and it is likely that the overall number of Roman soldiers and temple police would have exceeded 600. The fact that such a large number of forces was employed to arrest one man shows how panicked the religious leaders were about Jesus escaping "from their midst" again.

So when the combined cohort of Roman soldiers and temple police arrived to arrest Jesus that night, the hillside where the Garden of Gethsemane is located was *swarming* with hundreds of Roman soldiers and highly trained militia from the Temple Mount.

A Great Multitude

To confirm that such a large multitude of Roman soldiers and temple police came to arrest Jesus in the Garden of Gethsemane, let's see what the other gospel writers tell us about this incident.

- As Matthew related the story, he clearly stated that "a great multitude" of soldiers came to arrest Jesus (*see* Matthew 26:47). The words "a great multitude" in the original language unmistakably mean *a huge multitude of soldiers*.

- As Mark related the story, he reported that "a great multitude" came to arrest Jesus (*see* Mark 14:43). Once again, the original language emphatically and unquestionably means it was a massive crowd.

- As Luke related the story, he used the same Greek word — here translated "multitude" — to again inform us of the colossal quantity of soldiers who came that night (*see* Luke 22:47).

- As we have already seen, John wrote that on the night Jesus was arrested, a *cohort* of soldiers were also accompanied by temple police (*see* John 18:3).

The biblical narrative is clear that an *enormous* group of Roman soldiers and temple police went with Judas and the religious leaders to arrest Jesus. Again, the overall combined number likely exceeded 600. That would be a lot of soldiers even if the chief priests and religious leaders were worried Jesus might try to escape. It makes one wonder what Judas Iscariot had told them about Jesus to make them think they would need an army to arrest Him.

We can speculate that Judas may have forewarned the chief priests and religious leaders that Jesus and His disciples would put up a fight. Or perhaps the chief priests and religious leaders were already nervous that Jesus might release divine power to resist them and, therefore, they would be ready for a fight.

These assumptions are speculation, but the vast number of soldiers who swarmed the hillside of the Garden makes one wonder what they were so afraid of and what Judas had told them about Jesus.

Jesus was certainly known for His miraculous power. By this time, He had been ministering for three years, and countless miracles occurred wherever He went. The stories of Jesus' power were already so legendary during His lifetime that even Herod Antipas had heard of Jesus' power and longed to be an eyewitness of a miracle performed by Him (*see* Luke 23:8).

I have already noted the apostle John's words that the world could not contain all the books necessary to record every one of Jesus' miracles, and it's simply a fact that nearly everyone in Jesus' day had heard stories of the extraordinary power that flowed through Him.

Isn't it thrilling to think of the power of Jesus Christ!

Just as thrilling is to think that the same Holy Spirit who anointed Jesus to fulfill His ministry has been sent to empower you as a believer to do the same works He did *if* you will allow that power to operate in you.

This truth is so powerful that it would do you well to remind yourself every day that the same power that raised Jesus from the dead now resides within you (*see* Romans 8:11) and is at your disposal 24 hours a day. In fact, the next time you're faced with a situation that

needs to be turned around with supernatural power, let that divine power flow!

I don't know what stories were being repeated about Jesus, but they must have been sufficient to cause the religious leaders to think it would take 300 to 600 Roman soldiers and scores of temple police to arrest Him that night in the Garden of Gethsemane. And not only were there hundreds of these men, but they were ready to intensely search for Jesus — *and they were armed to the max!*

Bright-Shining Lamps and Long-Burning Torches

Remember, the religious leaders had unsuccessfully tried to catch Jesus on many occasions, but each time, He supernaturally slipped through the crowd to safety (*see* Luke 4:30 and John 8:59).

When you look at the vast number of soldiers dispatched to search for Jesus — and the weaponry, lamps, and torches they were carrying in the Garden that night — it seems likely that they were fearful Jesus and the disciples would either put up a fight or slip away again and try to hide from them.

John 18:3 tells us, "Judas then, having received a band of men and officers from the chief priests and Pharisees, cometh thither with *lanterns* and *torches* and weapons."

I want you to especially notice the words "lanterns" and "torches" here. Since there were hundreds of soldiers and temple police — and if the majority of them were carrying lanterns and torches — there

would have been hundreds of lanterns and torches, or enough to light up the entire hillside that night.

It's also important to note that all these events occurred at the time of Passover, which always happens at the time of a full moon. This means on the night Jesus was arrested, the sky was already well lit. But the religious leaders didn't want to take the risk that Jesus and His disciples wouldn't be found, so they dispatched these armed forces with equipment to *search*, *hunt*, and *track them down* if necessary with the aid of "lanterns" and "torches."

The word "lantern" in the original language refers to *a bright and shining light*. It can portray some kind of light that is intended to "light up" a dark room so you can see things better. In reality, this word "lantern" pictures a light that was the equivalent of a First-Century flashlight. This lamp produced a beam so brilliant that it could penetrate darkened areas and reveal things hidden in darkness. But because such lamps were short-lived, John 18:3 says the Roman soldiers and temple police also brought along *long-burning lamps* called *torches*.

The word "torches" is from a word that describes *a long-burning oil lamp*. These so-called "torches" were oil-based, had a long wick, and could burn all night if necessary. The fact that these soldiers came with such torches suggests the soldiers and police were prepared to search all night if necessary.

Thus, when the Roman soldiers and temple police came to the Garden of Gethsemane that night, they carried enough *bright-shining lights* and *long-burning oil lamps* to nearly light up the entire hillside so they could hunt for Jesus all night long. Just imagine the scene that night, as hundreds of soldiers and temple police entered the hillside,

carrying brightly lit lamps, in case they needed to *search and search and search* for Jesus!

If one wanted to hide, it would have been easy to do in the Garden of Gethsemane, where there were a great number of caverns, holes, and caves scattered all over the hill where it was located. That hillside also had many graves with large tombstones, behind which a person or even a group of people could have easily hidden. And as we have seen, the Garden of Gethsemane had many great olive trees with massive, twisted trunks and huge branches, and these, too, would have provided places for someone to easily hide.

But why would hundreds of soldiers and temple police need so many brilliantly lit lights to find Jesus — *unless* they thought He would try to hide or escape from them?

These Soldiers Were Armed for a Fight

John 18:3 also tells us the Roman soldiers who came to arrest Jesus brought "weapons" with them. The word for "weapons" in the original language is the very word used to depict *the full weaponry of a Roman soldier* that is referred to in Ephesians 6:13-18. This means a whole cohort of Roman soldiers came attired in *full weaponry — belt, breastplate, greaves, spikes, shoes, oblong shield, a brass helmet, a sword,* and *a lance*. These 300 to 600 soldiers were armed for *a huge skirmish* and *intense confrontation*!

But in addition to these weapons carried by the Roman soldiers that night, Mark 14:43 tells us the accompanying temple police also came ready for a fight. It says, "And immediately, while he yet spake,

cometh Judas, one of the twelve, and with him a great multitude with swords and staves, from the chief priests and the scribes and the elders." Although the temple police were not armed in Roman military gear, Mark said they were carrying "swords" and "staves."

The word "sword" refers to *a deadly type of sword* that was used for stabbing someone at close range. *Does this mean the temple police were ready to stab and draw blood that night?* The word "stave" is from a word that describes *a thick, heavy stick made of wood*. It was a heavy-duty, dangerous, hard-hitting club intended to beat someone.

If you consider the combined list of weapons that the cohort of Roman soldiers carried, plus the swords and clubs that the temple police brought to the Garden of Gethsemane that night, it is clear these Roman soldiers and temple police were prepared to be militarily engaged.

As noted previously, the stories of Jesus' power were already legendary at that time — and Judas Iscariot knew of Jesus' power and had seen its miraculous abilities firsthand. Despite what he or the religious leaders must have thought, Jesus wasn't going to fight. He knew it was the Father's will for Him to lay down His life and die as the Lamb of God to take away the sin of the world. But it does make one wonder why Jesus' betrayer, after he had walked with Jesus for three years, had a false perception about how Jesus would respond to such an event.

Jesus Neither Hid Nor Fought

That night Jesus did *not* hide, and He did *not* fight. After being supernaturally strengthened by the angel that God sent to help Him,

Jesus arose and greeted Judas and the vast number of troops that he brought with him into the Garden. But when Jesus saw Judas with hundreds upon hundreds of soldiers and temple officers with lanterns, torches, and weapons, don't you think He was surprised to discover how erroneously Judas had perceived Him?

Remember that the next time you hear someone has a wrong perception about you. If this could happen to Jesus, it can happen to you, too, so I urge you not to let it ruffle your feathers too much.

When Judas came with all those soldiers, Jesus didn't say, *"How dare you think so preposterously about Me!"* Instead of arguing or trying to change their opinion or false perception about Him, Jesus simply surrendered and allowed the soldiers to bind Him. They didn't know it then, but Jesus was in the process of giving His life for them — the very men who were arresting Him.

In the next chapter, you will see that Judas stepped forward and gave Jesus a kiss of betrayal. What did that kiss really mean? Why did Judas know he could give Jesus a kiss? What kind of signal did that kiss represent to the cohort of Roman soldiers and temple police who were sent to arrest Jesus that night? That's what you are about to discover in the pages to come!

QUESTIONS TO PONDER
AND DISCUSS

1. When people wrongfully judge us, we often want to retaliate with our words. But the best response comes from the way we live. What is your life saying about you? Think about a time when the quality of your character invalidated a negative perception someone held about you. Did that misunderstanding affect the way you presented yourself and, in turn, perceived others?

2. Have you ever misunderstood another person and then discovered you were wrong? What caused your initial perception of that person? What eventually proved it to be wrong? How could you have prevented such a misunderstanding in the first place?

3. A spirit of fear will always prompt people to overreact as Judas and the religious leaders did. Think about your own life for a moment. Are you facing an absurdly disproportionate amount of opposition against you right now because of your stand for God? If so, consider why the enemy is so afraid of what God plans to do through you!

4. How many times has the devil sought to destroy your life, your family, your business, or your ministry — but each time, you eluded the enemy's grasp? What God-ordained purpose have you been preserved to fulfill? What has God instructed you to do in diligent preparation for that purpose to come to pass?

Because the grotto where Jesus and His disciples spent so much of their time held such an important role in the final hours of Christ's life, it was converted into a chapel in the Fourth Century. The grotto can still be accessed today, but there is now an altar, chairs for worshipers, and several paintings depicting famous biblical scenes that took place there.

It seems that before Judas led a throng of soldiers armed with weapons into the grotto where Jesus and His other disciples had gathered, he warned the chief priests and religious leaders about Jesus' phenomenal power. This may explain why they felt they needed a distinct signal to identify their target and let the troops know they should move in swiftly to make their arrest.

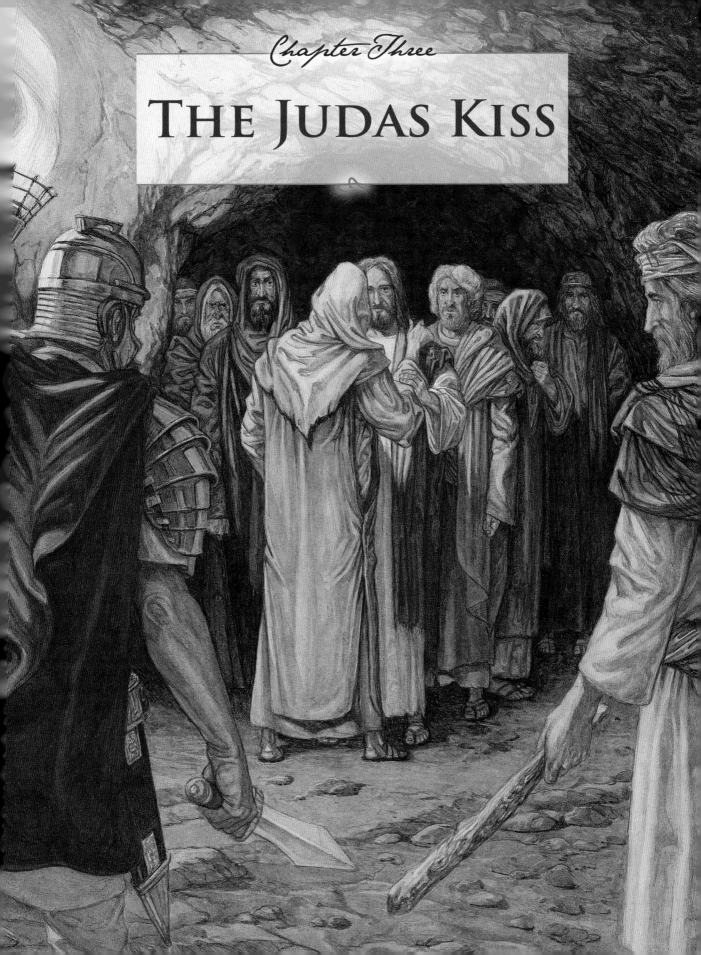

Chapter Three

THE JUDAS KISS

In the last chapter, we saw that a cohort of Roman soldiers — somewhere between 300 to 600 fully armed soldiers — along with a vast number of temple police came into the Garden of Gethsemane to arrest Jesus on the night He was betrayed. The disciples who stood with Jesus must have been shocked to be swarmed by so many Roman soldiers and temple police armed to the maximum. But the most shocking sight was likely the man who led this incursion — Judas, their companion in ministry — and his kiss on the face of Jesus just before the authorities stepped forward to arrest the Lord.

Before Judas led the cohort of Roman soldiers and temple police to the grotto in the Garden of Gethsemane to arrest Jesus, he had privately convened with the Jewish religious leaders to negotiate a deal for handing Jesus over to them. This means there was nothing accidental about this event. It was a premeditated betrayal that was thought out and meticulously executed by Judas Iscariot. During a clandestine meeting with religious leaders, Judas had disclosed information about where Jesus prayed, where He met with His disciples, and precisely where they could arrest Him apart from the watchful eyes of the crowds.

In those undercover meetings with the religious leaders, Judas agreed to receive a payment of 30 pieces of silver for betraying the Lord Jesus into their hands (see Matthew 26:15; 27:9).

As we have seen in the previous chapter, it seems Judas warned the chief priests and religious leaders about Jesus' phenomenal power, which may explain why so many soldiers came with weapons to arrest

Jesus on the night of His betrayal. But many of the Roman soldiers and temple police had never actually seen Jesus themselves, so Judas knew he needed to devise a special signal that would alert them to know who to take into custody on that historic night.

In Mark 14:44, that special signal is called a *token*: "And he that betrayed him had given them a *token*, saying, Whomsoever I shall kiss, that same is he; take him, and lead him away safely." The word "token" in the original text describes *a signal previously agreed upon*, and it makes it unquestionably clear that the kiss Judas gave Jesus was nothing more than a signal devised to let the troops know they needed to move in swiftly to make their arrest.

Thus, Jesus was to be betrayed by the kiss of a so-called friend.

Think about how confused Judas must have been. On the one hand, he seemed to have warned the religious leaders about Jesus' supernatural power so effectively that the Roman soldiers and temple police arrived on the scene with weapons of murder, ready to put up a serious fight. But on the other hand, Judas was sure that he could easily deliver Jesus into their hands with a mere kiss.

A deceived person is always a confused person, and clearly, Judas was very confused.

What Kind of Relationship Did Jesus and Judas Have?

In the Garden that night, Judas led a throng of soldiers armed with weapons into the grotto where Jesus and His other disciples had gathered. Because the space in the grotto would have been limited to a hundred people or more, we can assume it must have been filled from one side to the other, as men prepared to fight in that space no matter how densely packed.

During the three years of Jesus' ministry, Judas Iscariot had been the treasurer for the ministry, which meant he and Jesus had a close working relationship. It is probable that Judas and Jesus spent many hours together, side-by-side, as they discussed ministry projects and expenditures. Thus, on that night when Jesus saw Judas leading the pack, Jesus no doubt stepped forward to greet His longtime team member and treasurer. Matthew 26:50 tells us, "And Jesus said unto him, *Friend*, wherefore art thou come…?"

The word "friend" in this verse is not used anywhere else in the four gospels to depict Jesus' relationships with any of the other disciples. It is a word that depicts *a buddy, a companion, a comrade, a confidante,* or *an enjoyable friend.* It would only be used to describe someone with whom one had spent much time and had learned to enjoy. It is clear that the use of this word meant Jesus had worked so closely with Judas that He could call him *a buddy, a companion, a comrade, a confidante,* or *an enjoyable friend.* However, Judas' loyalty to Jesus was fatally flawed.

Remember, Judas had previously told the Roman troops and temple police, "…Whomsoever I shall *kiss*, that same is he; take him, and lead him away safely" (Mark 14:44).

In the original text, the word "kiss" speaks of *strong emotion, affection,* and *love.* It represents such strong affection that it is primarily used only between people who had a *strong bond* or a *deeply felt obligation* to each other, such as husbands and wives or family members. Still later, it came to be used as a form of greeting between especially dear and cherished friends. During the time the gospels were written,

40

this word depicted *friends who were bound by some kind of obligation or covenant and who cherished each other very deeply*. It also became the word for *a kiss* that a man would give his wife, *a kiss* that parents and children might give to each other, or *a kiss* that a brother or sister might give to his or her siblings.

So the word "kiss" used in Mark 14:44 clearly means that the kiss Judas gave Jesus was a symbol of *deep love, affection, obligation, covenant,* and *relationship*. This kind of kiss was such a powerful signal to everyone who saw it that strangers never greeted each other with such a kiss. Indeed, it was a special kiss reserved only for the most treasured relationships. And Judas was well aware that he could give Jesus such a kiss — which lets us know that he and Jesus had a working relationship that was close. Even though Jesus knew Judas had issues and was His betrayer, He nevertheless remained faithful, loving Judas to the point that He called him "friend" as he and the authorities approached Jesus in the Garden that night.

However, the kiss Judas gave Jesus was a *false kiss* that revealed insincerity, bogus love, and a phony commitment. The fact that his betrayal of Jesus and this phony kiss were premeditated made it even worse. Again, this was no accidental betrayal, but one that was well-planned and very deliberate. The facts show that Judas played the game all the way to the end, working closely with Jesus and remaining part of His inner circle. And then — at the pre-appointed time — he drove the dagger in as deeply as he could in his moment of betrayal in the Garden of Gethsemane. Betraying Jesus with a kiss was about as low as a person could go. It was like saying, *"You and I are friends forever. Now please turn around so I can sink my dagger into your back!"*

People often feel betrayed in life by someone they loved and trusted. After opening their hearts, sharing their secrets, and giving a part

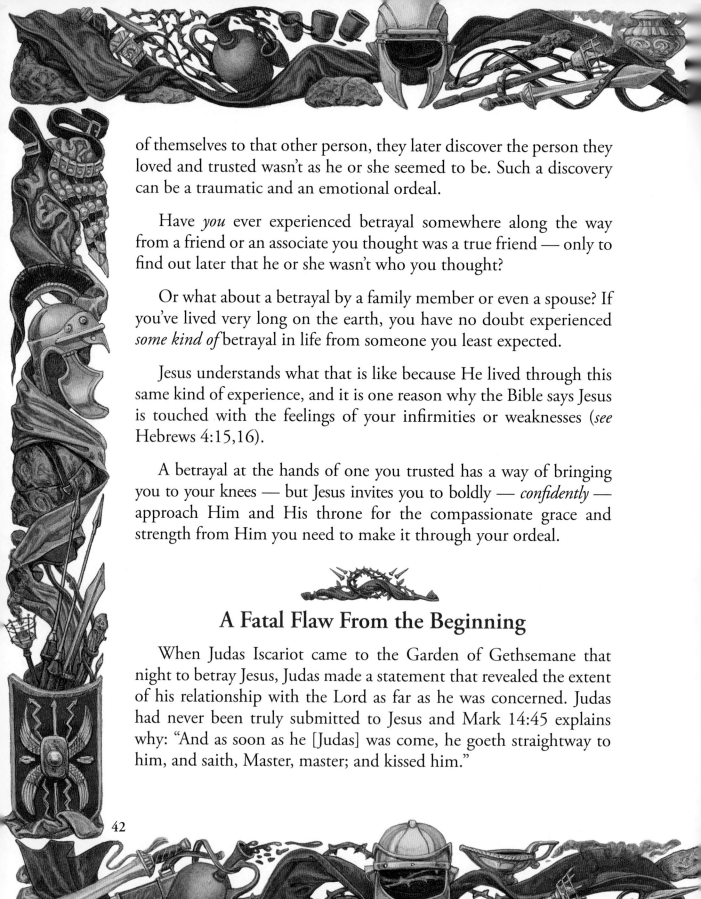

of themselves to that other person, they later discover the person they loved and trusted wasn't as he or she seemed to be. Such a discovery can be a traumatic and an emotional ordeal.

Have *you* ever experienced betrayal somewhere along the way from a friend or an associate you thought was a true friend — only to find out later that he or she wasn't who you thought?

Or what about a betrayal by a family member or even a spouse? If you've lived very long on the earth, you have no doubt experienced *some kind of* betrayal in life from someone you least expected.

Jesus understands what that is like because He lived through this same kind of experience, and it is one reason why the Bible says Jesus is touched with the feelings of your infirmities or weaknesses (*see* Hebrews 4:15,16).

A betrayal at the hands of one you trusted has a way of bringing you to your knees — but Jesus invites you to boldly — *confidently* — approach Him and His throne for the compassionate grace and strength from Him you need to make it through your ordeal.

A Fatal Flaw From the Beginning

When Judas Iscariot came to the Garden of Gethsemane that night to betray Jesus, Judas made a statement that revealed the extent of his relationship with the Lord as far as he was concerned. Judas had never been truly submitted to Jesus and Mark 14:45 explains why: "And as soon as he [Judas] was come, he goeth straightway to him, and saith, Master, master; and kissed him."

Notice Judas called Jesus, "Master, master." These words were very revealing, for they showed the type of relationship that *really* existed in Judas' heart and mind toward Jesus.

The word "master" is from a Greek word that means *teacher*. When it is translated "master," as it is in this verse, it gives the idea of *one who is a fabulous, masterful teacher*, and it is the Greek equivalent of the Hebrew word *rabbi*.

A *rabbi* is a teacher who is honored and respected because of his understanding of and ability to explain the Scriptures. So when Judas greeted Jesus in the Garden that night, he called Him, "Master, master," which meant, *"Teacher, teacher."*

Titles are very important because they define relationships. For instance, the words "Daddy" and "Mother" define the unique relationship between a child and a parent. The word "boss" defines the relationship between an employee and his or her employer — a relationship much different than the one that exists between the employee and his or her fellow employees. The word "President" defines the relationship between a nation and its leader. And the word "pastor" defines the relationship between a congregation and their pastor. A world without titles would be a world with confusion, for titles give rank, order, and definition to relationships.

Jesus Himself told the disciples, "Ye call me Master and Lord: and ye say well; for so I am" (John 13:13). Therefore, even Jesus acknowledged it was correct for His disciples to call Him "Lord" and "Master." In fact, there isn't a single occurrence in the gospels in which the disciples casually called Him "Jesus." They were respectful, honoring, and deferential when they spoke of Him or to Him.

43

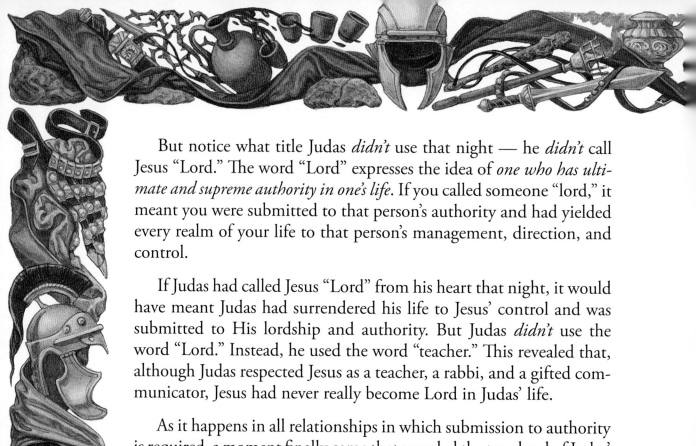

But notice what title Judas *didn't* use that night — he *didn't* call Jesus "Lord." The word "Lord" expresses the idea of *one who has ultimate and supreme authority in one's life.* If you called someone "lord," it meant you were submitted to that person's authority and had yielded every realm of your life to that person's management, direction, and control.

If Judas had called Jesus "Lord" from his heart that night, it would have meant Judas had surrendered his life to Jesus' control and was submitted to His lordship and authority. But Judas *didn't* use the word "Lord." Instead, he used the word "teacher." This revealed that, although Judas respected Jesus as a teacher, a rabbi, and a gifted communicator, Jesus had never really become Lord in Judas' life.

As it happens in all relationships in which submission to authority is required, a moment finally came that revealed the true level of Judas' submission to Jesus, and it revealed that there was a fatal flaw in his relationship with the Lord. Right there in the Garden that night, it became apparent to everyone that, even though Judas followed Jesus as a teacher, he had never really made Jesus the Lord of his life.

Even with all the love, patience, and time Jesus had sown into Judas, it was Judas who ultimately had to determine the level of relationship between himself and Jesus. Jesus was willing to be Judas' Lord — but Judas was the one who had to open his heart and submit his life fully to Jesus' authority. Instead, it finally became clear that Judas had only authorized Jesus to be a gifted teacher in his life and not his Lord.

The same is true in our lives. Jesus paid a high price to save us and redeem us to Himself and to the Father in a supernatural, divine act of reconciliation. And He has the power to sustain us, the wisdom to govern us, and the majesty and glory to exercise lordship in every

realm of our life and existence. He was and is willing to be our Lord — but *we* are the ones who must decide in our hearts to accept His sacrifice and commitment and to return that commitment to Him in willing submission and obedience to His plan and purpose for our lives.

Just as Judas made apparent the true nature of his relationship with Jesus on that night in the Garden, it is likely that experiences we've had in life show that it takes time to really get to know who people are. Have you ever been shocked to discover someone you thought was with you all the way really wasn't with you at all? *If this has ever happened to you, please remember that it happened to Jesus too.* And just as God used Jesus to extend mercy, grace, and patience to Judas Iscariot, it may be that God will use you to give such a person in your life an opportunity to have a change of heart before it's too late.

- Can God count on *you* to be His extension of kindness to such a person?

- Are *you* called to be God's mercy outstretched to give that person a magnificent opportunity to make a true turn-around in his heart, mind, and character?

- Are *you* supposed to be that kind of person to someone close to you right now who is demonstrating disloyalty?

It's easy to fixate on a "kiss" of betrayal that you've received from an unfaithful person or friend — but instead, stop and think about how much God loves that "problem person" by giving him a friend like you to help him get it right.

If such a person chooses *not* to respond to the mercy, grace, and patience that are being poured out to him through you, he will have

to live with the results of his own decision. But make sure that you fulfill what God is requiring of *you* in such a relationship. Pray and ask God for wisdom concerning how to proceed. It may seem difficult to do, but it is possible that God has entrusted you with the responsibility of giving a person who has been unfaithful another chance to get it right.

Paralyzed by His Presence

After Jesus received Judas' kiss of betrayal, He stepped forward and asked the crowd of militia, "…Whom seek ye?" (John 18:4). They answered Him, "…Jesus of Nazareth…," and Jesus responded: "…I am he…" (v. 5). Verse 6 says, "As soon then as he had said unto them, I am he, *they went backward, and fell to the ground.*"

In that moment, Jesus stepped forward to address all the various religious and military forces that had gathered in that space to arrest Him. Just as the Roman soldiers and temple police were stepping in to make their arrest, a supernatural power was suddenly released so strong that it literally threw the entire band of 300 to 600 soldiers or more backward and down onto the ground. In the flash of a second, it looked as if an invisible bomb had been detonated. So much explosive strength was released that it knocked all those religious leaders and various types of soldiers flat on their backs. But where did that discharge of power come from, and what released it?

Again, Jesus asked, "Whom seek ye?" (John 18:4), and they responded, "Jesus of Nazareth" (v. 5). As soon as they responded, Jesus answered them, saying, *"I am He,"* and, immediately, "they went backward, and fell to the ground" (v. 6).

Jesus Is the Great *'I AM!'*

They were seeking Jesus of Nazareth, and Jesus answered them, "I am He." These mighty words come from Greek words that are more accurately translated, *"I AM!"*

This was not the first time Jesus used this particular phrase to identify Himself. He also used these very words in John 8:58 and John 13:19. In those passages, when Jesus said those particular words, the hearers recognized them as the very words God used to identify Himself when He spoke to Moses on Mount Horeb and said, "I AM THAT I AM!" (*See* Exodus 3:14.)

For example, we read in John 8:58 that Jesus said, "…Verily, verily, I say unto you, Before Abraham was, I am." Those final words in the verse, "I am," are the very Greek words used in the Old Testament Greek Septuagint that are translated, *"I AM!"*

We also read in John 13:19 that Jesus said, "Now I tell you before it come, that, when it is come to pass, ye may believe that *I am he.*" If you read this verse in the *King James Version* of the Bible, you will notice that the word "he" is italicized, which means it was supplied by the *KJV* translators and is not in the original text. The original text simply says, "…That…ye may believe that I AM!" In both of these cited texts, Jesus uses the very words that God used to describe Himself in Exodus 3:14. Therefore, by using this well-known phrase, Jesus was declaring that He was, and is, the Great "I AM" of the Old Testament!

The soldiers who came to arrest Jesus that night probably expected Him to answer, "I am *Jesus of Nazareth*" — but instead, Jesus remarkably

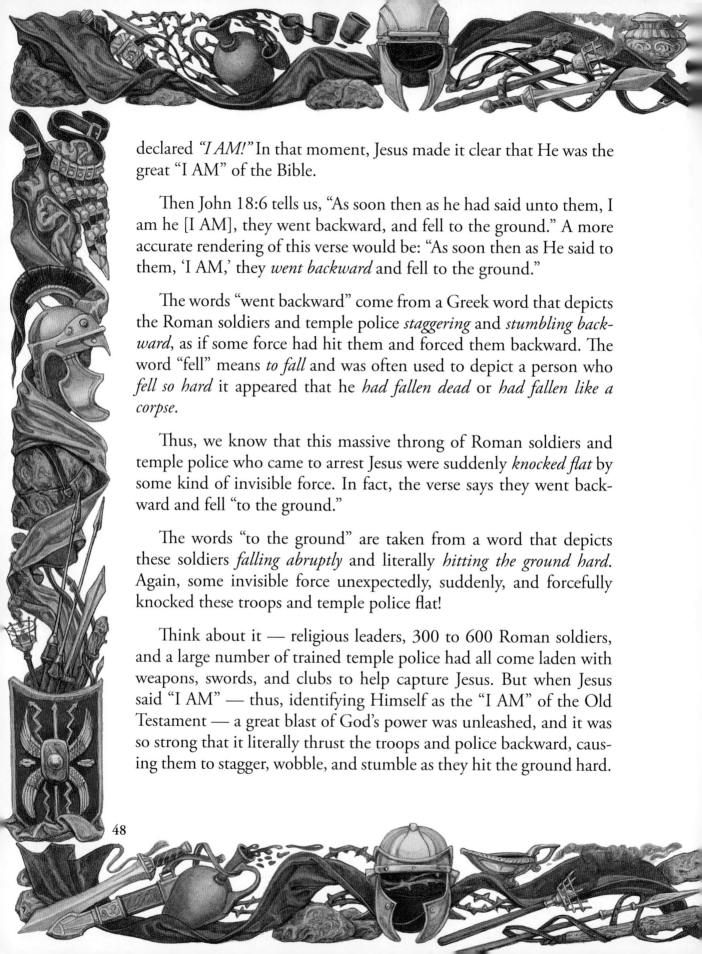

declared *"I AM!"* In that moment, Jesus made it clear that He was the great "I AM" of the Bible.

Then John 18:6 tells us, "As soon then as he had said unto them, I am he [I AM], they went backward, and fell to the ground." A more accurate rendering of this verse would be: "As soon then as He said to them, 'I AM,' they *went backward* and fell to the ground."

The words "went backward" come from a Greek word that depicts the Roman soldiers and temple police *staggering* and *stumbling backward*, as if some force had hit them and forced them backward. The word "fell" means *to fall* and was often used to depict a person who *fell so hard* it appeared that he *had fallen dead* or *had fallen like a corpse.*

Thus, we know that this massive throng of Roman soldiers and temple police who came to arrest Jesus were suddenly *knocked flat* by some kind of invisible force. In fact, the verse says they went backward and fell "to the ground."

The words "to the ground" are taken from a word that depicts these soldiers *falling abruptly* and literally *hitting the ground hard*. Again, some invisible force unexpectedly, suddenly, and forcefully knocked these troops and temple police flat!

Think about it — religious leaders, 300 to 600 Roman soldiers, and a large number of trained temple police had all come laden with weapons, swords, and clubs to help capture Jesus. But when Jesus said "I AM" — thus, identifying Himself as the "I AM" of the Old Testament — a great blast of God's power was unleashed, and it was so strong that it literally thrust the troops and police backward, causing them to stagger, wobble, and stumble as they hit the ground hard.

48

What a shock it must have been for those religious leaders and military men to discover the mere words of Jesus were enough to overwhelm and overpower them. The legendary tales they had heard about Jesus' supernatural power were correct. He really was strong enough to overcome an army. After all, He was, and still is, the Great "I AM"!

But after Jesus proved He couldn't be taken by force, He willfully surrendered to the soldiers because He knew it was a part of the Father's plan for the redemption of mankind.

It's important to understand that no one took Jesus. It was His voluntary choice to go with the troops. You see, my friend, the Jesus we serve is powerful! And He was lovingly and willingly intent on offering Himself as the ultimate Sacrifice for the sin of all mankind, and that included you and me.

There is no force strong enough to resist Jesus' power. No sickness, financial turmoil, relational problems, or political force — absolutely nothing has enough power to resist the supernatural power of Jesus Christ! When Jesus — the Great "I AM" — opens His mouth and speaks, every power that attempts to defy Him or His Word is pushed backward and shaken until it staggers, stumbles, and falls to the ground!

So what is your need today? Why not present your needs to Jesus, who is the Great "I AM"? Let Him speak to your heart and direct you to the promises in His Word, and once you see the promise you need for the specific situation you're facing, pray in agreement with His Word. As you do, you will see the mighty power of God unleashed against the evil forces that have been trying to defy you!

QUESTIONS TO PONDER
AND DISCUSS

1. Accidental betrayal is one thing, but premeditated disloyalty is another. Jesus knew that Judas would betray Him; nevertheless, Jesus continued to work closely with Judas. Have you ever been in a situation in which you knew a person was flawed, yet you felt led to extend mercy and love to that person and maintain a relationship anyway?

2. The act of betrayal reveals the quality of a person's character, whether he is the betrayer or the one betrayed. Have you ever betrayed someone or been betrayed by another? If so, what did you learn about yourself as a result of that experience? How has it changed you?

3. People who do not effectively understand submission and authority can be difficult to deal with in business, in marriage, in ministry, and in life. If such a person is in your life, how are you responding to help that individual grow and change for the better? What have you discovered about your own heart in the process?

4. Think about the mentors God has brought into your life through the years to teach and train you so you can fulfill your divine purpose. What are some significant ways you can express honor to these mentors for their role in your life? Have you allowed an offense to separate you from any of these individuals? If so, what steps can you take to mend that breach?

Jesus asked the armed guards who had come with Judas to take Him away, "...Whom seek ye? They answered him, Jesus of Nazareth. Jesus saith unto them, I am he..." (John 18:4,5). As soon as He said those words, a great blast of power knocked those troops and police back so they hit the ground hard. In that moment, Jesus made it clear that He was the great "I AM" of the Bible.

Gripping a sword, Peter swung it with all his might and lopped off the right ear of the high priest's servant, Malchus, who had arrived with the authorities to arrest Jesus. But in demonstration of the Father's love even to someone who would be instrumental in leading Him to His crucifixion, Jesus miraculously healed Malchus' ear.

Chapter Four

PETER'S MESS AND THE NAKED BOY IN THE GARDEN OF GETHSEMANE

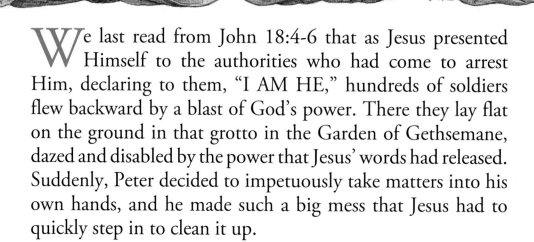

We last read from John 18:4-6 that as Jesus presented Himself to the authorities who had come to arrest Him, declaring to them, "I AM HE," hundreds of soldiers flew backward by a blast of God's power. There they lay flat on the ground in that grotto in the Garden of Gethsemane, dazed and disabled by the power that Jesus' words had released. Suddenly, Peter decided to impetuously take matters into his own hands, and he made such a big mess that Jesus had to quickly step in to clean it up.

A Hotheaded Moment
Followed by the Lord's Rescue

Before we look at Peter's serious error in judgment, stop and think of a time when you decided to take matters into your own hands and ended up making a big mess of things. Perhaps you were trying to get things moving a little faster, or you felt trapped in a situation and, rather than hold yourself in a calm frame of mind, you came out of that "trap" fighting. Were you regretful for your spur-of-the-moment, impetuous, or hotheaded actions?

At one time or another, we all have been guilty of acting rashly and thoughtlessly. For example, just think of how many times you've said something you later regretted. Oh, how you probably wished you could have retracted those words, but it was too late! Or perhaps you've been guilty of acting spontaneously on an issue before you had enough time to really think things through or gather all the facts.

Or have you ever gotten so angry at someone that you "popped off" and vocalized your dissent before the other person was finished talking? When you later realized that person wasn't even saying what you thought he said, did you feel like a fool for reacting too quickly? Did you have to apologize for making a rash statement, all the while wishing you had just kept your mouth shut a few minutes longer?

Impetuous and hotheaded moments rarely produce good fruit. In fact, when we act rashly, we usually end up loathing the stupidity of our words or actions. The truth is, we all need a good dose of patience at times in our lives.

But perhaps no story better demonstrates the mess that impatience produces than that night in the Garden of Gethsemane when Peter unwisely seized the moment and brought hurt and harm to someone in the crowd — and it was a move that could have cost Peter his future ministry and perhaps even his life.

Peter must have seen this moment as his great chance to show himself brave, but what he did was simply shocking. While all those soldiers and other authorities were still flat on their backs, as we just read — their bodies and minds yet stunned and dazed — Peter decided to take matters into his own hands, and he did something unthinkable.

Gripping a sword, Peter swung it with all his might and lopped off the ear of the high priest's servant, who was present with the authorities who'd come to arrest Jesus!

This spontaneous, hasty behavior earned Peter a place in history that no one has ever forgotten. However, to see the full picture of what happened that night, it is essential to piece the story together from both Luke's and John's gospels, for each gospel writer tells a different part of the story.

While the soldiers and temple police were lying on their backs, Peter looked around and realized that the armed men were disabled. So he pulled out a sword, and with the weapon in hand, inquired, "…Lord, shall we smite with the sword?" (*see* Luke 22:49).

But before Jesus had an opportunity to answer, Peter swung into action and did something outrageous and utterly bizarre! He impulsively swung down, slicing right past the head of the high priest's servant, and cutting his ear off. Imagine how shocked Jesus must have been to see Peter lop off this poor man's ear and then watch the severed ear fall into the dirt on the ground!

John 18:10 tells us that Peter "…*smote* the high priest's servant, and cut off his right ear…." The word "smote" in the original text is a word that means *to strike*, as a person who viciously strikes someone with a dangerous tool, weapon, or instrument.

It can also be translated *to sting*, like a scorpion that strongly injects its stinger into a victim. In addition, it means *to beat with the fist*. In this verse, the word is used to picture *the force* of Peter's swinging action. This tells us that Peter put all his strength into the swinging of his sword, fully intending to cause some kind of bodily impairment.

But do you really think Peter was aiming for the servant's ear? Why would anyone attack an ear? Furthermore, it wouldn't take that much "smiting" force to cut off an ear.

No, it seems that Peter was aiming for the man's head and missed, swiping his ear by mistake. When that sword missed its target, it slipped down the side of the servant's head and took his ear with it.

When John 18:10 says Peter *cut off* his right ear, the words "cut off" are from the Greek word that describes *a downward swing that*

cuts something off. In this case, Peter swung downward so hard that he completely removed the ear of the servant of the high priest.

Some people insinuate that Peter merely nicked this man's ear, but the Greek word used here shows that the swing of Peter's sword caused the ear's complete removal. The Greek word for "ear" refers to *the entire outer ear.* The Bible is so detailed about the events that occurred, it even tells us it was the servant's *right* ear. The servant of the high priest lost his entire right ear when Peter swung in his direction!

As Jesus stood in the midst of His own arrest, He watched as Peter impetuously cut off a man's ear. Then, suddenly, a wounded man had blood pouring from the side of his head. Can you imagine the wounded man putting pressure on the side of his head to try to stop the blood from pouring onto the ground around him — and the shock shown on his face as he looked at his severed ear lying on the ground to his side?

Who Was the Man Peter Assaulted?

John 18:10 tells us the servant's name was *Malchus.* Who was Malchus? Did Peter indiscriminately select Malchus as his target that night? Or was there a particular reason Peter chose this man as the focus of his wrath?

The name Malchus has two meanings: *ruler* and *counselor.* We don't know that this was the servant's original name, as it may have been a name given to him because of his close position to the high priest, who at that time was a man named Caiaphas.

Caiaphas was a member of the Sadducees, a sect of Jewish religious leaders that was particularly opposed to the reality of supernatural

happenings and viewed most supernatural events of the Old Testament as myths and legends. This is one reason Caiaphas was so antagonistic to the ministry of Jesus, which, of course, was overflowing with miraculous events every day.

But some believe it's likely that as spokesman for the high priest, Malchus had been a public voice for Caiaphas and that it was Malchus who had previously issued atrocious statements about Jesus and His disciples. If that was the case, when Peter saw Malchus in the Garden of Gethsemane, it no doubt brought back memories of the many times he had seen Malchus standing at the side of the high priest or the times this servant had issued damning public statements about Jesus.

Although the man is referred to as the servant of the high priest, his was a very prominent position in the religious order of the priesthood. As a high-ranking officer of the religious court, Malchus would have been regally dressed and would have carried himself with pride and dignity.

To Peter's eye, he probably represented everything that belonged to the realm of the priesthood, an order of religious men that had instigated numerous problems for Jesus and His disciples.

Because Malchus was present at the time of Jesus' arrest, scholars conclude that he was there at that moment to be the personal representative of the high priest, charged to officially oversee the activities connected with Jesus' arrest.

As impetuous as Peter's actions appeared, few scholars believe that Peter singled Malchus out by chance. Although it can't be said with absolute certainty, Malchus may have become the intended target because of Peter's deep resentment and long-held grudge toward the

high priest and his entourage, all of whom had been continually hostile toward Jesus' ministry.

It is also important to note that one who was disfigured was not allowed certain functions in holy sites, and such a disfigurement would have prohibited Malchus from serving further in the Temple premises. But rather than leave him disfigured, Jesus healed him, thus protecting his reputation and ability to serve in his profession alongside the high priest.

It is amazing that the healing of Malchus' ear was the last miracle Jesus performed before His death, burial, and resurrection. What a statement this makes to us about Jesus, for just before He went to the Cross, He reached out to heal and help one who had been His publicly declared and avowed foe!

Malchus was part of a group that had been menacing and antagonistic toward Jesus for a long time. But when Peter assaulted him, Jesus didn't say, "Finally, one of you guys got what you deserve!" Instead, Jesus reached out to the man in his need, touched him, and *supernaturally* healed him. Keep in mind that the high priest, a Sadducee, was vehemently opposed to Jesus' supernatural ministry. Yet it was the high priest's own servant who received *a supernatural touch* from the Lord!

What a contrast Jesus' actions were to Peter's behavior. More than likely, Peter acted out of a long-held offense, but Jesus demonstrated love and genuine care even to those who opposed Him and were instrumental in leading Him to His crucifixion.

But let's see what Jesus did for Peter that night in the Garden of Gethsemane after Peter chopped off Malchus' ear. There is something else we can learn from the example of Jesus and His actions that night.

Jesus Cleaned Up Peter's Mess

What Peter did to Malchus was not only scandalous — it was against the law and, therefore, punishable. Peter's wrongdoing was *criminal* — sufficient to ruin his entire life! He could have been sentenced for physically injuring a fellow citizen. And this wasn't just any citizen. As the servant of the high priest, Malchus was an extremely well-known man in the city of Jerusalem. Peter would have certainly been imprisoned for injuring a person of such stature.

Not long before all this happened, Jesus had been sweating blood from an intense spiritual battle He had fought in prayer while in the Garden of Gethsemane. Then He received the kiss of betrayal from a so-called friend and was, therefore, facing the prospect of the Cross and three days in the grave.

Now a new problem had been thrust upon Him because of Peter's impetuous, unauthorized behavior. Jesus had to put everything on hold for a moment so He could step forward and fix the mess Peter had inconceivably created in a heated moment.

As blood poured from the side of Malchus' head and dripped from the blade in Peter's hand, Jesus said to the soldiers, "…Suffer ye thus far…" (Luke 22:51). This was the equivalent of saying, *"Let Me just do one more thing before you take Me!"*

Then Jesus reached out to Malchus and "…touched his ear, and healed him" (v. 51). Rather than allow Himself to be taken away while Peter was still subject to arrest, imprisonment, and possible execution, Jesus stopped the entire process to fix the mess Peter had made.

The Bible says that Jesus "touched" the servant. The Greek word for "touch" is a word that means *to firmly grasp* or *to hold tightly*. This is very important, as it lets us know that Jesus didn't just lightly touch Malchus. He firmly grabbed the servant's head and held it tightly. This is significant because it tells us the tenacity with which Jesus prayed. When Jesus laid His hands on people, they *knew* that hands had been laid on them!

The Bible doesn't tell us whether Jesus touched the stump that remained from the severed ear and grew a new ear or retrieved the old ear from the ground and miraculously set it back in its place. Regardless of how the miracle occurred, however, the word "touched" lets us know that Jesus was aggressive in the way He touched the man. And as a result of Jesus' touch, Malchus was completely "healed" (v. 51).

The word "healed" is a Greek word which means *to cure*, *to restore*, or *to heal*. Before the soldiers bound Jesus and led Him out of the Garden, He completely restored Malchus' ear! And He rescued Peter from the terrible punishment that would have surely ensued for assaulting the servant of the high priest.

What a night in the Garden of Gethsemane!

- Jesus' mere words literally knocked 300 to 600 soldiers off their feet and flat on their backs.

- Although Jesus didn't need Peter's help and never requested Peter's intervention, nevertheless, Peter suddenly jumped in the middle of God's business and tried to instigate a revolt.

- Rather than walk off and leave Peter in the mess he had made of his own doing, Jesus stopped everything that was happening and intervened on Peter's behalf.

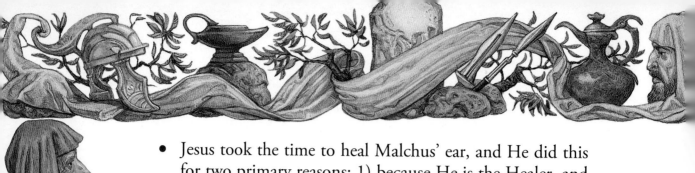

- Jesus took the time to heal Malchus' ear, and He did this for two primary reasons: 1) because He is the Healer, and 2) because He didn't want Peter to be arrested for his impulsive actions.

So the next time you think you are too busy or too important to get involved in a friend's problem, remember this example that Jesus gave us on the night of His arrest. That night, Jesus had a lot on His mind, but He nevertheless stopped everything to help His friend. He could have said, "Peter, you've made this mess by yourself; now you can fix it by yourself." But it was clear that Peter would have never gotten out of this trouble without assistance, so Jesus stepped in to help Peter get things back in order again.

When you are tempted to be judgmental about other people's impetuous behavior and self-imposed problems, it would be good to remember the many times God's mercy has intervened to save you from messy situations that you created yourself. Even though you deserved to be in trouble, God loved you enough to come right alongside you and help you pull things together so you could get out of that mess. Now whenever you see others in trouble, you have the opportunity to be an extension of God's mercy to them.

I also want to encourage you that if you see a friend in trouble, stop a moment to put your own concerns on hold so you can reach out to a friend in trouble. Then do whatever you can to help restore the situation. Since this was important enough for Jesus to do, you have time to do it as well. Make it a priority today to be a faithful friend to the end, just as Jesus was to Peter in the Garden of Gethsemane!

Jesus didn't need Peter's undersized, insignificant sword to deal with His situation. What good would a single sword have been against all the troops assembled in the grotto in the Garden of Gethsemane

that night, anyway? Peter's actions were a perfect example of how the flesh tries in vain to solve its own problems but cannot. Jesus had all the power that was needed to conquer those troops, yet He chose to surrender to them because He knew it was the Father's will to do so.

As you face your own challenges in life, always keep in mind that Jesus has the power to fix any problem you'll ever face. Before you jump in and make things worse by taking matters into your own hands, remember the story of Peter! If you're tempted to "grab a sword and start swinging," take a few minutes to remind yourself that Jesus can handle the problem without your intervention. Wait for Him to show you what to do or for Him to act on your behalf.

So the next time you're facing trouble, before you do anything else, pray and ask the Lord what you are supposed to do. Then after you receive your answer and follow His instructions, just watch His supernatural power swing into action to solve the dilemma you are facing!

Jesus Could Have Called Upon Twelve Legions of Angels

That night when the Roman soldiers and temple police arrested Him, Jesus also told them, "Thinkest thou that I cannot now pray to my Father, and he shall presently give me more than twelve legions of angels?" (Matthew 26:53) — but He forfeited His right to do so in order that God's plan of redemption could be fulfilled.

To fully understand the magnitude of what Jesus said here, we need to know:

- What is a "legion"?
- How many angels would there be in 12 legions?
- What would be the combined strength of this number of angels?

It is important to answer these questions because the answers reveal the full might that was available to Jesus had He requested supernatural help in the Garden of Gethsemane.

When we take into account the power that was already demonstrated in the Garden and then add the potential assistance and impact of 12 legions of angels, it becomes obvious that there was no human force on earth strong enough to take Jesus against His will. The only way He was going to be taken was if He *allowed* Himself to be taken!

This is why Jesus later told Pilate, "…Thou couldest have no power at all against me, except it were given thee from above…" (John 19:11).

So let's begin with the first question: *What is a "legion"?*

The word "legion" is a military term that was taken from the Roman army. A legion denoted a group of at least 6,000 Roman soldiers; although, the total number could be higher. This means that anytime we read about a "legion" of anything, we know it always refers to at least 6,000 of something.

An amazing example of this is found in Mark 5:9, in which the Bible tells us that the demon-possessed man of the Gadarenes had a legion of demons. That means this man had an infestation of at least 6,000 demons residing inside him!

But let's also answer the second question: *How many angels would there be in 12 legions?*

Since the word "legion" refers to *at least* 6,000, it means a single legion of angels would be *at least* 6,000 angels. But Jesus said that the Father could give Him "more than" 12 legions of angels if He requested it. Because it would be pure speculation to try to figure out how many "more than" 12 legions would be, let's just stick with the figure of 12 legions to see how many angels that entails.

So let's say that one legion is at least 6,000 angels. If you multiply that number by 12, you will discover that 12 legions of angels would include a minimum of *72,000 angels*. However, Jesus said the Father could give Him *more than* 12 legions of angels, so we can conclude that there were potentially many additional thousands of angels available to Jesus the night He was arrested!

Now let's look at our third question: *What would be the combined strength of this number of angels?*

Angels are so very powerful that Isaiah 37:36 tells us a single angel obliterated 185,000 men in one night. So if one angel had that much strength, how much combined strength would there be in 12 legions of angels?

Considering a single angel was able to obliterate 185,000 men in one night, we can reasonably conclude the combined strength in a legion of 6,000 angels would be enough to destroy 1,110,000,000 men (that is, 1 billion, 110 million men). But that's just the combined power in *one* legion of angels!

Let's multiply the number 185,000 by 12 legions — or at least 72,000 angels — which was the number of angels that Jesus said was available to Him on the night of His arrest. When we do, we discover that there was enough combined strength at Jesus' disposal to have annihilated at least 13,320,000,000 men (that is, 13 billion,

320 million men) — which is more than twice the number of people living on the earth right now!

Of course, all these figures assume that the angel spoken of in Isaiah 37:36 had *maxed out* his power at 185,000 men (which is unlikely). Simply put, angels are *powerful*, and Jesus had a *huge* number of angels at His disposal!

So, you see, Jesus really didn't need Peter's sword that night. If the Master had chosen to do so, He could have summoned 72,000 magnificent, mighty, dazzling, glorious, overwhelmingly powerful angels to the Garden of Gethsemane to obliterate the Roman soldiers and temple police who had come to arrest Him. In fact, the combined strength in 12 legions of angels could have wiped out the entire human race!

But Jesus *didn't* call on the supernatural help that was available to Him because He knew it was time for Him to voluntarily lay down His life for the sin of humanity.

Have you ever stopped to think about the magnitude of God's power compared to that of man — and that, *literally*, no man had the power to take Jesus' life from Him? Jesus had to willingly lay His life down to rescue and redeem you and me.

Oh, what a Savior Jesus Christ was, is, and forevermore will be!

But wait — there's more! Besides the army of Jewish and Roman authorities that showed up to arrest Jesus — and Peter's impetuous actions that caused an interruption in the chain of events — there's even more that happened in the Garden of Gethsemane on the night of Jesus' arrest. And this event further demonstrates the raw, heavenly power in the name of Jesus the Great "I AM"!

Who Was the Naked Boy
in the Garden of Gethsemane?

Just as Jesus finished healing the ear of the servant of the high priest, we are told in Mark 14:51 and 52, "And there followed him a certain young man, having a linen cloth cast about his naked body; and the young men laid hold on him: and he left the linen cloth, and fled from them naked."

- Who was this young man?
- Why was he following Jesus?
- Why was he naked?
- Why was he draped in a linen cloth instead of wearing normal clothes?
- Why was the Holy Spirit so careful to include this in Mark's account of the events that night?
- What is the significance of this event?

The key to identifying this young man lies in the "linen cloth" he had lightly draped about his body. The Greek word that is used for this "linen cloth" is used in only one other event in the New Testament — to depict the "linen cloth" in which the body of Jesus was wrapped for burial (*see* Matthew 27:59, Mark 15:46, and Luke 23:53). Thus, the only reference we have for this kind of cloth in the New Testament is that of a burial shroud used for covering a dead body in a grave.

Indeed, the answer to this naked young man's identity lies in the cloth he had wrapped around his body. You see, when a body was

prepared for Jewish burial, it was washed, made ceremonially clean, and buried naked in a linen cloth exactly like the one described here in the gospel of Mark. Furthermore, the Garden of Gethsemane was situated on the side of the Mount of Olives, and toward the base of that mount is a heavily populated cemetery, with many of its graves today dating back to the time of Jesus.

When Jesus said, "I AM," the power released was so tremendous that it knocked the soldiers backward, but evidently it also caused a rumbling in the local cemetery! When that blast of power was released, a young boy, draped in a linen burial cloth in accordance with the tradition of that time, *crawled out from his tomb — raised from the dead!*

The Boy 'Continuously Followed' Jesus

The reason this young boy who had crawled out of his grave "followed" Jesus was to get a glimpse of the One who had resurrected him. The word "followed" here means *to continuously follow.* This tells us that this resurrected young man trailed the soldiers as they took Jesus through the Garden on the way to His trial.

When the soldiers discovered the young man who was following Jesus, they tried to apprehend him. But when they reached out to grab him, he broke free from their grip and fled, leaving the linen cloth in their possession.

Please reflect again on the amazing power that was active at the time of Jesus' arrest in the Garden of Gethsemane. He later told Pilate,

"…Thou couldest have no power at all against me, except it were given thee from above…" (John 19:11). Indeed, there was so much power present that *no one* could have withstood Jesus had He chosen to resist. Jesus was not taken by the will of man; He was delivered by the will of the Father.

Think how marvelous it is that Jesus freely gave His life for us! So much power was at work in Him, even at the time of His arrest, that no one had sufficient power to forcibly take Him. The only reason Jesus was taken was that He chose to willingly lay down His life for you and for me.

In the next chapter, we will see what happened after Jesus demonstrated His phenomenal power and permitted the soldiers to take Him into custody. In a certain sense, it was simply an *act* or *formality* so that Jesus could fulfill God's plan to redeem mankind as the consummate Lamb led away "to the slaughter" (*see* Isaiah 53:7). Jesus, who is Lord over all, had already vividly proven that they didn't have the adequate power to take Him.

QUESTIONS TO PONDER AND DISCUSS

1. In a moment of rashness, Peter cut off a man's ear. Similarly, we can all probably think of times when we have acted out of haste without thinking through the results of our own actions. But when we refuse to wait on God, impatience will always produce a problem in our lives. Are you making choices today that will produce the results you want tomorrow?

2. Can you think of a time when you were in trouble and someone helped you without smothering you in judgment for what might have been a self-imposed problem? How did that person's intervention affect you then, and how does his or her example of love continue to influence you today?

3. When we think about the divine power available to Jesus that night in the Garden, it seems almost laughable that Peter thought his little sword offered protection. What pitifully inadequate substitutes for God's power have you attempted to rely on in the past when you faced a difficult situation and were in need of divine help or deliverance?

4. No foe could have withstood the power in Jesus if He had chosen to resist His enemies. And if *you* resist the devil, he can't withstand the power of God that resides in *you* either. Is there an area of your life where the devil is seeking to overtake you? Take a moment to remind yourself of the overwhelming power of the Greater One within you and then use your authority in Jesus' name to actively *resist* the enemy!

When Jesus said, "I AM," the power released was so tremendous that evidently it caused a rumbling in the local cemetery. When that blast of power was released, a young boy, draped in a linen burial cloth *crawled out from his tomb — raised from the dead!* When the soldiers discovered the young man, they tried to apprehend him, but he broke free from their grip and fled.

This illustration demonstrates Jesus being led to the home of the high priest Caiaphas, where He received horrific treatment at the hands of religious leaders. Caiaphas and the scribes and elders humiliated Jesus by spitting on His face — a strong form of shaming someone in a demeaning, debase, and hateful way — and violently struck Him with their fists.

Chapter Five

SPITTING IN JESUS' FACE AND PLAYING GAMES WITH JESUS

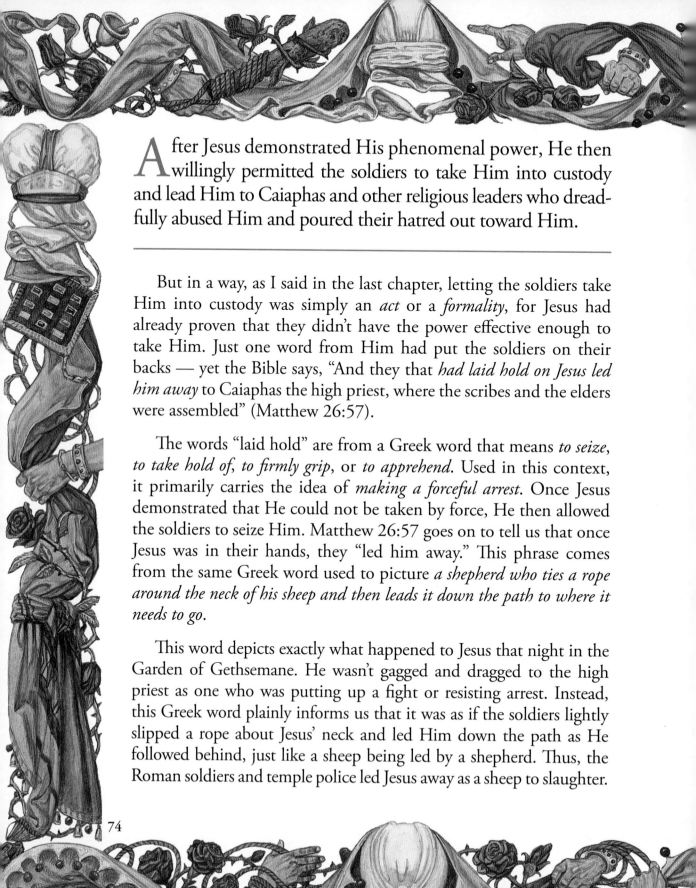

After Jesus demonstrated His phenomenal power, He then willingly permitted the soldiers to take Him into custody and lead Him to Caiaphas and other religious leaders who dreadfully abused Him and poured their hatred out toward Him.

But in a way, as I said in the last chapter, letting the soldiers take Him into custody was simply an *act* or a *formality*, for Jesus had already proven that they didn't have the power effective enough to take Him. Just one word from Him had put the soldiers on their backs — yet the Bible says, "And they that *had laid hold on Jesus led him away* to Caiaphas the high priest, where the scribes and the elders were assembled" (Matthew 26:57).

The words "laid hold" are from a Greek word that means *to seize, to take hold of, to firmly grip,* or *to apprehend.* Used in this context, it primarily carries the idea of *making a forceful arrest.* Once Jesus demonstrated that He could not be taken by force, He then allowed the soldiers to seize Him. Matthew 26:57 goes on to tell us that once Jesus was in their hands, they "led him away." This phrase comes from the same Greek word used to picture *a shepherd who ties a rope around the neck of his sheep and then leads it down the path to where it needs to go.*

This word depicts exactly what happened to Jesus that night in the Garden of Gethsemane. He wasn't gagged and dragged to the high priest as one who was putting up a fight or resisting arrest. Instead, this Greek word plainly informs us that it was as if the soldiers lightly slipped a rope about Jesus' neck and led Him down the path as He followed behind, just like a sheep being led by a shepherd. Thus, the Roman soldiers and temple police led Jesus away as a sheep to slaughter.

Isaiah 53:7 prophesied this scenario many centuries earlier, saying, "…He [Jesus] is brought as a lamb to the slaughter, and as a sheep before her shearers is dumb, so he openeth not his mouth." On that night, as the soldiers led Jesus to the house of Caiaphas, the high priest, this verse was further fulfilled as Jesus refused to open His mouth and defend Himself as religious leaders blasphemed, screamed, and abused Him.

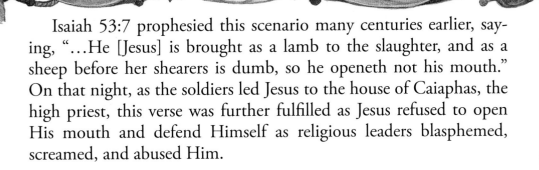

Who Was Caiaphas?

Caiaphas was appointed high priest in the year 18 AD. As high priest, he became so prominent in Israel that even when his term as high priest ended, he wielded great influence in the business of the nation, including its spiritual, political, and financial affairs.

As a young man, Caiaphas married Anna, the daughter of Annas who was serving as high priest at that time. Annas served as Israel's high priest for nine years. The title of high priest had fallen into the jurisdiction of this family, and they held this high-ranking position firmly in their grip, passing it among the various members of the family and, thus, keeping the reins of power in their hands.

Flavius Josephus, the famous Jewish historian, even reported that five of Annas' sons served in the office of the high priest.[1] It was a spiritual monarchy, and the holders of this coveted title retained great political power, controlled public opinion, and owned vast wealth.

After Annas was removed from his position by the Romans, the title of high priest eventually passed to his son-in-law Caiaphas, and Annas continued to exercise control over the nation through his son-in-law.

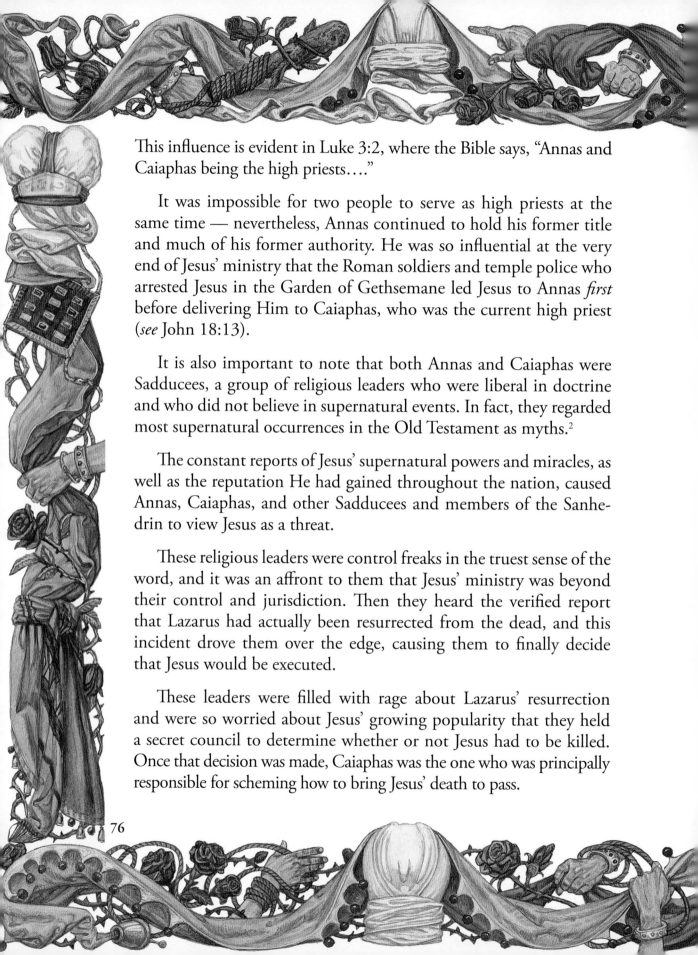

This influence is evident in Luke 3:2, where the Bible says, "Annas and Caiaphas being the high priests…."

It was impossible for two people to serve as high priests at the same time — nevertheless, Annas continued to hold his former title and much of his former authority. He was so influential at the very end of Jesus' ministry that the Roman soldiers and temple police who arrested Jesus in the Garden of Gethsemane led Jesus to Annas *first* before delivering Him to Caiaphas, who was the current high priest (*see* John 18:13).

It is also important to note that both Annas and Caiaphas were Sadducees, a group of religious leaders who were liberal in doctrine and who did not believe in supernatural events. In fact, they regarded most supernatural occurrences in the Old Testament as myths.[2]

The constant reports of Jesus' supernatural powers and miracles, as well as the reputation He had gained throughout the nation, caused Annas, Caiaphas, and other Sadducees and members of the Sanhedrin to view Jesus as a threat.

These religious leaders were control freaks in the truest sense of the word, and it was an affront to them that Jesus' ministry was beyond their control and jurisdiction. Then they heard the verified report that Lazarus had actually been resurrected from the dead, and this incident drove them over the edge, causing them to finally decide that Jesus would be executed.

These leaders were filled with rage about Lazarus' resurrection and were so worried about Jesus' growing popularity that they held a secret council to determine whether or not Jesus had to be killed. Once that decision was made, Caiaphas was the one who was principally responsible for scheming how to bring Jesus' death to pass.

As high priest and the official head of the Sanhedrin, Caiaphas was also responsible for arranging Jesus' illegal trial before the Jewish authorities. At first, he charged Jesus with the sin of blasphemy. But because the accusation Caiaphas brought against Him was not really provable, the high priest delivered Jesus to the Roman authorities, who then found Jesus guilty of treason for claiming to be King of the Jews, over whom only the emperor of Rome would have uncontested rulership in that vast Roman-occupied territory.

Caiaphas was so powerful that even after the death of Jesus, he continued to persecute believers in the Early Church. For instance, after the crippled man at the Beautiful Gate was healed (*see* Acts 3), Peter and John were seized and brought before the council (Acts 4:6). Caiaphas was the high priest at that time and continued to serve as high priest until 36 AD. This means Caiaphas was also the high priest who interrogated Stephen in Acts 7:1. In addition to this, Caiaphas was also the high priest we read about who gave Saul of Tarsus written authorization to arrest believers in Jerusalem and later in Damascus (*see* Acts 9:1,2).

Because of political events in the year 36 AD, Caiaphas was finally removed from the office of high priest. Of the 19 men who served as high priests in the First Century, this evil man ruled the longest. But the title of high priest remained in the family and was eventually passed to his brother-in-law Jonathan, another son of Annas. In a certain sense, this family ruled religious affairs like a "religious mafia" who refused to yield influence or control to anyone else.

Although Jesus had never sinned (*see* 2 Corinthians 5:21), no guile had ever been found in His mouth (1 Peter 2:22), and His entire life was devoted to doing good and to healing all who were oppressed of the devil (Acts 10:38), He was placed temporarily into the hands of these evil spiritual vipers who were ruling in Jerusalem at the time. However, Jesus never questioned the Father's will or balked at the mission assigned to Him.

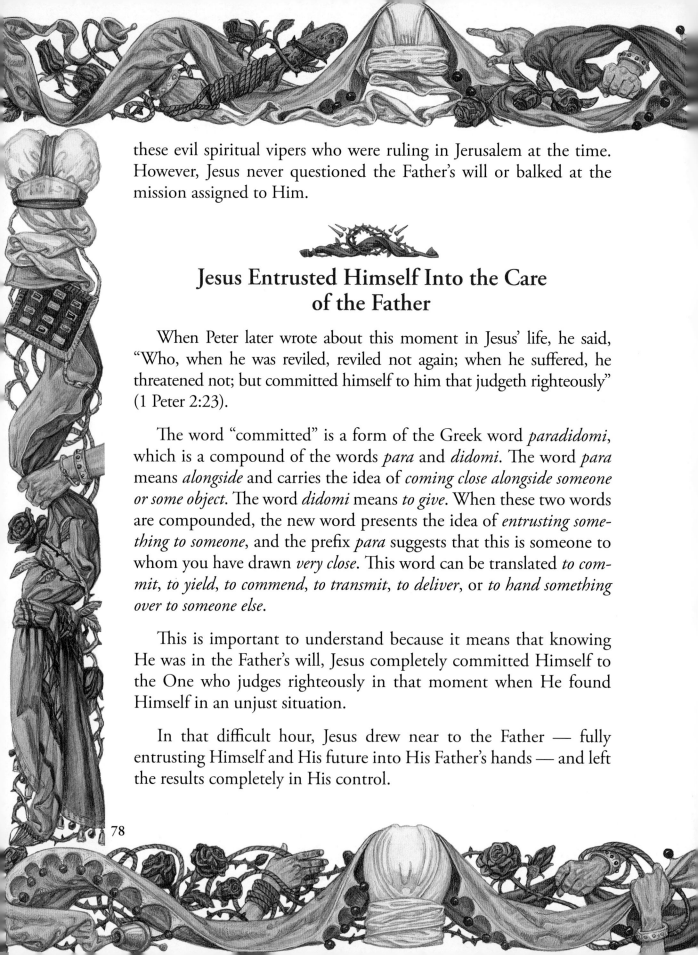

Jesus Entrusted Himself Into the Care of the Father

When Peter later wrote about this moment in Jesus' life, he said, "Who, when he was reviled, reviled not again; when he suffered, he threatened not; but committed himself to him that judgeth righteously" (1 Peter 2:23).

The word "committed" is a form of the Greek word *paradidomi*, which is a compound of the words *para* and *didomi*. The word *para* means *alongside* and carries the idea of *coming close alongside someone or some object*. The word *didomi* means *to give*. When these two words are compounded, the new word presents the idea of *entrusting something to someone*, and the prefix *para* suggests that this is someone to whom you have drawn *very close*. This word can be translated *to commit*, *to yield*, *to commend*, *to transmit*, *to deliver*, or *to hand something over to someone else*.

This is important to understand because it means that knowing He was in the Father's will, Jesus completely committed Himself to the One who judges righteously in that moment when He found Himself in an unjust situation.

In that difficult hour, Jesus drew near to the Father — fully entrusting Himself and His future into His Father's hands — and left the results completely in His control.

Spitting in Jesus' Face

That night after Jesus was arrested, He was led to the home of the high priest Caiaphas, where Caiaphas and the scribes and elders had assembled to wait for His arrival. It was within those palace walls that Jesus was put through horrific treatment at the hands of these religious leaders.

Eventually a trial took place before the high priest and religious elders, and those religious leaders charged Jesus with the crime of declaring Himself the Messiah. Jesus replied by telling them that they would indeed one day see Him sitting on the right hand of power and coming with clouds of glory (*see* Matthew 26:64).

Upon hearing this, the high priest ripped his clothes and screamed, *"Blasphemy!"* as all the scribes and elders lifted their voices in anger, demanding that Jesus suffer the penalty of *death* (*see* Matthew 26:66).

After that, the religious scribes and elders did the *unthinkable*!

In Matthew 26:67 and 68 we read, "Then did they spit in his face, and buffeted him; and others smote him with the palms of their hands, saying, Prophesy unto us, thou Christ, Who is he that smote thee?"

Notice the Bible says, "…*They* spit in his face…." The word "they" refers to all the scribes and elders who were assembled for the meeting that night.

One scholar notes that there could have been many men in this crowd, and one by one, each of these so-called spiritual leaders, clothed in his religious garments, walked up to Jesus and spit in His face!

In that culture and time, spitting in someone's face was considered to be the strongest thing you could do to show utter disgust, repugnance, dislike, or hatred. When someone spattered his spit on another person's face, that spit was meant to humiliate, demean, debase, and shame that person. To make it worse, the one spitting would spit hard and close to the person's face to make it more humiliating.

By the time Caiaphas and his scribes and elders had finished taking turns spitting on Jesus, their spit would have been dripping down from Jesus' forehead into His eyes, dribbling down His nose, His cheekbones, and His chin, and even oozing down onto His clothes. It was certainly an extremely disrespectful, humiliating scene!

And remember, the men who were acting so hatefully and spitefully toward Jesus were religious leaders! Their hideous conduct was something Jesus definitely didn't deserve. And what makes this entire scene even more amazing is that Malchus — the servant whom Jesus had just healed — in all probability was standing at the side of Caiaphas, watching it all happen and even participating in this horrific behavior.

But these religious leaders didn't stop with just humiliating Jesus. After spitting on Him, they each doubled up their fists, and one by one, they hit Him violently in the face! Matthew 26:67 says, "Then did they spit in his face, *and buffeted him....*"

The word "buffet" in the original text means *to strike with the fist*. It is usually used to picture a person who is *violently beaten*. As if it wasn't insulting enough to spit on Jesus, the use of this word tells us that this large number of men viciously and cruelly struck Him with their fists. Not only was this *brutal — it was sadistic!* Humiliating Jesus with their spit and curses didn't satisfy the hatred of these men,

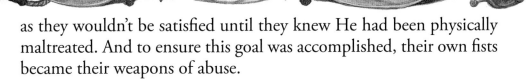

as they wouldn't be satisfied until they knew He had been physically maltreated. And to ensure this goal was accomplished, their own fists became their weapons of abuse.

Spitting on the Anointing

From this horrific display of humiliation and violence, it appears that these scribes and elders were so paranoid about Jesus getting more attention than themselves that they simply wanted to destroy Him.

Every time they spat on Jesus, they were spitting on the anointing on His life. Every time they struck Him, they were leveling a punch against the anointing. They hated Jesus and the anointing that operated through Him to such an extent that they voted to *murder* Him. But first they wanted to take some time to personally make sure He suffered before He died. What a strange way to render "thanks" to One who had done so much for them!

When you get disappointed at the way others respond to you or to what you have done for them, it would be good for you to recall what happened to Jesus on that night when He was brought before those Jewish leaders. But even though these men who spat on and hit Jesus refused to acknowledge Him, He still went to the Cross and died for *them*. His love for them was unwavering — unshaken and unaffected by their behavior.

- When you think about the way people have wronged you in the past, how does it affect your desire to love them?

- Is your love for those unkind people consistent, unwavering, unshaken, and unaffected?

- Or have conflicts revealed that you have a fickle love, which you quickly turn off when people don't respond to you the way you wished they would?

Remember that the same Holy Spirit who lived in Jesus now lives in you, and just as the Spirit of God empowered Jesus to love people consistently, regardless of what they did or didn't do, the Holy Spirit will empower you to do the same. Now it is your opportunity to walk as Jesus walked regarding those who have let you down or disappointed you in your life.

Why not take a few minutes to identify the individuals who fit this description and then *pray* for them. Forgive each person, one by one, and release them from their sin against you. Make the choice to follow your Master's example, loving those who have wronged you the way Jesus loved those who so grievously wronged Him.

But wait — there's still more that happened that night, which you need to understand.

Playing Games at Jesus' Expense

To get the full picture of what happened when the religious leaders were spitting on Jesus and striking Him in the face with their fists, we need to include the pieces of this story from the gospels of Matthew and Luke.

Luke 22:63 says, "And the *men* that held Jesus *mocked* him, and smote him."

The word "men" refers to the *guards* that held Jesus for the religious leaders. So now we find that the guards in the room also entered into the brutal treatment of Jesus. But I want you to particularly notice the word "mocked" in this verse. It comes from a Greek word that meant *to play a game*. It was often used for *playing a game with children* or for *amusing a crowd by impersonating someone in a silly and exaggerated way*.

For instance, this word could be used to depict a game of charades when someone intends to *comically portray someone or even make fun of someone*. This gives us an important piece of the story.

In addition to everything else that was going on that night, the guards in the religious court decided they, too, would take advantage of the moment. The Bible doesn't tell us how these men mimicked and impersonated Jesus, but the use of this particular Greek word categorically lets us know that these men turned a few minutes of that nightmarish night into a stage of comedy at Jesus' expense.

They put on quite a show, hamming it up, as they almost certainly pretended to be Jesus and the people He ministered to. Perhaps they laid hands on each other as if they were healing the sick; or lay on the floor "quivering," as if they were being liberated from devils; or wobbled around, acting as if they had been blind but now could suddenly see. Whatever these guards did to mock Jesus, it was a game of charades to mimic and make fun of Him.

When the guards were finished making sport of Jesus, Luke 22:63 tells us that these same guards "smote him." The word "smote" is from a Greek word used frequently to refer to *the grueling and barbaric practice of beating a slave*. This word is so dreadful that it is also often translated *to flay*, such as *to flay the flesh from an animal or human being*. The use of this word tells us that in addition to what the scribes and elders did to Jesus, the guards also put Him through a terrible ordeal.

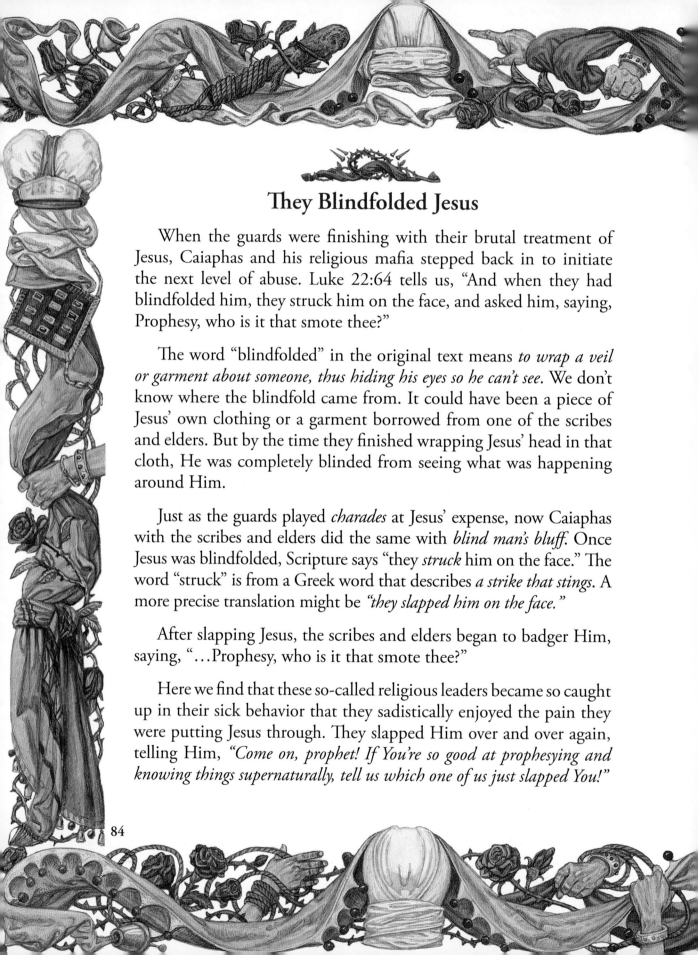

They Blindfolded Jesus

When the guards were finishing with their brutal treatment of Jesus, Caiaphas and his religious mafia stepped back in to initiate the next level of abuse. Luke 22:64 tells us, "And when they had blindfolded him, they struck him on the face, and asked him, saying, Prophesy, who is it that smote thee?"

The word "blindfolded" in the original text means *to wrap a veil or garment about someone, thus hiding his eyes so he can't see.* We don't know where the blindfold came from. It could have been a piece of Jesus' own clothing or a garment borrowed from one of the scribes and elders. But by the time they finished wrapping Jesus' head in that cloth, He was completely blinded from seeing what was happening around Him.

Just as the guards played *charades* at Jesus' expense, now Caiaphas with the scribes and elders did the same with *blind man's bluff.* Once Jesus was blindfolded, Scripture says "they *struck* him on the face." The word "struck" is from a Greek word that describes *a strike that stings.* A more precise translation might be *"they slapped him on the face."*

After slapping Jesus, the scribes and elders began to badger Him, saying, "…Prophesy, who is it that smote thee?"

Here we find that these so-called religious leaders became so caught up in their sick behavior that they sadistically enjoyed the pain they were putting Jesus through. They slapped Him over and over again, telling Him, *"Come on, prophet! If You're so good at prophesying and knowing things supernaturally, tell us which one of us just slapped You!"*

They Blasphemously Spoke to Jesus

Finally, Luke 22:65 tells us, "And many other things *blasphemously* spake they against him." The word for "blasphemy" used here means *to slander*, *to accuse*, *to speak against*, or *to speak derogatory words for the purpose of injuring or harming one's reputation*. It also signifies *profane, foul, unclean language*.

When Luke said they "blasphemously spake," he was talking about Caiaphas with his scribes and elders! Once these religious leaders "took off the lid," every foul thing that was hiding inside them came to the top. It was as if a monster had been let out, uninhibited, and they couldn't get it back in its cage!

Jesus had previously told these religious leaders, "Woe unto you, scribes and Pharisees, hypocrites! for ye are like unto whited sepulchres, which indeed appear beautiful outward, but are within full of dead men's bones, and of all uncleanness" (Matthew 23:27). In the end, the filth and uncleanness in their souls came raging to the top as they screamed and yelled at Jesus using profane, foul, unclean language.

I'm sure if the people of Israel had been allowed to peek into that room that night, they would have been shocked to see their supposedly godly leaders slapping Jesus, spitting on Him, slapping Him again, and then screaming words of profanity right in His face! Here these leaders were — all dressed up in their religious garb on the outside, but inwardly they were so rotten that they could not hide their true nature anymore.

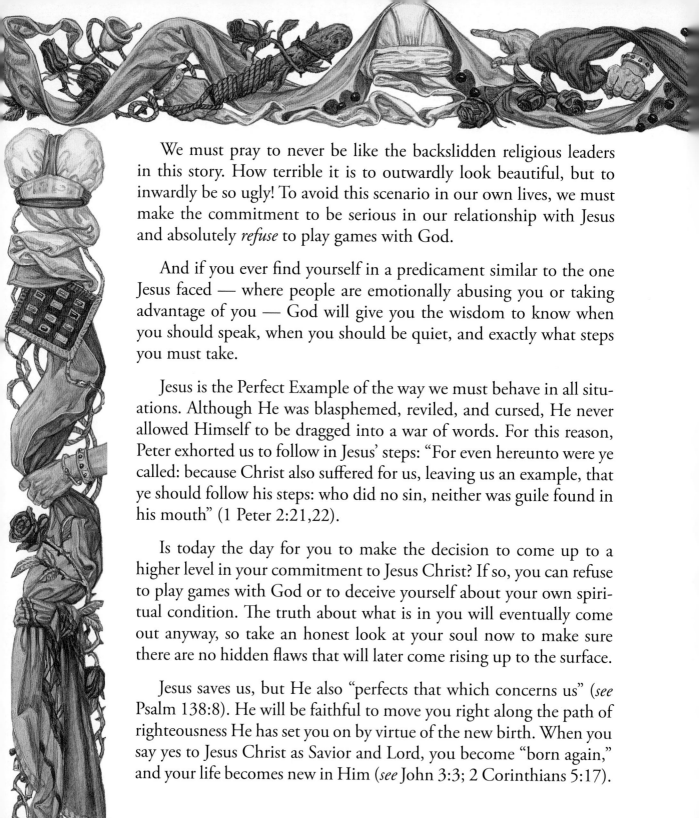

We must pray to never be like the backslidden religious leaders in this story. How terrible it is to outwardly look beautiful, but to inwardly be so ugly! To avoid this scenario in our own lives, we must make the commitment to be serious in our relationship with Jesus and absolutely *refuse* to play games with God.

And if you ever find yourself in a predicament similar to the one Jesus faced — where people are emotionally abusing you or taking advantage of you — God will give you the wisdom to know when you should speak, when you should be quiet, and exactly what steps you must take.

Jesus is the Perfect Example of the way we must behave in all situations. Although He was blasphemed, reviled, and cursed, He never allowed Himself to be dragged into a war of words. For this reason, Peter exhorted us to follow in Jesus' steps: "For even hereunto were ye called: because Christ also suffered for us, leaving us an example, that ye should follow his steps: who did no sin, neither was guile found in his mouth" (1 Peter 2:21,22).

Is today the day for you to make the decision to come up to a higher level in your commitment to Jesus Christ? If so, you can refuse to play games with God or to deceive yourself about your own spiritual condition. The truth about what is in you will eventually come out anyway, so take an honest look at your soul now to make sure there are no hidden flaws that will later come rising up to the surface.

Jesus saves us, but He also "perfects that which concerns us" (*see* Psalm 138:8). He will be faithful to move you right along the path of righteousness He has set you on by virtue of the new birth. When you say yes to Jesus Christ as Savior and Lord, you become "born again," and your life becomes new in Him (*see* John 3:3; 2 Corinthians 5:17).

But Jesus not only willingly died to save you — He ever lives and will remain faithful to you for the rest of your life.

I encourage you to open your heart, allow the Holy Spirit to shine His glorious light into every crevice and cranny of your soul, and ask Him to reveal those areas of your life where you need to yield to His cleansing work. As you do, you will find yourself becoming more and more transformed into the image of Jesus, who left you an example so you could follow in His steps.

After Jesus was treated so horrifically, He was then led to Pontius Pilate. What happened to Him next, and how Jesus responded to it, is what we will learn in the next chapter.

QUESTIONS TO PONDER AND DISCUSS

1. Imagine how Jesus felt, knowing that He was giving His life for people who not only mocked His purpose, but also wanted Him to suffer and feel humiliated even as He gave to them. What kinds of attitudes and actions do you think serve as a "spit in the face" toward another individual?

2. Disrespect and dishonor are far too easy to find in our modern society, while honor and respect are rare, yet so valuable. Jesus endured deliberate mental and emotional abuse from His enemies, in addition to the unthinkable, sadistic physical abuse they inflicted on His body. If you are in a similar predicament, call out to God! Not only will He strengthen you, but He will also give you the wisdom you need concerning the steps you must take.

3. Our flesh always wants to retaliate when we've been wronged, but Jesus gave us the perfect example to follow. When He was cursed, He refused to be dragged down to the level of His attackers. No guile was found in His mouth. How can you pattern your responses to wrong treatment to be more in line with how Jesus responds? What inward and outward adjustments can you make in your own life?

4. Jesus told the scribes and religious leaders that they were like beautiful tombs — lovely to look upon, but full of filth and uncleanness. Are there any areas of your life that look lovely to others, yet are hiding motives and behavior that are unclean?

After spitting on, striking, and mocking Jesus, Caiaphas and the religious leaders blindfolded Him and began playing a degrading game of asking Him to prophesy who among them had beaten Him. Despite all the vicious mistreatment they put Him through, Jesus still went to the Cross and died for them.

Illustrated here is Jesus when He was brought before Pontius Pilate, the Roman procurator or governor of Israel. Pilate interrogated Jesus and listened to the accusations of the religious leaders while Jesus remained silent. At the end of the interrogation, Pilate asked Jesus, "Art thou the King of the Jews?" And Jesus responded, "Thou sayest it" (Luke 23:3).

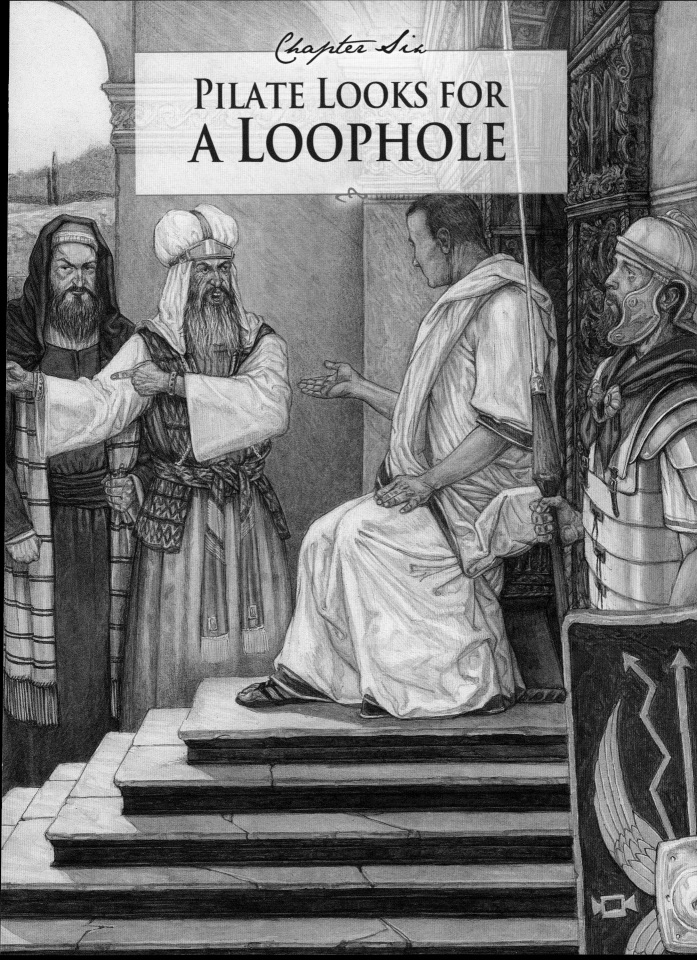

Chapter Six

PILATE LOOKS FOR A LOOPHOLE

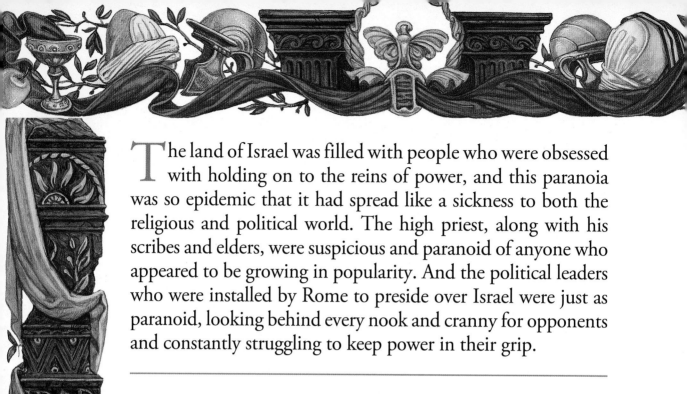

The land of Israel was filled with people who were obsessed with holding on to the reins of power, and this paranoia was so epidemic that it had spread like a sickness to both the religious and political world. The high priest, along with his scribes and elders, were suspicious and paranoid of anyone who appeared to be growing in popularity. And the political leaders who were installed by Rome to preside over Israel were just as paranoid, looking behind every nook and cranny for opponents and constantly struggling to keep power in their grip.

Israel was under the enemy control of Rome, an occupying force that the Jews despised. They hated the Romans for their pagan tendencies and for pushing the Roman language and culture on them, and they also hated the taxes they were required to pay to Rome. That's only a few of the reasons the Jews despised the Romans and their rule over them.[1]

Because of the political turmoil in Israel, very few political leaders from Rome held power for long, and those who succeeded remaining in power a long time did it by using cruelty and brutality. The land of Israel was full of revolts, rebellions, insurgencies, assassinations, and endless political upheavals. The ability to rule long in this environment required a ruthless, self-concerned leader who was willing to do anything necessary to maintain a position of power.

This leads us to *Pontius Pilate*, who was just that type of man.

Pilate remarkably ruled as governor for ten years. He was the Roman ruler who finally gave the order for Jesus' scourging and crucifixion.

Although Pilate was governor of Israel, the fact is that he loathed the Jewish religious atmosphere of Jerusalem. For that reason, most of the time, he stayed at a lavish palace built by King Herod that was situated on the shores of the Mediterranean Sea at Caesarea Maritima. However, during religious feasts, he traveled to Jerusalem with specially trained military forces and stayed there to help maintain calm and order in the city. When Pilate was in Jerusalem, he stayed at his palace in the city, which plays importantly into the story of Jesus' crucifixion.

But let's see what else we can learn about Pontius Pilate.

Who Was Pontius Pilate?

After one of King Herod the Great's sons named Herod Archelaus was removed from power, the territory of Judea was placed into the care of a Roman procurator. This was a natural course of events, because the Roman Empire was already divided into approximately 40 provinces, which were each governed by a *procurator* — a position that was the equivalent of a *governor*.

It was normal for a procurator in most provinces to serve in his position for 12 to 36 months. However, Pilate governed Judea for *ten years*, beginning in the year 26 AD and concluding in the year 36 AD. This ten-year span of time is critical, for it tells us Pilate was governor of Judea throughout the entire length of Jesus' ministry. The Jewish historian, Flavius Josephus, noted that Pilate was ruthless and unsympathetic and that he failed to comprehend and appreciate how important the Jews' religious beliefs and convictions were to them.

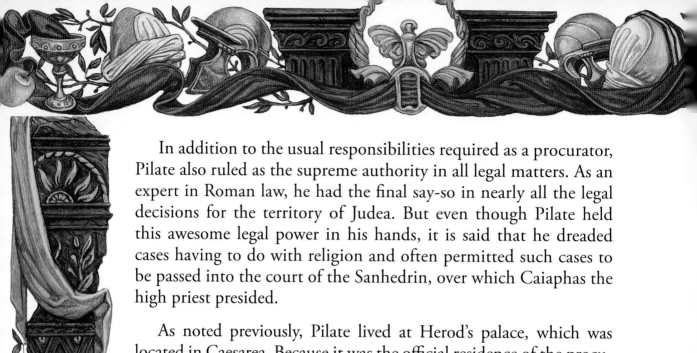

In addition to the usual responsibilities required as a procurator, Pilate also ruled as the supreme authority in all legal matters. As an expert in Roman law, he had the final say-so in nearly all the legal decisions for the territory of Judea. But even though Pilate held this awesome legal power in his hands, it is said that he dreaded cases having to do with religion and often permitted such cases to be passed into the court of the Sanhedrin, over which Caiaphas the high priest presided.

As noted previously, Pilate lived at Herod's palace, which was located in Caesarea. Because it was the official residence of the procurator, a military force of about 3,000 Roman soldiers was stationed there to protect the Roman governor. Pilate so disliked the city of Jerusalem that he recoiled from making visits there — but, as stated, at the time of feasts when the city of Jerusalem was filled with guests, travelers, and strangers, there was a greater potential of unrest, turbulence, and disorder, so Pilate and his troops would go into the city of Jerusalem to guard and protect the peace of the population. This is the reason Pilate was in the city of Jerusalem at the time of Jesus' crucifixion.

As a highly political man, Pilate knew how to play the political game, but the Jewish leadership in Jerusalem also learned how to play political games. At one point, so many complaints had been filed in Rome about Pilate's unkind and ruthless style of ruling that the threat of an additional complaint was all that was needed for the Jews to manipulate Pilate to do their bidding. Although Pilate despised intermeddling in Jewish religious affairs, in the end, this political predicament no doubt affected his decision to crucify Jesus.

But on the day the high priest, the Sanhedrin, and the entire mob insisted that Jesus be crucified, Pilate wanted to know the reason for

this demand, so they answered him, "…We found this fellow perverting the nation, and forbidding to give tribute to Caesar, saying that he himself is Christ a King" (Luke 23:2).

The Jewish Leaders' Motivation: They Were Jealous of Jesus and Despised Pilate for His Cruelty

Of course, Pilate knew that the Jews were jealous of Jesus, but politically, the charges they brought against the Lord put Pilate in a very bad position. What if the news reached Rome that Jesus had perverted the nation, teaching the people to withhold their taxes, and that He had claimed to be a counter-king in place of the Roman emperor?

It would be political suicide for Pilate to do nothing about that kind of situation. The Jewish leaders were well aware of this when they fabricated these charges against Jesus. They knew exactly what political strings to pull to get Pilate to do what they wanted — and they were pulling every string they held in their hands.

The Jewish people despised Pilate for his cruelty and inadequate care of his subjects. The kind of brutality that made him so infamous and hated can be seen in Luke 13:1, where Scripture mentions that Pilate slaughtered a number of Galileans and then mixed their blood together with the sacrifices. As appalling and sick as this may sound, it was on par with many other vicious actions instigated under Pilate's rule as procurator of Judea.

Another example of Pilate's callousness can be seen in an incident that occurred when a prophet claimed to possess a supernatural gift

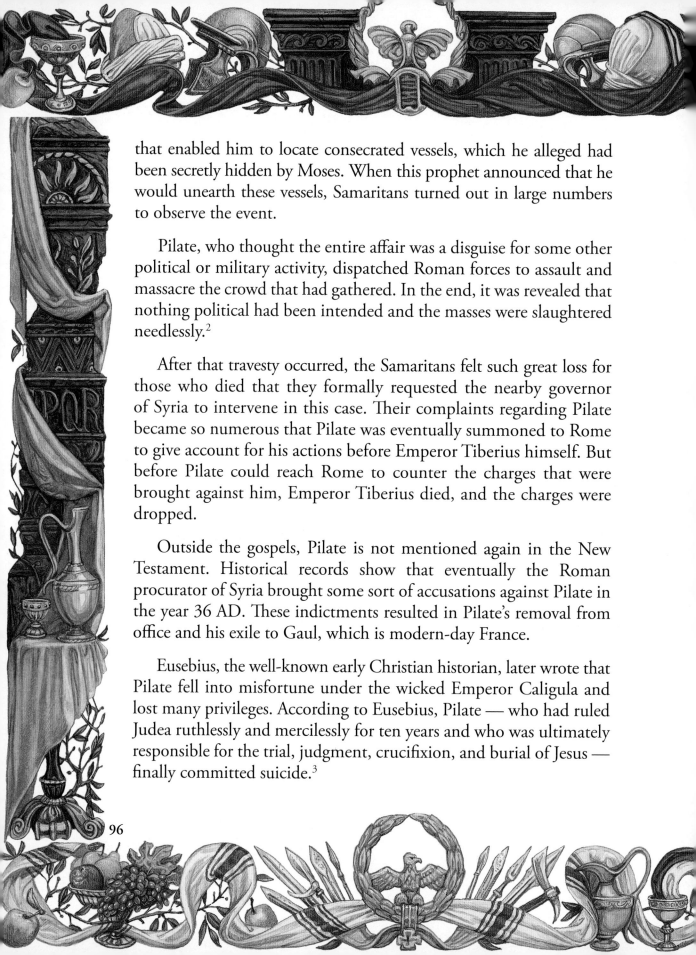

that enabled him to locate consecrated vessels, which he alleged had been secretly hidden by Moses. When this prophet announced that he would unearth these vessels, Samaritans turned out in large numbers to observe the event.

Pilate, who thought the entire affair was a disguise for some other political or military activity, dispatched Roman forces to assault and massacre the crowd that had gathered. In the end, it was revealed that nothing political had been intended and the masses were slaughtered needlessly.[2]

After that travesty occurred, the Samaritans felt such great loss for those who died that they formally requested the nearby governor of Syria to intervene in this case. Their complaints regarding Pilate became so numerous that Pilate was eventually summoned to Rome to give account for his actions before Emperor Tiberius himself. But before Pilate could reach Rome to counter the charges that were brought against him, Emperor Tiberius died, and the charges were dropped.

Outside the gospels, Pilate is not mentioned again in the New Testament. Historical records show that eventually the Roman procurator of Syria brought some sort of accusations against Pilate in the year 36 AD. These indictments resulted in Pilate's removal from office and his exile to Gaul, which is modern-day France.

Eusebius, the well-known early Christian historian, later wrote that Pilate fell into misfortune under the wicked Emperor Caligula and lost many privileges. According to Eusebius, Pilate — who had ruled Judea ruthlessly and mercilessly for ten years and who was ultimately responsible for the trial, judgment, crucifixion, and burial of Jesus — finally committed suicide.[3]

Jesus Was Literally Led Like a Lamb to the Slaughter

With this history of Pilate behind us, let's look at Matthew 27:2, which says, "And when they had *bound* him, they *led him away*, and delivered him to Pontius Pilate the governor." The word "bound" is a Greek word that describes *the binding, tying up, or securing of an animal*.

We can be confident that "a lamb led to the slaughter" was precisely the image Matthew had in mind, because the next phrase in verse 2 uses a word that was common in the world of animal caretakers. It says they "led him away." These words in the original text depict *a shepherd who ties a rope around the neck of his sheep and then leads it down the path to where it needs to go*. Just as the soldiers had led Jesus to Caiaphas, now they similarly slipped a rope about His neck and walked the Lamb of God to the residence of Pontius Pilate in Jerusalem.

This again reminds us of Isaiah 53:7 that prophesied this moment in Jesus' life. It says, "He was oppressed, and he was afflicted, yet he opened not his mouth: he is brought as a lamb to the slaughter, and as a sheep before her shearers is dumb, so he openeth not his mouth."

Jesus' Interrogation Before Pontius Pilate

Once Jesus was in Pilate's jurisdiction, the Bible tells us that they "…delivered him to Pontius Pilate the governor" (*see* Matthew 27:2).

This means that when the high priest ordered Jesus to be "delivered" to Pilate, he officially made Jesus a problem for Pilate to handle. In that moment, the high priest took Jesus to Pilate, delivered Him fully into Pilate's hands, and then left Pilate with the responsibility of finding Him guilty and crucifying Him.

Matthew 27:11 says, "And Jesus stood before the governor: and the governor asked him, saying, Art thou the King of the Jews? And Jesus said unto him, Thou sayest." Pilate asked a direct question, but Jesus refused to directly answer him.

Matthew 27:12 goes on to say, "And when he was accused of the chief priests and elders, he answered nothing." So for a second time, Jesus refused to answer or refute the charges that were brought up against Him.

Matthew 27:13,14 tells us, "Then said Pilate unto him, Hearest thou not how many things they witness against thee? And he answered him to never a word; insomuch that the governor marvelled greatly."

Notice that the Bible says Pilate "marveled greatly" at Jesus' silence. In Greek, this phrase is a word that means *to wonder, to be at a loss of words*, or *to be shocked and amazed*. But why did Jesus' silence leave such an impression on Pilate?

Three Legal Chances To Answer

The reason Pilate was dumbfounded by Jesus' silence is that Roman law permitted prisoners three chances to open their mouths to defend themselves. If a prisoner passed up those three chances to speak in his own defense, he would be automatically charged as "guilty."

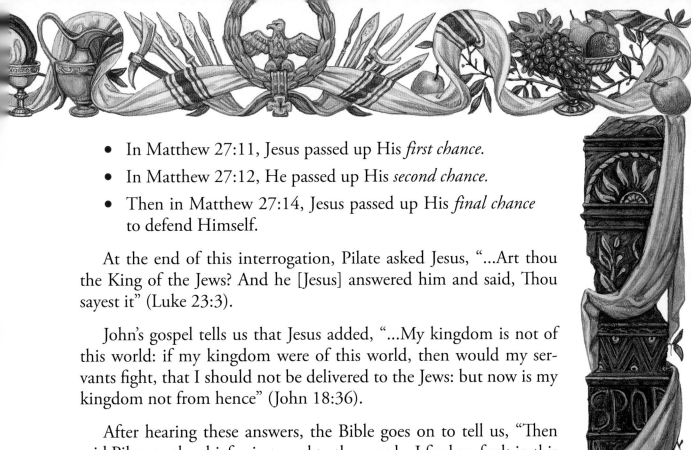

- In Matthew 27:11, Jesus passed up His *first chance.*
- In Matthew 27:12, He passed up His *second chance.*
- Then in Matthew 27:14, Jesus passed up His *final chance* to defend Himself.

At the end of this interrogation, Pilate asked Jesus, "...Art thou the King of the Jews? And he [Jesus] answered him and said, Thou sayest it" (Luke 23:3).

John's gospel tells us that Jesus added, "...My kingdom is not of this world: if my kingdom were of this world, then would my servants fight, that I should not be delivered to the Jews: but now is my kingdom not from hence" (John 18:36).

After hearing these answers, the Bible goes on to tell us, "Then said Pilate to the chief priests and to the people, I find no fault in this man" (Luke 23:4). The word "fault" in the original language means *no causable, legal reason to take action against him*, which tells us Pilate could not find any legal reason to execute Jesus.

Pilate Looks for a Loophole!

And because Pilate could find no reason to execute Jesus, he searched diligently for a legal loophole so he wouldn't have to kill Him. That is why John 19:12 tells us, "And from thenceforth Pilate sought to release him...."

But nothing Pilate could do was able to stop the Father's plan from being implemented. Even Jesus passed up His three chances to defend Himself because He knew that the Cross was a part of His

purpose in being sent to Earth. When Jesus finally answered Pilate's question, He didn't defend Himself because He knew it was the appointed time for Him to be slain as the Lamb of God who would take away the sins of the world (*see* John 1:29).

The fact is, Pilate didn't want to crucify Jesus, so the Roman governor began looking for a loophole — for some way to escape putting this Man to death.

Pilate had never had a problem causing bloodshed in the past, so it is unusual that he balked at the thought of crucifying Jesus. As governor and the chief legal authority of the land, Pilate had been vested by Rome with the power to decide who would live or die. And remember that this Roman governor was infamous for his cold-hearted, insensitive, and cruel style of leadership and had never found it difficult to order the death of a criminal — *until now*.

There was something inside Pilate that recoiled at the idea of crucifying Jesus. The Bible doesn't state exactly why Pilate didn't want to crucify Him, but it makes one wonder if perhaps he saw something in Jesus' eyes while he interrogated Him. We know from Scripture that Pilate's wife had a dream about Jesus and urged Pilate not to hurt him (*see* Matthew 27:19). Whether Pilate was affected by his wife's dream — or he was simply amazed at the manner in which Jesus carried Himself — Matthew 27:14 nevertheless tells us that Pilate "marveled greatly" at Jesus.

Again, the words "marveled greatly" are from a Greek word that means *to wonder, to be at a loss of words*, or *to be shocked and amazed*. Never before had a man like Jesus stood before Pilate, and the governor was obviously disturbed at the thought of murdering Him. Pilate was *so* disturbed, in fact, that he decided to probe deeper by asking questions. He was looking for a loophole that would enable him to escape this trap the Jews had set both for Jesus and for himself as well.

The Religious Leaders in Jerusalem
Devised a Scheme To Get Rid of Either Jesus or Pilate

The crooked Jewish religious vipers in Jerusalem had carefully schemed a fool-proof trap with three potential results, any of which would have made them very happy. The three-fold purpose of this trap was as follows:

1. **To see Jesus judged by the Roman court, thus ruining His reputation and guaranteeing His crucifixion, while at the same time vindicating themselves in the eyes of the people.**

To ensure that this happened, the Jewish leaders falsified charges that made Jesus appear to be a bona fide political offender. The charges were that:

- Jesus had perverted the whole nation — a religious charge that was the responsibility of the Sanhedrin to judge.
- Jesus had commanded people not to pay their taxes to Rome.
- Jesus claimed to be the King of the Jews (*see* Luke 23:3).

According to Roman law, Jesus absolutely should have been crucified for claiming to be a king. And if these charges were proven to be true, Pilate was bound by law to crucify Him. If that was what followed, the first purpose of their scheme would have worked and they would have gotten rid of Jesus.

2. To see Pilate removed from power on the charge that he was unfaithful to the Roman emperor because he would not crucify a man who claimed to be a rival king to the emperor.

The Jewish leadership claimed that Jesus purported to be a rival king to the Roman emperor. If Pilate had declined to crucify Jesus, this would have given the Jewish leaders the ammunition they needed to prove to Rome that Pilate should be removed from power because he was a traitor to the emperor. News would have soon reached the emperor of Rome that Pilate permitted a rival king to live, and it is certain that Pilate would have been charged with treason (*see* John 19:12).

This charge most assuredly would have led to Pilate's removal and death or banishment. If Jesus had been freed by Pilate, the Jewish leadership would have been thrilled, for then they would have had a legal reason to see Pilate removed and expelled from their land. Thus, even if Pilate did not execute Jesus, they would at least get rid of Pilate!

3. If Pilate would not crucify Him, they intended to take Jesus back into their own court in the Sanhedrin, where they had the religious authority to stone Him to death for claiming to be the Son of God.

The truth is that the Jewish leaders never needed to deliver Jesus to Pilate, because the court of the Sanhedrin already had the religious authority to kill Jesus by stoning for claiming to be the Son of God. Even if Pilate refused to crucify Jesus, they fully intended to kill Him, anyway (*see* John 19:7). Jews had the right to stone an offender to death, but they did not possess the legal authority to carry out a horrific Roman-style crucifixion — which is what they desired for Jesus — so they shifted this responsibility to Pilate.

So we see that the trip to Pilate's court was designed to turn Jesus' arrest into a political catastrophe so terrible that it would *possibly* help the Jewish leaders get rid of Pilate as well. But if Jesus had been freed by the Roman court, they nevertheless intended to kill Him, anyway.

The solution to this ugly mess was easy! If Pilate gave the order to crucify Jesus, he would have happy Jewish elders on his hands, no charges of treason leveled against him in Rome, strengthened ties to the religious community, and a guarantee of remaining in power. All Pilate would have had to do would be to simply say, "CRUCIFY HIM!" and this political game would be over. But for some reason, this harsh, brutal, power-grabbing Roman governor couldn't bring himself to utter those words!

Instead, as we have seen, Pilate gave Jesus three opportunities to speak up in His own defense. But Jesus said nothing. Isaiah 53:7 confirms that He "opened not his mouth" in his own defense.

So according to Roman law, Jesus should have *automatically* been declared "guilty" because He passed up His three chances to defend Himself, but Pilate simply could not permit himself to follow the due course of judicial process. Instead, he sought to find a way out of this dilemma. As noted before, perhaps Pilate saw something in Jesus' eyes that affected him. Or maybe Jesus' kind and gracious behavior tugged at Pilate's heart.

Some have speculated that Pilate's wife may have secretly been a follower of Jesus who told her husband about His goodness and about the miracles that followed His life. Matthew 27:19 reports that Pilate's wife was so upset about Jesus' impending death that she even had upsetting dreams about Him in the night, and she sent word about her dreams to Pilate and begged him not to crucify Jesus.

Hooray! A Way Out of This Dilemma — or So It Seemed

As Pilate probed deeper in his interrogation of Jesus, he suddenly discovered that Jesus was from Galilee!

At long last, Pilate could breathe a sigh of relief. He'd found a loophole that shifted the full weight of the decision to his old enemy — *Herod Antipas!* Galilee was under the legal jurisdiction of Herod. *What a coincidence!* And Herod just "happened" to be in Jerusalem that week to participate in the Feast of Passover!

Upon discovering that Jesus was from Galilee, Pilate promptly ordered Jesus to be transferred to the other side of Jerusalem to the residence where Herod was staying with his royal entourage.

The Bible tells us, "And when Herod saw Jesus, he was exceeding glad: for he was desirous to see him of a long season, because he had heard many things of him; and he hoped to have seen some miracle done by him" (Luke 23:8). However, it didn't take long before Herod lost his temper with Jesus and sent Him back to Pilate!

Can you imagine? Jesus first stood before a Roman governor, then before a Jewish tetrarch — only to be shipped back to the Roman governor all over again?

If you have ever — or are right now — being knocked around and passed from one authority figure to another at home, at church, in the workplace, or in the governmental system, you can talk to Jesus about it, because He really understands the predicament you find yourself

in right now. Hebrews 4:15 and 16 says, "For we have not an high priest which cannot be touched with the feelings of our infirmities; but was in all points tempted like as we are, yet without sin. Let us therefore come boldly unto the throne of grace, that we may obtain mercy, and find grace to help in time of need."

Jesus completely understands such a dilemma, and you can speak freely to Him about the emotional ups and downs you feel as a result of your situation. His throne is a throne of grace — a place where you can obtain mercy and find grace to help in your time of need.

In the next chapter, we'll see the shocking details about what happened to Jesus when he appeared for a brief period before Herod Antipas at his palace in Jerusalem.

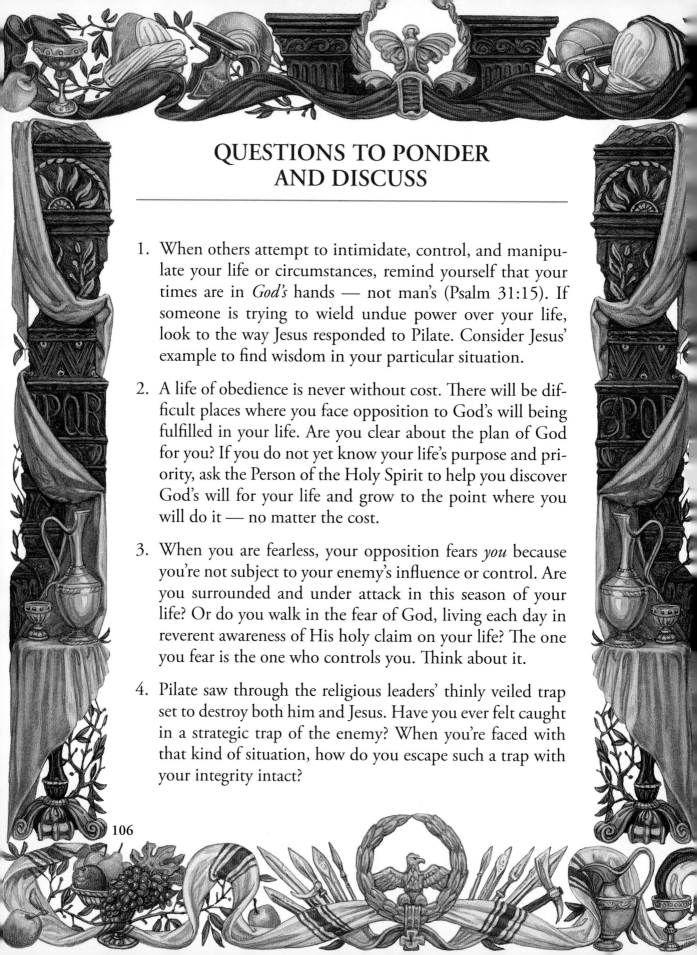

QUESTIONS TO PONDER
AND DISCUSS

1. When others attempt to intimidate, control, and manipulate your life or circumstances, remind yourself that your times are in *God's* hands — not man's (Psalm 31:15). If someone is trying to wield undue power over your life, look to the way Jesus responded to Pilate. Consider Jesus' example to find wisdom in your particular situation.

2. A life of obedience is never without cost. There will be difficult places where you face opposition to God's will being fulfilled in your life. Are you clear about the plan of God for you? If you do not yet know your life's purpose and priority, ask the Person of the Holy Spirit to help you discover God's will for your life and grow to the point where you will do it — no matter the cost.

3. When you are fearless, your opposition fears *you* because you're not subject to your enemy's influence or control. Are you surrounded and under attack in this season of your life? Or do you walk in the fear of God, living each day in reverent awareness of His holy claim on your life? The one you fear is the one who controls you. Think about it.

4. Pilate saw through the religious leaders' thinly veiled trap set to destroy both him and Jesus. Have you ever felt caught in a strategic trap of the enemy? When you're faced with that kind of situation, how do you escape such a trap with your integrity intact?

After Pontius Pilate heard Jesus' answers to his questions, Pilate could find no legal reason to execute Him. Despite being a cruel and harsh leader, Pilate didn't want to crucify Jesus — something inside him balked at the thought of it. So he began to search for a loophole to release Him and eventually sent Jesus to Herod.

Herod Antipas was ecstatic to finally meet Jesus. Luke 23:8 tells us he was "exceeding glad" because he had desired to meet Jesus for a long time and hoped to see a miracle done by Him. But when Jesus refused, Herod unleashed his rage against Him and instructed his soldiers to mock and abuse Him with the greatest cruelty, which we see pictured here.

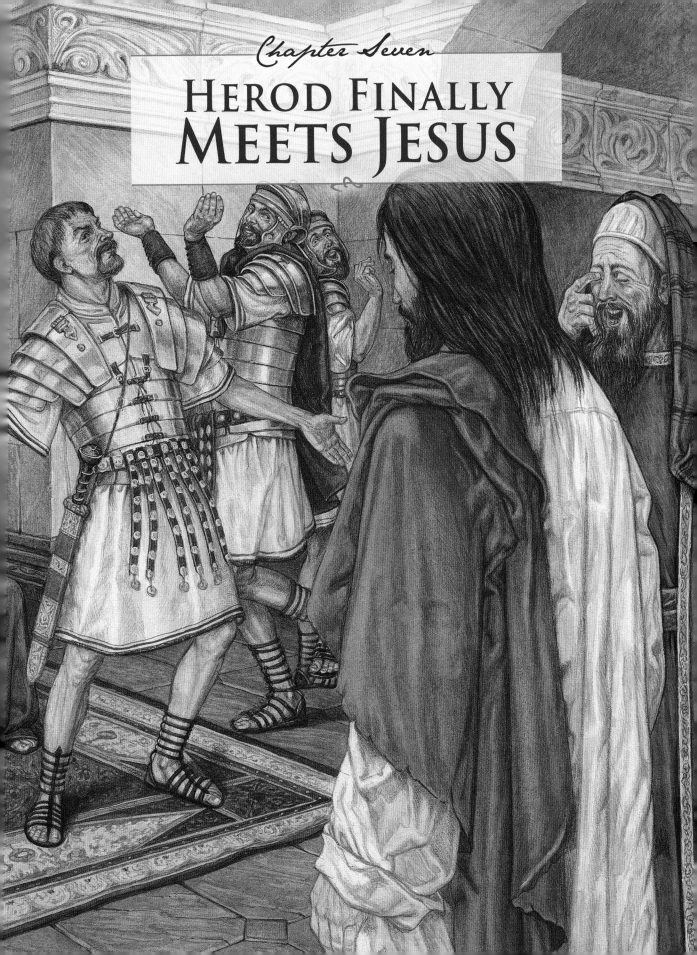

Chapter Seven

HEROD FINALLY
MEETS JESUS

Today when visitors come to the Old City of Jerusalem, often they enter through a gate near what is referred to as the Tower of David — a tower built directly above the ruins of King Herod's massive palace in Jerusalem. The lower parts of the so-called Tower of David are constructed of original stones from Herod's palace in Jerusalem. Today only the ruins remain, but at the time of Jesus trial, Herod's palace was a massive fortress complex with towers that stood ubiquitously along the western city wall in Jerusalem. Herod Antipas, one of the sons of King Herod, was staying at that palace during the time of Jesus' trial because he had come from Galilee to Jerusalem to celebrate the Passover with the Jewish people.

As we have seen, when Pilate discovered Jesus was from Galilee, which fell under the jurisdiction of Herod, he saw it as his legal loophole to make Jesus someone else's problem. Pilate quickly sent Jesus off to see Herod on the other side of the city, and because Herod was there to celebrate the Feast of Passover, it made transferring Jesus to Herod very easy. Herod was thrilled to finally meet Jesus face to face, but before we get into why Herod was so excited to meet Jesus, let's first take a closer look at *which Herod* Luke 23:8 is talking about.

You see, in history there were several men named Herod who ruled Israel. The first and most famous was "Herod the Great," who was made the first governor of Galilee when he was 25 years old. His kingship was launched by the order of Octavius and Marc Antony — and, as we've seen, he was the same Marc Antony who was famously in a relationship with Cleopatra the Queen of Egypt. Flavius Josephus, the well-known Jewish historian, recorded that Herod the Great died

110

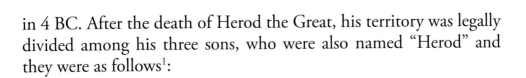

in 4 BC. After the death of Herod the Great, his territory was legally divided among his three sons, who were also named "Herod" and they were as follows[1]:

HEROD ARCHELAUS

Herod Archelaus was made governor of Samaria, Judea, and Idumea in 4 BC when his father died, and he ruled until approximately 6 AD. This makes him the Herod who was ruling when Mary, Joseph, and Jesus returned from their flight to Egypt (*see* Matthew 2:22).

When Herod Archelaus ascended to the throne in 4 BC, things almost immediately went sour for him. The first problem he confronted was a rebellion incited among Jewish students by their teachers. Because the Ten Commandments forbade graven images, these teachers encouraged their students to tear down and destroy the imperial golden eagle that Rome had ordered to be hung on the entrance to the Temple.

As punishment, Herod Archelaus ordered these teachers and students to be burned alive. The massacre continued until 3,000 Jews had been slaughtered during the Feast of Passover. Soon afterward, Herod Archelaus journeyed to Rome where he was crowned by the Emperor Augustus. But fresh riots ensued in his absence, resulting in more than 2,000 people being crucified by this treacherous ruler.

The gospel of Matthew tells us that Joseph and Mary were troubled about settling in the territories ruled by Herod Archelaus and that is why they made their home in Galilee after they returned from Egypt (*see* Matthew 2:22). Herod Archelaus was so despised that the Jews and Samaritans, who were usually foes, united together and corporately appealed to Rome to request that he be removed from power. In 6 AD, Herod Archelaus was banished to Gaul, which is modern-day France, and he died before the year 18 AD.

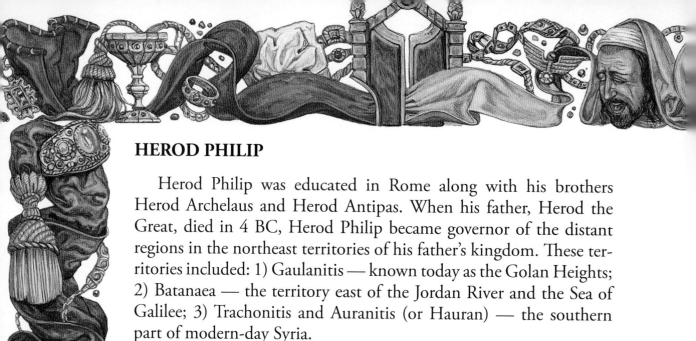

HEROD PHILIP

Herod Philip was educated in Rome along with his brothers Herod Archelaus and Herod Antipas. When his father, Herod the Great, died in 4 BC, Herod Philip became governor of the distant regions in the northeast territories of his father's kingdom. These territories included: 1) Gaulanitis — known today as the Golan Heights; 2) Batanaea — the territory east of the Jordan River and the Sea of Galilee; 3) Trachonitis and Auranitis (or Hauran) — the southern part of modern-day Syria.

The Jews were a minority among Herod Philip's subjects. Most people under his rule were of Syrian or Arabian ancestry, but he had Greek and Roman subjects as well, usually living in the cities. Herod Philip died in the year 34 AD after having ruled his kingdom for 37 years. Since he left no heir, the Roman Emperor Tiberius directed his territories to be added to the region of Syria.

Flavius Josephus wrote that Herod Philip was moderate and quiet in the conduct of his life and government.[2] And when Tiberius died in 37 AD, his successor, Emperor Caligula, restored the principality almost in its entirety and appointed Herod Philip's nephew, Herod Agrippa, as the new ruler.

HEROD ANTIPAS

We finally come to the third son of Herod the Great — *Herod Antipas*, the same Herod before whom Jesus appeared in Luke 23:8 and who had long desired to personally meet Jesus.

What do we know of this Herod? Herod Antipas was assigned tetrarch of Galilee and Peraea (a territory located on the east bank of the Jordan River). The Roman Emperor Augustus affirmed this decision, and the reign of Herod Antipas began in the year 4 BC when his father died.

112

The name "Antipas" is a compound of two Greek words, *anti* and *pas*. The word *anti* means *against*, and the word *pas* means *all* or *everyone*. Once compounded into one word, it means *one who is against everything and everyone*. This name alone should tell us something about the personality of this demented and wicked ruler.

In the year 17 AD, Herod Antipas founded the city of Tiberias — a new capital he built on the shores of the Sea of Galilee to honor the Roman Emperor Tiberius. But when his Jewish subjects discovered the new city was being built on top of an old Jewish graveyard, it caused an enormous disturbance. Because these ancient graves were desecrated in the building process, devout Jews refused to even enter the city of Tiberias for a very long time.

Herod Antipas tried to style himself in a way that would appeal to the Jewish people, even participating in national Jewish celebrations — but people were not convinced by this act and viewed him as an insincere fraud.

Even Jesus compared Herod Antipas to a *fox* — an animal that was considered to be the epitome of *trickery* and that was usually *unclean* and *infected with sickness*. So when Jesus called Herod a fox, it was the equivalent of saying Herod was a sneaky, lying, deceiving, dishonest, infected, and sick individual.

Herod Antipas' first marriage was to the daughter of an Arabian leader, but he divorced her so he could marry the ex-wife of his half-brother, a woman named *Herodias*. Taking the ex-wife of one's brother was not uncommon, but Herodias was also the daughter of Herod's other half-brother, Aristobulus, making her his niece.

In Roman law, marriage to one's niece was permitted, but marriage to a woman who was both one's sister-in-law and one's niece was most

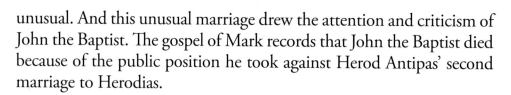

unusual. And this unusual marriage drew the attention and criticism of John the Baptist. The gospel of Mark records that John the Baptist died because of the public position he took against Herod Antipas' second marriage to Herodias.

Later, in the year 37 AD, Herodias (Herod Antipas' new wife) disagreed when her brother Herod Agrippa became king in place of Herod Philip. She thought that the royal title should not be given to Herod Agrippa but to her husband, and she made plans accordingly for Herod Antipas to be appointed king. Because the Roman emperor adamantly disagreed with Herodias, the emperor exiled both her and her husband to live the rest of their lives in Gaul, which again was located in what is today modern-day France.

Herod Was Jubilant To Meet Jesus

But in Herod Antipas' earlier reign, Luke 23:8 tells us that he was jubilant to finally meet Jesus. It says, "And when Herod saw Jesus, he was exceeding glad: for he was desirous to see him of a long season, because he had heard many things of him; and he hoped to have seen some miracle done by him." Notice the verse says, "And when Herod *saw* Jesus…." The word "saw" is from a word that means *to see, to behold, to delightfully view, to look with scrutiny,* or *to look with the intent to examine.*

This word paints a very important picture for us of exactly what happened when Jesus finally stood before Herod Antipas. It conveys the idea that Herod was *excited* and *delighted* to finally behold the miracle-worker he had heard so much about. Once Jesus stood before him, Herod literally *looked Him over, scrutinizing and examining every detail* of the Man who appeared before him.

The next part of Luke 23:8 confirms the exhilaration and jubilation Herod Antipas felt about seeing Jesus. It says "he was *exceeding glad*." In Greek, these words mean *much, great,* or *exceedingly* and suggest *extreme excitement*, depicting someone who is *ecstatic* about something. In other words, Herod Antipas was so "hyper" about having the chance to meet Jesus that he was nearly jumping up and down on the inside!

This should tell us how well-known Jesus had become during His ministry. Since even Herod Antipas was this excited to meet Him, it's no wonder that the scribes and elders were apprehensive about Jesus' widespread popularity. You see, even nobility longed for a chance to see Jesus and to experience His miracles! But the next part of Luke 23:8 importantly says that "…he [Herod Antipas] was desirous to see him of a long season, because he had heard many things of him…." The word "desirous" in the original text means *to will* or *to wish*. However, the construction used in this Greek phrase intensifies the *wish*, making it *a very strong wish or desire*. According to this verse, Herod had this strong desire for "a long season" — a phrase in Greek that could be translated *for many years*, *for a long time*, or *for many seasons*.

The Story of Jesus Was Legendary in the Herod Family

Why had Herod Antipas longed to see Jesus for so many years? Verse 8 says, "…Because he had heard many things of him…."

Actually, Jesus was a name the Herod household had heard for years!

I'm sure all three Herod boys — *Archelaus*, *Philip*, and *Antipas* — heard tales about:

1. Jesus' supernatural birth.

2. The Magi from the East who had come to acknowledge and worship Him. (I write extensively about the Magi in my book *Christmas — The Rest of the Story*.)

3. The attempt of their father, Herod the Great, to kill Jesus by ordering all the babies in Bethlehem to be murdered.

4. Jesus and His parents slipping into Egypt and waiting for the right moment to come back into Israel.

5. The ministry of Jesus that was touching the nation with healing and delivering power.

Stories of Jesus must have been very familiar to the Herod household. In fact, the Bible tells us that Herod Antipas had longed for a chance to meet this famous personality for many years. Jesus was a living legend, and now He was standing in Herod Antipas' presence!

Herod Longed To See Jesus Perform a Miracle

At the end of Luke 23:8, we read the reason that Herod Antipas was most excited to meet Jesus. The verse continues, saying, "…He hoped to have seen some miracle done by him."

The Greek word for "hoped" means *to hope*, but the construction used in this verse means *to wish*. Just as Herod's *wish* to see Jesus was *a very strong wish*, now his *hope* was to see some miracle performed by Jesus — and it was *a very strong hope* or *an earnest expectation*.

Herod Antipas was really wishing to "...*have seen* some miracle done by him." The word "seen" is the same word used in the first part of this verse when we are told that Herod was *excited to see* Jesus. Now this word is used to let us know Herod was *euphoric* about his chance to see some "miracle" done by Jesus.

The word "miracle" denotes *a sign, a mark, or a token that verifies or authenticates an alleged report*. It is used in the gospels primarily to depict *miracles and supernatural events*, which means the purpose of such miracles and supernatural events is *to verify and authenticate* the message of the Gospel. Jesus was known for performing miracles, which Herod had heard so much about, and now this ruler wanted to personally see a miracle performed by Jesus!

Herod and the Religious Leaders Accused Jesus of Being a Fraud

But Luke 23:9 tells us that Jesus didn't work miracles on-demand for Herod, nor did He answer the numerous questions Herod put to Him that day. Verse 10 tells us that as a result of Jesus' silence, "...The chief priests and scribes stood and vehemently accused him."

Wait...this verse says that the chief priests and scribes were there, which means they followed Jesus from Pilate's palace to Herod's residence! When Jesus performed no miracle for Herod, the scribes and elders, most of whom belonged to the sect of the Sadducees who didn't believe in the supernatural, seized the moment to start screaming and yelling uncontrollably.

The word "vehemently" in the original text means *at full pitch*, *at full volume*, *strenuously*, or *vigorously*. In other words, these religious leaders weren't just slightly raising their voices; they were what we might call "screaming their heads off"! Most likely they were screaming accusations right in Jesus' face, saying things like, *"Some miracle worker You are! You have no power! You're a fraud! If You can work miracles, why don't You work one right now! You're nothing but a charlatan!"*

Because Jesus didn't perform "on demand" as Herod insisted, this governor's expectations were dashed, and it caused him to unleash his rage against Jesus. In the short time that followed, Jesus took the full brunt of this wicked ruler's wrath. Yet in the midst of all the abuse Jesus suffered, He again remained quiet and held Himself calm.

- Have you ever been in situations when you've been railed at because you failed to meet someone's demands?

- Did you yell and scream back when that person vented his or her anger at you?

- Or were you able to remain quiet and controlled like Jesus did that day as He stood before Herod Antipas and the chief priests and elders?

Life occasionally takes us through difficult places — such as times when you discover that people are disappointed with your performance, even at no fault of your own. If you find yourself in this kind of predicament, remember that Jesus failed to meet the expectations of Herod Antipas (although that was probably the *only* person whose expectations Jesus ever failed to meet). If you find yourself in such a situation, I encourage you to hide yourself away for a few minutes and call out to the Lord. He has been there, He understands, and He will help you know how to respond according to His wisdom.

Herod Mocked the King of Kings and Lord of Lords

Once the screaming stopped and the volume of the men's voices had lowered enough for Herod's voice to be heard, Herod gave the official order for his "men of war" to begin humiliating, mocking, making fun of, and heckling Jesus. Suddenly the men in Herod's residence turned into a booing, hissing, mocking, laughing mob with all their venom directed toward Jesus. Luke 23:11 tells us about this event, "And Herod with his men of war set him at nought, and mocked him, and arrayed him in a gorgeous robe, and sent him again to Pilate." Notice that Herod was gathered that day with his "men of war." Who were these men of war, and why were they at Herod's side when Jesus stood before him?

The word for "men of war" depicts *a small detachment of soldiers*, but it suggests these men were Herod's personal bodyguards who were selected from a larger group of soldiers because they were exceptionally trained and prepared to fight if called upon — thus, the reason the *King James Version* refers to them as "men of war."

The Bible informs us that Herod — with the assistance of his bodyguards — took Jesus and *"set him at nought."* These words "set him at nought" are developed from a Greek word that means *to make one out to be nothing*. It can be translated *to make light of, to belittle, to disdain, to disregard, to despise,* or *to treat with maliciousness and contempt.*

Jesus had already endured the insane yelling and screaming that the chief priests and elders unleashed on Him. But now Herod and his bodyguards entered center stage to start their own brand of humiliating Jesus.

Luke used this very specific language to let us know they were *malicious* and *vindictive* and that their behavior was *nasty* and *ugly*. But then Luke went on to say that Herod and his men "*mocked* him." This gives us an idea of how low they sank in their ridiculing of Jesus.

The word "mocked" is the same Greek word used in Luke 22:63 to portray the mocking behavior of the soldiers who guarded Jesus before He was taken into Caiaphas' high court.

As we saw in Chapter 5, this word meant *to play a game* and was often used for *playing a game with children* or *to amuse a crowd by impersonating someone in a silly and exaggerated way*. As noted earlier, it might be used in *a game of charades* in which someone intends *to comically portray or even make fun of someone*.

Herod Antipas, a governor, was supposedly an educated, cultured, and refined man. He was surrounded by finely trained Roman soldiers who were supposed to be professional in their conduct and appearance. But now these men of war, along with their boss and ruler, descended deep into depravity as they began to put on quite a show, mockingly impersonating Jesus and the people He ministered to.

As we saw in a previous chapter, they probably hammed it up, acting as if they were healing the sick — and lying on the floor and quivering as if they were being liberated from devils or groping around as if they were blind and then suddenly able to see. It was all a game of charades intended to mock and make fun of Jesus.

120

They Arrayed Jesus in a Royal Robe

Luke 23:11 then tells us, "...[They] arrayed him in a gorgeous robe...." The word "arrayed" is a word that means *to throw about* or *to drape about*, as to drape around one's shoulders. The words "gorgeous robe" depicts *something that is resplendent, glistening, or magnificent*. It was frequently used to depict *a garment made of sumptuous, brightly colored materials*.

In all likelihood, this was a garment worn by a politician, because when candidates were running for public office, they wore beautiful and brightly colored clothes. It is even likely that this was one of Herod's own sumptuous garments that he permitted to be draped around Jesus' shoulders so they could pretend to adore Him as "king" as part of their mockery of Him.

Jesus Was Returned to Pilate's Court

Although Herod apparently enjoyed this maltreatment and abuse of Jesus, Luke 23:14,15 tells us that he could find no crime in Jesus worthy of death, so after the conclusion of these shameful events, Herod "...sent him again to Pilate" (*see* Luke 23:11).

When Herod sent Jesus back to Pilate, he sent Him clothed in that royal robe. One scholar notes that since this garment was one usually worn by a candidate running for office, Herod's decision to send Jesus to Pilate in this robe was the equivalent of saying, *"This is no king! It's only another candidate, a pretender, who thinks he's running for some kind of office!"*

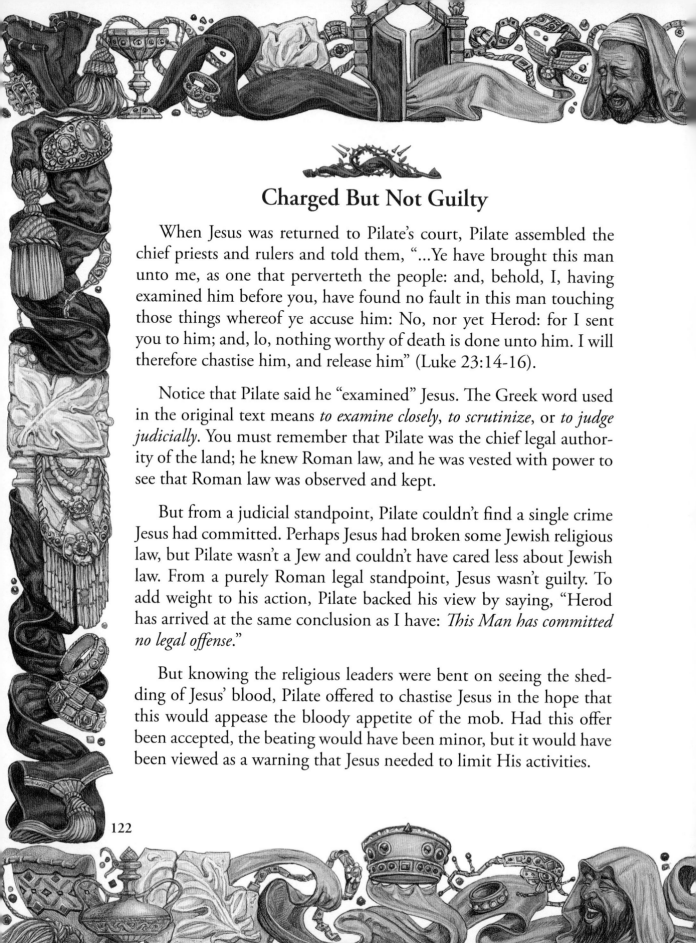

Charged But Not Guilty

When Jesus was returned to Pilate's court, Pilate assembled the chief priests and rulers and told them, "...Ye have brought this man unto me, as one that perverteth the people: and, behold, I, having examined him before you, have found no fault in this man touching those things whereof ye accuse him: No, nor yet Herod: for I sent you to him; and, lo, nothing worthy of death is done unto him. I will therefore chastise him, and release him" (Luke 23:14-16).

Notice that Pilate said he "examined" Jesus. The Greek word used in the original text means *to examine closely*, *to scrutinize*, or *to judge judicially*. You must remember that Pilate was the chief legal authority of the land; he knew Roman law, and he was vested with power to see that Roman law was observed and kept.

But from a judicial standpoint, Pilate couldn't find a single crime Jesus had committed. Perhaps Jesus had broken some Jewish religious law, but Pilate wasn't a Jew and couldn't have cared less about Jewish law. From a purely Roman legal standpoint, Jesus wasn't guilty. To add weight to his action, Pilate backed his view by saying, "Herod has arrived at the same conclusion as I have: *This Man has committed no legal offense.*"

But knowing the religious leaders were bent on seeing the shedding of Jesus' blood, Pilate offered to chastise Jesus in the hope that this would appease the bloody appetite of the mob. Had this offer been accepted, the beating would have been minor, but it would have been viewed as a warning that Jesus needed to limit His activities.

Pilate Attempts To Release Jesus

Pilate then announced that after Jesus was finished being chastised, he would "release" Him. But when the mob heard the word "release," they jumped on the opportunity to reverse Pilate's decision by dragging up a tradition that was carried out every year at that particular time.

It was a custom at that time of the year for one prisoner to be "released" from prison as a favor to the people. Because Israel hated the Roman occupation, many Jewish men had fought as "freedom fighters" to overthrow Roman rule. Therefore, each year when it came time for this big event, all of Jerusalem waited with anticipation to see which prisoner would be released.

By choosing to "release" Jesus at this moment, it was as if Pilate was making the choice himself which prisoner would be released — and his choice was Jesus. But when the people heard of Pilate's decision, they cried out, "...Away with this man, and release unto us Barabbas: (who for a certain sedition made in the city, and for murder, was cast into prison)" (Luke 23:18,19).

Who Was Barabbas?

Barabbas was a notorious rabblerouser who had been proven guilty of *"sedition"* in the city of Jerusalem. The word "sedition" used in Luke 23:19 comes from a Greek word for *treason*, which

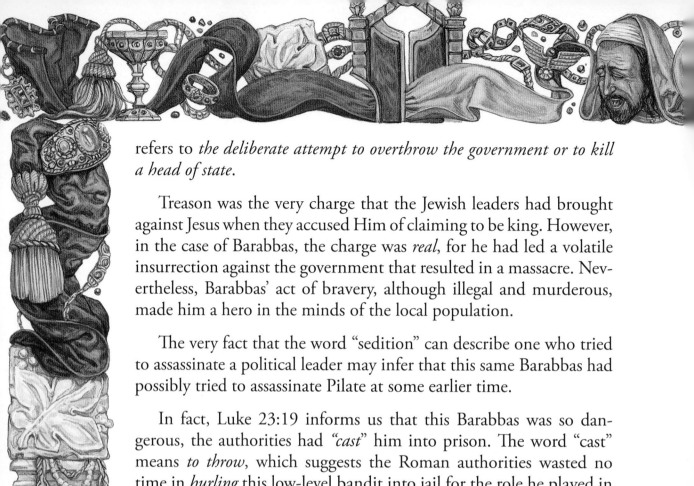

refers to *the deliberate attempt to overthrow the government or to kill a head of state.*

Treason was the very charge that the Jewish leaders had brought against Jesus when they accused Him of claiming to be king. However, in the case of Barabbas, the charge was *real*, for he had led a volatile insurrection against the government that resulted in a massacre. Nevertheless, Barabbas' act of bravery, although illegal and murderous, made him a hero in the minds of the local population.

The very fact that the word "sedition" can describe one who tried to assassinate a political leader may infer that this same Barabbas had possibly tried to assassinate Pilate at some earlier time.

In fact, Luke 23:19 informs us that this Barabbas was so dangerous, the authorities had *"cast"* him into prison. The word "cast" means *to throw*, which suggests the Roman authorities wasted no time in *hurling* this low-level bandit into jail for the role he played in the bloody uprising. This Barabbas was so dangerous that the Roman authorities wanted him off the streets and locked up forever!

'CRUCIFY HIM!'

But Luke 23:20 and 21 tells us, "Pilate therefore, willing to release Jesus, spake again to them. But they cried, saying, Crucify him, crucify him." The word "willing" would be better translated, *"Pilate therefore, wishing, longing, and desiring to release Jesus...."* Thus, although Pilate earnestly searched for a way to set Jesus free, the multitude continued to scream for His crucifixion — and this was the first time that *crucifixion* had been specifically demanded by the crowd.

Luke 23:21 says that the angry mob "cried" for Jesus to be crucified. The word "cried" in the original text means *to shout, to scream, to yell, to shriek,* or *to screech.* The Greek tense means they were hysterically *screaming* and *shrieking* at the top of their voices — totally out of control and without pause. Pilate appealed to them again in Luke 23:22, "...Why, what evil hath he done? I have found no cause of death in him: I will therefore chastise him, and let him go."

Again the Roman governor hoped that a beating might satisfy the people's bloody hunger, but "...*they were instant* with loud voices, requiring that he might be crucified. And the voices of them and of the chief priests prevailed" (Luke 22:23).

The words "they were instant" are from a Greek word that means the people began *to pile evidence on top* of Pilate, nearly *burying him* in reasons why Jesus had to be crucified. To finish this quarrel, they threatened Pilate, saying, "...If thou let this man go, thou art not Caesar's friend: whosoever maketh himself a king speaketh against Caesar" (John 19:12).

Pilate was taken aback by the threat of treason that these Jewish leaders were bringing against him. Once he heard these words, he knew they had him in a trap — and there was only one way legally for him to get out of the mess he was in. He could either set Jesus free and sacrifice his own political career, or he could deliver Jesus to be crucified and, thus, save himself.

Pilate Publicly Washed His Hands of the Matter

When confronted with these two stark choices, Pilate decided to sacrifice Jesus and save himself. But as he turned Jesus over to

the masses, Pilate first wanted to make it clear to everyone who was listening that he didn't agree with what they were doing. This is why Matthew 27:24 tells us, "When Pilate saw that he could prevail nothing, but that rather a tumult was made, he took water, and washed his hands before the multitude, saying, I am innocent of the blood of this just person: see ye to it."

Pay careful attention to the fact that Pilate "...took water, and washed his hands...." Water, of course, is symbolic of *a cleansing agent*, and hands are symbolic of *our lives*.

For instance, with our hands we touch people, we work, and we make money. In fact, nearly everything we do in life, we do with our hands. This is why Paul told us to "lift up holy hands" when we pray and worship (*see* 1 Timothy 2:8). When we lift our hands to God, it is the same as lifting our entire lives before Him, because our hands represent our lives.

But importantly, in New Testament times, the washing of hands was a ritual used symbolically for *the removal of one's guilt*. So when Pilate washed his hands in that basin of water and publicly declared, "I am clear of all guilt regarding the blood of this just person," he was demonstrating that he wanted everyone to know he was innocent of Jesus' blood.

Pilate Changed His Mind To Save Himself

When faced with the choice of enforcing the truth, yet sacrificing his career, or punishing an innocent man, Pilate caved and surrendered Jesus to the will of an angry mob. As long as Pontius Pilate thought he could stand with Jesus and keep his own position as well, he protected Jesus, but the moment Pilate realized that saving Jesus would mean he would have to sacrifice his own position, he quickly changed his tune and gave in to the demands of the mob of people who were screaming all around him.

Integrity comes with a price, but the consequences of abandoning integrity for self-preservation are even more costly. Pilate made an outward show of washing his hands to demonstrate what he considered to be his own innocence. But he only did it in an attempt to distance himself from the bloodthirsty crowd and to prove that he didn't support the decision he felt trapped into making. Yet as much as he tried to distance himself, Pilate's willing compromise with the crowd locked him solidly within their ranks.

Can you think of a time in your own life when your walk with Jesus put you in an unpopular position with your peers? What did you do when you realized your commitment to the Lord was going to jeopardize your job or your status with your friends? Did you sacrifice your friendship and your status, or did you sacrifice your commitment to the Lord?

Decide today to never make the mistake of sacrificing your relationship with Jesus for other people or other things. Instead, resolve to stand with Jesus regardless of the situation or the personal cost you may have to pay for staying faithful to Him.

In the next chapter, we will learn that Pilate ordered Jesus to be scourged and handed over for crucifixion. What do you know about a Roman scourging? In the pages that follow, you will learn what that brutal act of torture purchased for you in the redemptive plan of God.

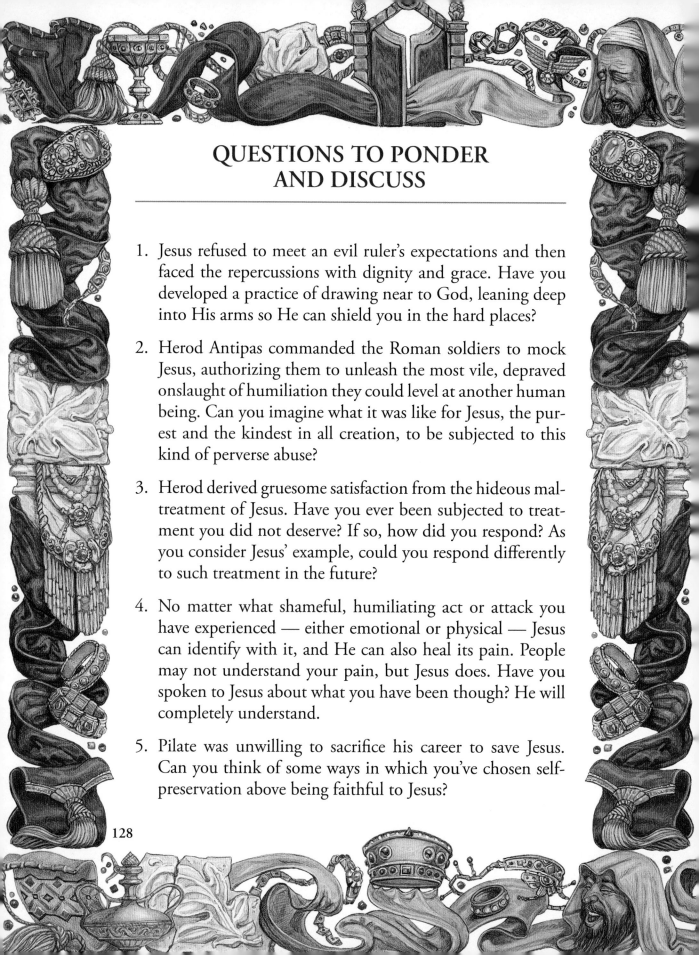

QUESTIONS TO PONDER
AND DISCUSS

1. Jesus refused to meet an evil ruler's expectations and then faced the repercussions with dignity and grace. Have you developed a practice of drawing near to God, leaning deep into His arms so He can shield you in the hard places?

2. Herod Antipas commanded the Roman soldiers to mock Jesus, authorizing them to unleash the most vile, depraved onslaught of humiliation they could level at another human being. Can you imagine what it was like for Jesus, the purest and the kindest in all creation, to be subjected to this kind of perverse abuse?

3. Herod derived gruesome satisfaction from the hideous maltreatment of Jesus. Have you ever been subjected to treatment you did not deserve? If so, how did you respond? As you consider Jesus' example, could you respond differently to such treatment in the future?

4. No matter what shameful, humiliating act or attack you have experienced — either emotional or physical — Jesus can identify with it, and He can also heal its pain. People may not understand your pain, but Jesus does. Have you spoken to Jesus about what you have been though? He will completely understand.

5. Pilate was unwilling to sacrifice his career to save Jesus. Can you think of some ways in which you've chosen self-preservation above being faithful to Jesus?

Pontius Pilate decided to spare himself by sacrificing Jesus. Illustrated here is Pilate when, as it says in Matthew 27:24, "…he took water, and washed his hands before the multitude, saying, I am innocent of the blood of this just person: see ye to it." Pilate made an outward show of what he considered to be his own innocence, but truthfully, his willing compromise with the bloodthirsty crowd solidly locked him within their ranks.

The Romans took great delight in the act of scourging, and as the bone-and-metal-laced whips tore into Jesus' flesh, Jesus' body was ripped to shreds and His blood poured out. Jesus went through this gruesome act of torture to pay the price for our physical healing. This is what Isaiah referred to as he wrote, "…And with his stripes we are healed" (Isaiah 53:5).

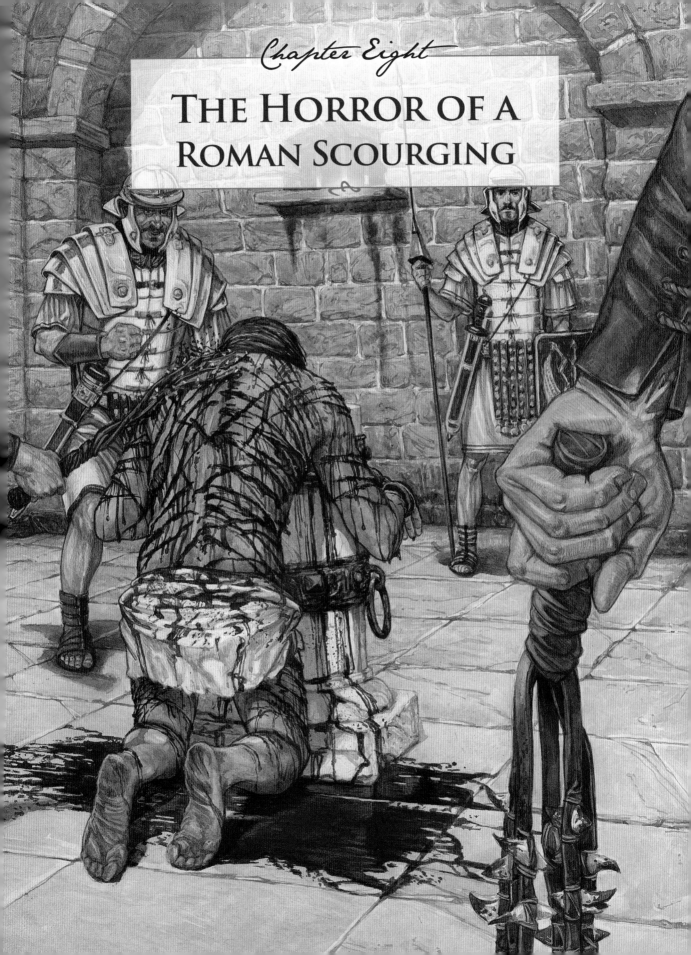

Chapter Eight

THE HORROR OF A ROMAN SCOURGING

In the Church of the Holy Sepulchre in Jerusalem are fragments of two stone columns dating back to the First Century that are disfigured by the marks of a Roman scourge. One column fragment, which is granite and whitish in color, rests behind a piece of glass in a niche that is located in a circular passageway, and it is overseen by the Roman Catholic Church. The other blackish-looking column is exhibited high on a shelf in the walls of an interior chapel in the same Church of the Holy Sepulchre, and it is overseen by the Orthodox Church.

This second column fragment, also marred by Roman scourging, had been broken into two fragments. Another piece of this dark-colored column is on display at the Patriarchal Cathedral Church of St. George, an Orthodox church in Istanbul, Turkiye. There, this treasured relic is located in the southeast corner of the church, described as a portion of the column where "our Lord was bound and whipped by Roman soldiers during His Passion and before His crucifixion."

Each of these historical churches claims "their" column is the actual column, or post, on which Jesus was scourged before He carried the cross to Golgotha. There are serious arguments to support that these respective columns are the authentic ones upon which Jesus was scourged — and the columns are so ancient that it is nearly certain they were used for scourging during the time period of Jesus' scourging.

The two short columns bear the scars of a Roman scourge and demonstrate how horrible a Roman scourging would be upon human flesh — for if the scourge of a torturer could shred and mar columns of stone, what would a scourge do to a human body?

In Matthew 27:26, we read Pilate "had scourged Jesus" before he delivered Him to be crucified. The word "scourge" was one of the most horrific words ever used in the ancient world because of the terrible images that immediately came to mind when a person heard it. It is essential for you to understand what it meant to be "scourged" so you can fully grasp what Jesus did for you and me even before He died on the Cross and was resurrected — raised to life again.

In this chapter, you will learn about the process of scourging and what it physically did to the human body. This is important so you can understand more completely what Jesus endured *before* He was taken to be crucified. In this chapter, we will see:

- What was it like for a person to be scourged?
- From what materials was a scourge made?
- How did it feel when the straps of a scourge ripped across a person's back and body?
- What effects did a scourging have on the human body externally and internally?

The Process of a Roman Scourging

When a decision was made to scourge an individual, the victim was first stripped *completely naked* so his entire flesh would be open and uncovered to the beating action of the torturer's whip. Then the victim was normally bound to a two-foot-high scourging post made of stone. His hands were tied over his head to a metal ring, and his wrists were securely shackled to that ring to restrain his body from movement.[1] When in this locked position, the victim couldn't wiggle, move, or dodge the lashes that were being laid across his body. Romans were professionals at scourging and took special delight in the fact that they were the "best" at punishing a victim with this brutal act.

Once a victim was harnessed to the post and stretched over it, Roman soldiers began to put him through unimaginable torture, so much so that one writer notes the mere anticipation of the whipping caused the victim's body to grow rigid, the muscles to knot in his stomach, the color to drain from his cheeks, and his lips to draw tight against his teeth as he waited for the first sadistic blow that would begin tearing his body open.

The scourge itself, as a weapon, consisted of a short, wooden handle with several 18- to 24-inch-long straps of leather protruding from it. The ends of these pieces of leather were knotted with sharp pieces of metal, wire, glass, and jagged fragments of bone. The scourge was considered to be one of the most feared and deadly weapons of the Roman world. It was so ghastly that the mere threat of scourging could calm a crowd or bend the will of the strongest rebel. Even the most hardened criminal recoiled from the prospect of being submitted to the vicious beating of a Roman scourging.

Most often two torturers were utilized to carry out this vicious punishment, simultaneously lashing the victim from two sides. As these dual whips struck the victim, the leather straps with their sharp, jagged objects extended over his entire back, and each piece of metal, wire, bone, or glass cut deeply through the victim's skin and into his flesh, shredding his muscles and sinews.

Every time the whip pounded across the victim, those straps of leather curled tortuously around his torso, biting painfully and deeply into the skin of his abdomen and upper chest. As each stroke lacerated the sufferer, even if he tried to thrash about, he was unable to move because his wrists were held so firmly to the metal ring fastened on the stone column. Helpless to escape the whip, most often victims would scream for mercy that this anguish might come to an end.

Every time the torturers struck a victim, the straps of leather that were attached to the wooden handle would cause multiple lashes as the sharp objects at the end of each strap sank into the flesh and then raked across the victim's body.

Then the torturer would jerk back, pulling hard in order to tear whole pieces of human flesh from the body. The victim's back, buttocks, back of the legs, stomach, upper chest, and face would soon be disfigured by the slashing blows of the whip.

The Physical Effects History Recorded About Roman Scourgings

Historical records describe a victim's back as being so mutilated after a Roman scourging that his spine could actually be exposed. Others recorded how the bowels of a victim could even spill out through the open wounds created by the whip. The Early Church historian Eusebius wrote: "The veins were laid bare, and the very muscles, sinews, and bowels of the victim were open to exposure."[2]

The Roman torturer would so aggressively strike his victim that he wouldn't even take the time to untangle the bloody, flesh-filled straps as he lashed the whip across the victim's mangled body over and over again. If the scourging wasn't stopped, the slicing of the whip would eventually flay the victim's flesh off his body.

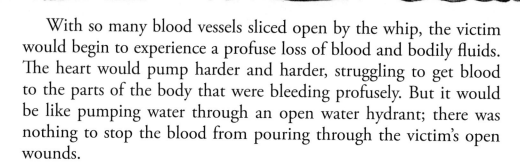

With so many blood vessels sliced open by the whip, the victim would begin to experience a profuse loss of blood and bodily fluids. The heart would pump harder and harder, struggling to get blood to the parts of the body that were bleeding profusely. But it would be like pumping water through an open water hydrant; there was nothing to stop the blood from pouring through the victim's open wounds.

This loss of blood caused the victim's blood pressure to drop drastically. Because of the massive loss of bodily fluids, he would experience excruciating thirst, often fainting from the pain and eventually going into shock. Frequently the victim's heartbeat would become so irregular that he would go into cardiac arrest.

This was a Roman scourging.

The Differences Between Jewish and Roman Scourgings

According to Jewish law described in Deuteronomy 25:3, Jews were permitted to give 40 lashes to a victim, but because the fortieth lash usually proved fatal, the number of lashes given was reduced to 39.

Romans, however, had no limit to the number of lashes they could give a victim, and the scourging Jesus experienced was at the hands of Romans, not Jews. So it is entirely possible that after the torturers pulled out their whips to beat Jesus, they may have laid more than 40 lashes across Jesus' body. In fact, this is probable in light of the explosive outrage the Jews felt for Jesus and the terrible mocking He had already suffered at the hands of Roman soldiers. And *think of*

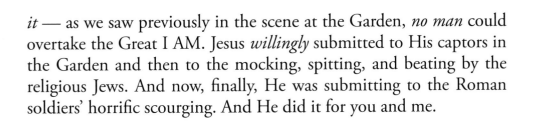

it — as we saw previously in the scene at the Garden, *no man* could overtake the Great I AM. Jesus *willingly* submitted to His captors in the Garden and then to the mocking, spitting, and beating by the religious Jews. And now, finally, He was submitting to the Roman soldiers' horrific scourging. And He did it for you and me.

Jesus' Appearance After a Brutal Roman Scourging

The New Testament doesn't tell us exactly what Jesus looked like after He was scourged, but Isaiah 52:14 gives us some idea, saying, "As many were astonied at thee; his visage was so marred more than any man, and his form more than the sons of men."

Taking this scripture literally for what it says, we can conclude that Jesus' physical body was marred nearly beyond recognition. As appalling as this sounds, it was only the overture to what was to follow, for Matthew 27:26 continues to tell us, "...And when he had scourged Jesus, *he delivered him to be crucified.*"

This scourging was only the preparation for Jesus' crucifixion.

By His Stripes, We Are Healed

When we think about the scourging Jesus received on that day, it is vital that we remember the promise God makes in Isaiah 53:5, "But he was wounded for our transgressions, he was bruised for our iniquities: the chastisement of our peace was upon him; and with his

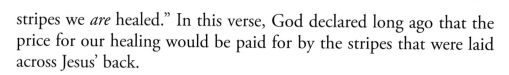

stripes we *are* healed." In this verse, God declared long ago that the price for our healing would be paid for by the stripes that were laid across Jesus' back.

In First Peter 2:24, Peter quoted Isaiah 53:5 as he told his readers, "...By whose stripes ye *were* healed." The Greek word for "stripes" in this verse describes *a full-body bruise*. It refers to *a terrible lashing that draws blood and that produces discoloration and swelling of the entire body*.

When Peter wrote this verse, he vividly remembered what happened to Jesus' body and what His physical appearance looked like after His scourging. After graphically reminding us of the beating, bleeding, and bruising that Jesus endured, Peter declared that it was by these same stripes that we were "healed."

The word "healed" is from a Greek word that clearly refers to *physical healing*, as it is a word borrowed from the medical term to describe *the physical healing or curing of the human body*. For those who think this promise refers to spiritual healing only, the Greek word emphatically speaks of *the healing of a physical condition*. This is a promise of bodily healing that belongs to all who have been redeemed, who are children of God by virtue of their acceptance of Christ's ultimate sacrifice and their belief in His resurrection as the King of kings and Lord of lords.

Just as Jesus willfully took our sins when He died on the Cross in our place, He willfully took our sicknesses and pains on Himself when they tied Him to a real scourging post and laid those lashes across His entire body. Jesus' broken body was the payment that guaranteed our physical healing.

It was that horrific scourging which paid for our healing!

This means if you need healing in your body or in your mind — and you are a redeemed child of God — you can go to the Father and ask for healing to come flooding into your system. Never forget that Jesus went through this agony for *you*, so don't let anyone tell you that it's God's will for you to be weak or sickly, vexed, or oppressed.

Considering the pain Jesus endured to bear your sicknesses that day, isn't that enough evidence to convince you how much He wants you to be physically well?

Pilate Delivered Jesus to the Roman Soldiers

After Jesus was horrifically scourged, Pilate then delivered Him to the Roman soldiers so they could initiate the crucifixion process. But first these Roman soldiers mercilessly dragged Jesus, in His near-mutilated state, through the worst mockery and humiliation of all.

Matthew 27:27-29 describes what Jesus went through at this stage of His ordeal:

Then the soldiers of the governor took Jesus into the common hall, and gathered unto him the whole band of soldiers. And they stripped him, and put on him a scarlet robe. And when they had platted a crown of thorns, they put it upon his head, and a reed in his right hand: and they bowed the knee before him, and mocked him, saying, Hail, King of the Jews!

Matthew 27:27 says that the soldiers "...took Jesus into the common hall, and gathered unto him the whole band of soldiers."

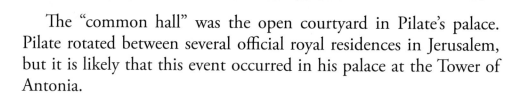

The "common hall" was the open courtyard in Pilate's palace. Pilate rotated between several official royal residences in Jerusalem, but it is likely that this event occurred in his palace at the Tower of Antonia.

What we know for sure is that the courtyard was so large it was able to hold "the whole band of soldiers" — and the phrase "band of soldiers" comes from a Greek word that refers to *a cohort* or *a group of 300 to 600 Roman soldiers.*

They Stripped Jesus Naked

Imagine the completely ravaged, bleeding, bruised, broken body of Jesus from the scourging that had just taken place at Pilate's charge. Jesus had been stripped naked and savagely assaulted with the Roman weaponry used in a typical scourging — so severely beaten that He was unrecognizable as the man He was before His judgment at the whipping post began.

To make Christ's humiliation even more severe, He was maneuvered from the whipping post to the central courtyard of Pilate's residence. Covered with a cloth of some kind after being severely scourged, one can imagine how that fabric meshed tightly to Jesus' open wounds — the blood seeping from His gaping lacerations drenching the cloth and acting as an adhesive, binding it tightly to His consumed flesh.

Suddenly, somewhere between 300 to 600 Roman soldiers filled that courtyard to participate in the events that followed. Matthew 27:28 says, "And they *stripped him*, and put on him a scarlet robe."

First, we read that the soldiers "stripped him." The word "stripped" means *to totally unclothe* or *to fully undress*. They didn't just strip Jesus to His underclothes; they stripped Him completely naked. In the Jewish world, nakedness was viewed as a disgrace, a shame, and an embarrassment. Public nakedness was associated with pagans — with their worship, their idols, and their statues — and the Jewish people believed it was a shameful disgrace to show human nakedness.

As children of God, the Jewish people honored the human body as being made in the image of God and believed that it should never be shamefully and nakedly displayed. Thus, to publicly parade someone's naked body was a great offense.

We can assume, then, that when Jesus was stripped naked in front of 300 to 600 soldiers, it went against the grain of His entire moral view regarding what was right and wrong. But in that moment when He was being so shamed, He was taking your shame upon Himself *so that you could be set free from shame forever!*

They Put a Scarlet Robe on Jesus

I can imagine the pain of humiliation Jesus experienced as well as the physical pain He felt once again as that cloth — tightly clinging to Him with the "glue" of His own blood — was *stripped away* from His body. As Jesus stood naked before them, the Bible lets us know the soldiers "...put on him a scarlet robe."

Here we find a Greek word for *a robe* or *a cloak*, which could refer to a soldier's cloak, but the next word makes it more probable that this was one of Pilate's old cloaks. The word "scarlet" in the original

141

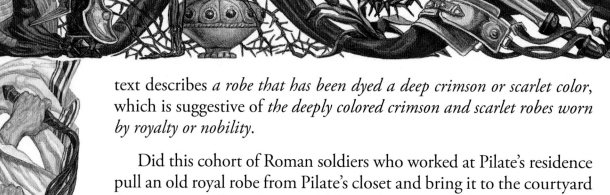

text describes *a robe that has been dyed a deep crimson or scarlet color*, which is suggestive of *the deeply colored crimson and scarlet robes worn by royalty or nobility.*

Did this cohort of Roman soldiers who worked at Pilate's residence pull an old royal robe from Pilate's closet and bring it to the courtyard for the party? If so, they would have done it in order to mock Jesus, not to honor Him.

They Put a Crown of Thorns on Jesus' Head

Matthew continues his account of this event, and we are told that the soldiers "...*platted* a crown of thorns, they put it upon his head...." (Matthew 27:29).

Thorns grew everywhere in Israel, including inside the imperial grounds of Pilate's palace, and these thorns were long and sharp like nails. The soldiers took vines that were loaded with sharp and dangerous thorns, and they carefully wove together those dangerous, razor-sharp, jagged vines until they formed a tightly woven circle that resembled the shape of a crown.

Matthew 27:29 goes on to say the soldiers "...put it upon his head...." In Matthew's gospel, he used a word that implies they *violently pushed* or *forcefully shoved* this crown of thorns onto Jesus' head.

These thorns would have been extremely painful and caused blood to flow profusely from His brow. Because the thorns were so jagged, they would have created terrible wounds as they scraped across Jesus' scalp and literally tore the flesh from His skull.

142

Matthew also called it a "crown" of thorns, and the word "crown" is from a Greek word that described a coveted *victor's crown*. These soldiers intended to use this crown of thorns to make fun of Jesus, but little did they know that Jesus was preparing to win the greatest victory of the ages! Not only did God bring life from death in Christ's resurrection, but He brought honor from dishonor, ultimately giving Jesus Christ the highest seat in Heaven and Earth! And God knows how to bring resurrection power to the situations of *your* life and to give *you* honor where the enemy has caused shame.

They Put a Reed in Jesus' Hand

After forcing the crown of thorns down onto Jesus' brow, the soldiers put "...a *reed* in his right hand..." (Matthew 27:29).

There were beautiful ponds and fountains in Pilate's inner courtyard where such long, tall, hard "reeds" grew. While Jesus sat there naked — only covered with a royal robe and with a crown of thorns on His head — one of the soldiers in the crowd decided the picture was not quite complete, so he pulled a "reed" from one of the ponds or fountains to put in Jesus' hand.

This reed represented a ruler's staff, and it was very similar to what is seen in the famous statue *Ave Caesar*, which depicts Caesar holding *a staff* or *a scepter* in his right hand. The same image, showing a scepter in the right hand of the emperor, also appeared on coins that were minted in the emperor's honor and were in wide circulation. There is no doubt that the soldiers were dressing Jesus like an emperor — but they were ignorantly mocking Him as a charlatan emperor.

They Mockingly Bowed Before Jesus

Once the soldiers draped that discarded royal robe about Jesus' shoulders, set a crown of thorns so deeply into His head that blood drenched His face, and stuck a reed from Pilate's ponds or fountains in Jesus' right hand, they then "...bowed the knee before him, and mocked him, saying, Hail, King of the Jews!" (*see* Matthew 27:29).

The word "bowed" means *to fall down upon one's knees*. Therefore, one by one, the cohort of 300 to 600 soldiers passed before Jesus — dramatically and comically dropping to their knees in front of Him as they laughed at and shamelessly mocked Him. The word "mocked" is the same word we saw in Chapter 7 that was used to describe the mocking of Jesus by Herod and his bodyguards.

As Pilate's soldiers mocked Jesus, they exclaimed, "Hail, King of the Jews!" The word "hail" was always used as an acknowledgment of honor when saluting Caesar. Thus, the soldiers shouted this out as a mock salute to Jesus, in the manner they normally would salute a king to whom their honor was due.

But for these soldiers, this was a further way to mock Jesus as He sat "enthroned" before them with a discarded politician's robe, a crown of thorns, and a reed from a fountain or pond for a scepter in His hands.

They Spit on Jesus and Struck Him

Then Matthew 27:30 tells us, "And they spit upon him, and took the reed, and smote him on the head."

The word "they" refers to the entire cohort of 300 to 600 soldiers who were present in Pilate's courtyard that night. As each soldier passed by Jesus, he mockingly bowed before Him, leaned forward to spit right in Jesus' blood-drenched face, and then grabbed the reed from Jesus' hand to strike Him as hard as possible on His already wounded head.

After each soldier was done, he would stick the reed back in Jesus' hand to make Him ready for the next soldier to repeat the whole process. And the Greek tense Matthew used means *the soldiers repeatedly struck Jesus again and again on the head.*

Here was another beating that Jesus endured, but this time it was with the slapping action of a hard reed. This must have been excruciatingly painful for Jesus. His body was already lacerated from the savage scourging, including His head that had been deeply gashed by the crown of thorns.

Matthew 27:31 tells us that when all 300 to 600 soldiers were finished spitting on Jesus and striking Him with the reed, "...they took the robe off from him, and put his own raiment on him, and led him away to crucify him."

The robe that was wrapped around Jesus had also no doubt meshed into His wounds as His blood dried. It would have taken a great amount of time for so many soldiers to parade before Him, and — finally — when they jerked this robe from Him, it must have been terrifically painful once again as the material ripped free from the dried blood that had coagulated on His open lacerations.

But this would not be the last act of torture Jesus would endure in this stage of His ordeal. After putting His own clothes back on Him, the soldiers led Jesus from the palace to the place of execution.

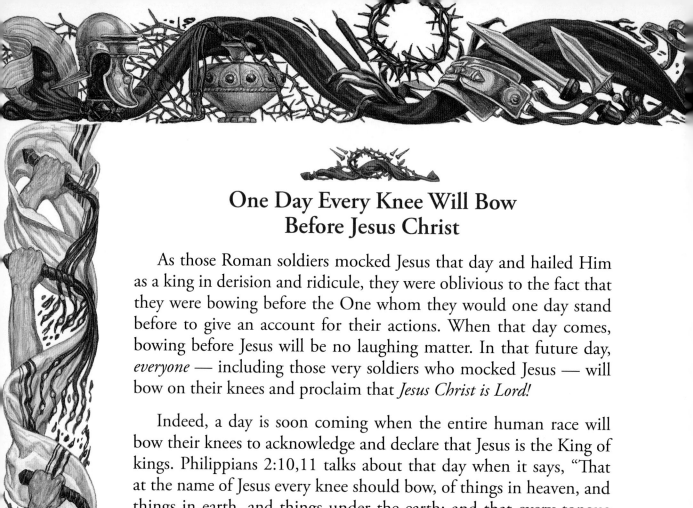

One Day Every Knee Will Bow
Before Jesus Christ

As those Roman soldiers mocked Jesus that day and hailed Him as a king in derision and ridicule, they were oblivious to the fact that they were bowing before the One whom they would one day stand before to give an account for their actions. When that day comes, bowing before Jesus will be no laughing matter. In that future day, *everyone* — including those very soldiers who mocked Jesus — will bow on their knees and proclaim that *Jesus Christ is Lord!*

Indeed, a day is soon coming when the entire human race will bow their knees to acknowledge and declare that Jesus is the King of kings. Philippians 2:10,11 talks about that day when it says, "That at the name of Jesus every knee should bow, of things in heaven, and things in earth, and things under the earth; and that every tongue should confess that Jesus Christ is Lord, to the glory of God the Father."

But the declaration of Jesus' absolute lordship on this side of eternity is critically important. If you have a friend or loved one who doesn't know Jesus, don't you think it's time for you to introduce that person to Christ?

It is our responsibility to help lead our family, friends, and acquaintances to Jesus — and it is certain that God's Spirit will empower you to speak the Gospel to that person *if* you are willing to be used as a vessel for God to speak through to them. And if you pray before you speak to them, the Holy Spirit will do His work to prepare their hearts to hear the message.

Do *you* know Jesus Christ as Savior and Lord? If you have never embraced Jesus as the spotless, sinless Lamb of God who was slain as a sacrifice for your sin, you can do that right now by praying the prayer for salvation in the back of this book on page 271.

In the next chapter, we'll see that Jesus was crucified at a place called Golgotha. You might be wondering, *what was the significance of that particular place* — and *why was Jesus crucified exactly there?* Remember, this magnificent plan of redemption through the Cross of Christ was God's plan and purpose from the very beginning, and He never does anything randomly or coincidentally. So read on to find the amazing answer in the next chapter.

QUESTIONS TO PONDER AND DISCUSS

1. The vicious, sadistic scourging Jesus experienced mutilated and disfigured His body beyond recognition. Meditate on how Jesus' body was scourged so your body could be healed. Consider how valuable you and your body must be to God that He would allow His Son to pay such a price for your healing.

2. The Roman whip ripped and gouged Jesus' body until His blood gushed forth like water through an open hydrant and spilled upon the ground. Jesus' broken body was the payment required to purchase our physical healing. Do you need healing? Think about the horrific scourging Jesus willfully endured so you could have every right to go before God and confidently expect to obtain your healing. Then honor the gift of Jesus' life by gratefully receiving His healing provision for your physical body.

3. The crown of thorns, the robe, and the pond-reed staff each depicted a ruler's symbols of authority. One day every eye will behold Jesus crowned with a royal diadem and robed in the splendor of the glory that is His alone. On that day, every knee will bow, of saints and scoffers alike. What are you doing to prepare others to meet Jesus on that day? What are you doing to prepare yourself?

4. Since God didn't spare Jesus from paying such a high price for your sin, have you considered how willing He is to provide for your every physical need through the redemptive work of Jesus?

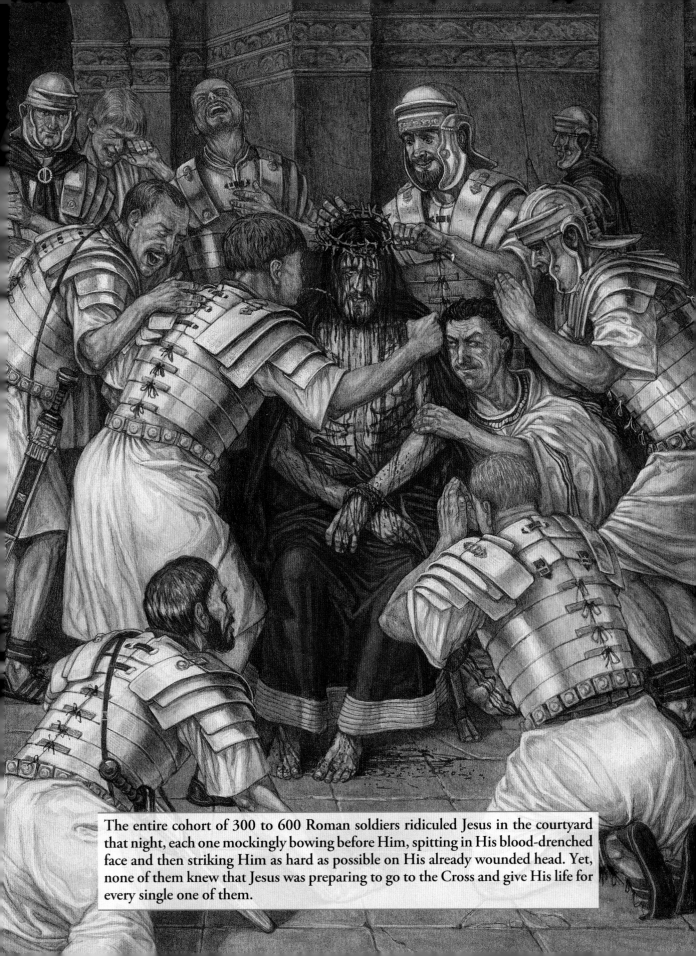

The entire cohort of 300 to 600 Roman soldiers ridiculed Jesus in the courtyard that night, each one mockingly bowing before Him, spitting in His blood-drenched face and then striking Him as hard as possible on His already wounded head. Yet, none of them knew that Jesus was preparing to go to the Cross and give His life for every single one of them.

Jesus was crucified like a criminal just outside the walls of the ancient city of Jerusalem, and although there is some debate on where this exact location is, there is no doubt in what Jesus accomplished — He surrendered His life to purchase our salvation. As Jesus lay on that wooden cross, Roman soldiers drove five-inch iron nails through His wrists and feet, securing Him to the place where He would ultimately give His life for mankind.

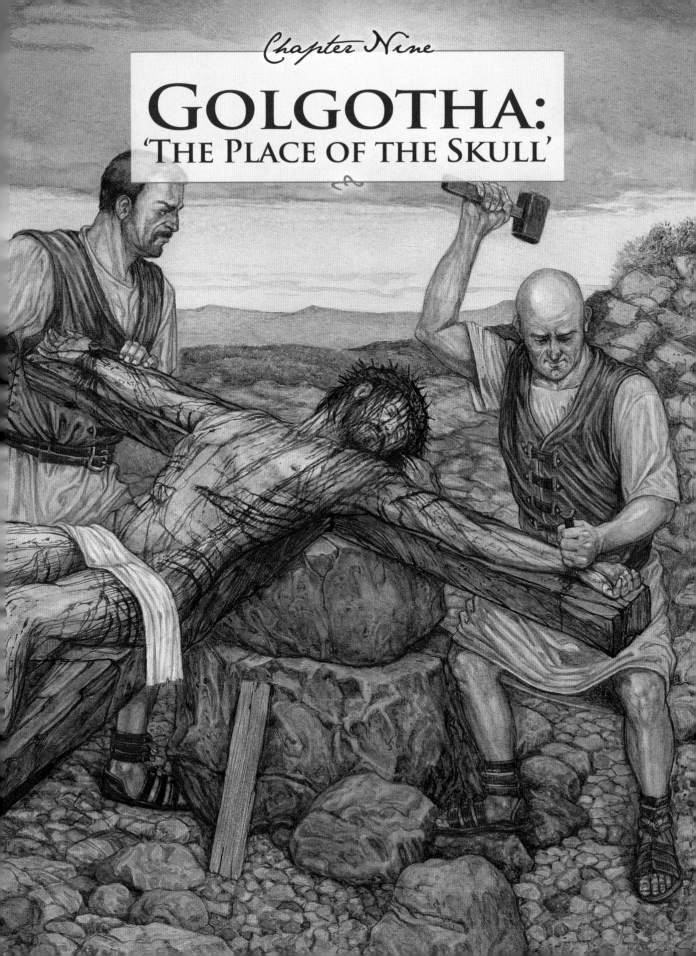

Chapter Nine

GOLGOTHA:
'THE PLACE OF THE SKULL'

When the Roman soldiers brought Jesus forth from the palatial residence of Pilate in Jerusalem, they gave Him a crossbeam to carry that would serve as the upper portion of His cross, and He carried it all the way to the place of His execution.

But just as we saw in the previous chapter that there are three fragments of ancient Roman columns that various historical churches claim are pieces of the real column on which Jesus was scourged, there are also two different alleged sites of Jesus' crucifixion, which was a place once referred to as *Golgotha*.

One of these two declared crucifixion locations is near what is called the Garden Tomb or Gordon's Tomb. The reason it is often referred to as Gordon's Tomb is, Major General Charles Gordon visited Jerusalem in 1883, and although some others had previously argued that it was the site of the real tomb of Jesus, Gordon's claim was much more publicized, so the site became associated with him. Today the site is controlled by The Garden Tomb Association, a charitable trust based in the United Kingdom and in Israel, that oversees volunteers who come from around the globe to help maintain the site.[1]

The Garden Tomb Association does not emphatically state that the Garden Tomb was Jesus' actual tomb, but that it was at least similar to the garden tomb where Jesus was placed after His crucifixion. Protestant Christians are especially attracted to this tomb because they do not like all the religious decorations at the other site — the other historical location that is believed to be where Jesus was both crucified and buried — which is called the Church of the Holy Sepulchre.

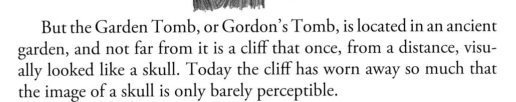

But the Garden Tomb, or Gordon's Tomb, is located in an ancient garden, and not far from it is a cliff that once, from a distance, visually looked like a skull. Today the cliff has worn away so much that the image of a skull is only barely perceptible.

And, as noted, the other historical site for Jesus' crucifixion — as well as His burial and resurrection — is found inside the Church of the Holy Sepulchre. And although this more traditional site is ostentatiously decorated with religious garb that especially puts off Protestant Christians, it has been recognized as the true site of Golgotha as well as of the authentic tomb of Jesus since the reign of Emperor Constantine.[2]

At the time of Constantine, his mother Helena conducted interviews with Christians in Jerusalem who affirmed that the site now preserved by the Church of the Holy Sepulchre was the authentic site of Golgotha and the tomb of Jesus. From the earliest records of Christian history, this traditional site has been commemorated for the eternally significant events that occurred there, but because it is covered with religious decorations and ornamentation, many Christians prefer to visit the Garden Tomb instead. However, history is solidly on the side of the historical, traditional site at the Church of the Holy Sepulchre.

Christian pilgrims have regularly visited the Church of the Holy Sepulchre for nearly 2,000 years, believing it is the true site of Jesus' crucifixion. Although today it is indeed ostentatiously embellished with age-old, religious ornamentations, this site is much changed from the way Golgotha and Jesus' tomb actually appeared 2,000 years ago. And therein lies another mystery: Why is the ancient site of the real Golgotha and the real tomb where Jesus was buried and resurrected obscured and nearly imperceptible today?

To find the answer to this mystery, one need only travel to Pisa, Italy! I have been there, so let me walk you through the scenario I'm referring to that will help answer the question of the diminished crucifixion and tomb site in Jerusalem.

In approximately 1173, Italian architects began construction of the renowned Tower of Pisa, but because the foundation was defective, the tower began to lean. With each subsequent floor, the tower leaned more off center and further off balance. Today it is famously called the Leaning Tower of Pisa, and millions of tourists from around the world travel to see it. However, those tourists are so focused on the Leaning Tower of Pisa that they miss the most important thing to see in Pisa — which is, amazingly, *Golgotha*.

You see, the same architects who constructed the Tower of Pisa also constructed a cathedral which stands adjacent to the Tower of Pisa. That cathedral is called the Cathedral of Pisa, and its construction began in 1063 and was finished in 1092. At that time in the Middle Ages, wealthy religious families in Pisa wanted to be buried on holy ground, and because no holier ground could be imagined than Golgotha itself, they dispatched workers from Pisa to Jerusalem to chip away at the location where Jesus was crucified. During the Fourth Century, these workers loaded the soil of Golgotha into five ships that transported the sacred soil from the Holy Land to the cathedral in Pisa where it was used to build a cemetery so that wealthy, religious families could be buried on the holy ground of Golgotha, albeit in Pisa, Italy.[3]

For this reason, when visitors travel to see the traditional site of Golgotha in Jerusalem that is visible inside the Church of the Holy Sepulchre, they are often disappointed, as it fails to meet their imagination of what it looked like when Jesus was crucified 2,000 years ago.

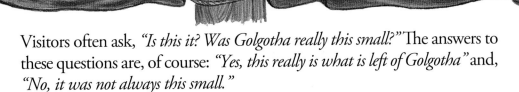

Visitors often ask, *"Is this it? Was Golgotha really this small?"* The answers to these questions are, of course: *"Yes, this really is what is left of Golgotha"* and, *"No, it was not always this small."*

Because of these "excavation" events that occurred in the Fourth Century, if one wants to see the remainder of the sacred soil of Golgotha today, he must travel from Jerusalem to Pisa, where the sacred soil of Golgotha composes the cemetery at the Cathedral of Pisa.

The Cross Jesus Carried

After Jesus was scourged and endured intense mockery from Roman soldiers, He then carried the upper portion — the crossbeam — of His cross all the way to a hill that was called Golgotha, a place located just outside the city of Jerusalem.

Today when people think of a cross, they visualize the typical kind of crosses that adorn churches, jewelry, or even the walls of people's homes. During the First Century, Romans did not use crosses shaped like the traditional crosses that most people see and know today. But the shape of the cross is not what's important — the good news that Christ died on it for you and me is what's important. The fact is, the crosses we're used to seeing displayed are an image that was created by painters during the Middle Ages and was carried over into modern times.

In reality, Roman crosses were shaped like a "T." They were made of a tall, upright post that had a notched groove at the top, into which a crossbeam was placed after a victim had been tied or nailed to it. The crossbeam usually weighed about 100 pounds and was carried on the back of the criminal to the place of execution.

Roman law dictated that once a criminal was convicted and ordered to be crucified, he was to carry his own cross to the place of execution if his crucifixion was to occur somewhere other than the place of the trial. The purpose of this practice was to remind bystanders of Roman military power and the people's need to comply with Roman authority lest they suffer a similar fate.

A Sign in Hebrew, Greek, and Latin To Declare One's Crime

After a person was declared guilty, a crossbeam was laid across his back and a herald walked ahead of him to proclaim his crime to those who were standing by the sides of the road to watch this "death parade." A sign with the person's crime was written on it, and it was later hung on the cross above his head. Sometimes the sign bearing the person's crime would be hung from his neck so that all the spectators who lined the streets to watch him walk by would know exactly the crime for which he was charged and convicted.

This was the very type of sign that was publicly displayed on the Cross above Jesus' head, with the crime He was charged with — "King of the Jews" — written in Hebrew, Greek, and Latin. But as Jesus walked to Golgotha, the place of His crucifixion, this sign dangled from His neck so that all who saw Him knew exactly what charges had been leveled against Him.

Carrying such a heavy weight for a long distance would be difficult for any man, and especially for one who had been as severely beaten as Jesus. The heavy crossbeam on which He was destined to be nailed pressed into His torn back as He carried it to the place of execution. Although the Bible does not state the reason why, we may assume that

156

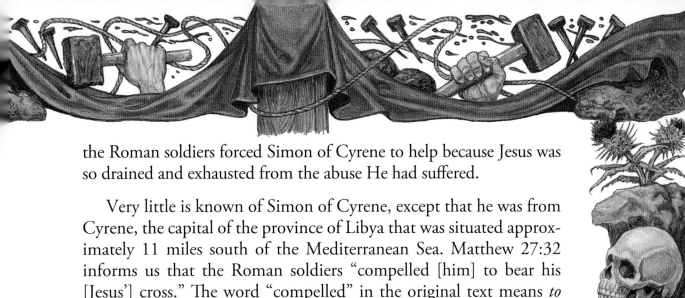

the Roman soldiers forced Simon of Cyrene to help because Jesus was so drained and exhausted from the abuse He had suffered.

Very little is known of Simon of Cyrene, except that he was from Cyrene, the capital of the province of Libya that was situated approximately 11 miles south of the Mediterranean Sea. Matthew 27:32 informs us that the Roman soldiers "compelled [him] to bear his [Jesus'] cross." The word "compelled" in the original text means *to compel, to coerce, to constrain, to make,* or *to force someone into some kind of compulsory service.*

Finally, at the death-permeated place of execution, it was common to see vultures flying overhead, as they waited to swoop down and start devouring the dying carcasses left hanging on crosses. In the nearby wilderness, wild dogs also anxiously waited for the newest dead bodies that would eventually be dumped by executioners and become the dogs' next meal.

Everything about a crucifixion site was disgusting and wretched.

Golgotha — 'a Place of a Skull'

But what else do we know about the place where Jesus was crucified? Matthew 27:33 tells us that the Roman soldiers led Jesus to "a place called Golgotha, that is to say, a place of a skull."

This scripture has been the center of controversy for several hundred years, and many have attempted to use this verse to geographically identify the exact location of Jesus' crucifixion. But early Christian writings extensively describe the place where Jesus was crucified, and inside the modern-day Church of the Holy Sepulchre

157

is likely the true location. Again, it is difficult for some Protestants to appreciate that site because it is so ornately decorated with religious entrapments — they therefore prefer to visit the other site, the Garden Tomb, or Gordon's Tomb, because it seems to match what they imagine the crucifixion site would have looked like 2,000 years ago.

But very early writings of Church fathers state interestingly that the phrase "a place of a skull" refers to something different than what most people imagine!

Writings by Early Church Leaders About Golgotha

An early Christian leader named Origen, one of the most important Early Church fathers, who lived from 185-254 AD, wrote that Jesus was crucified on the spot where Adam was buried. Whether or not this is true, it's important to note that there really *was* an early, widespread Christian belief that Jesus was crucified above the place where Adam was buried.

As this early story goes, when the earthquake occurred as Jesus hung on the Cross (*see* Matthew 27:51), Christ's blood ran down the Cross into a crack in the rock below and it drained through that crevice until it fell on the skull of Adam. This belief is so entrenched in early Christian tradition that Jerome, who was one of the most prominent scholars of the Early Church, also referred to it in a letter he wrote in 386 AD.[4]

Jewish tradition states that Noah's son, Shem, buried Adam near the city of Jerusalem. And although this is unknown to most Western believers, this is so accepted in early Christian history that it is a major

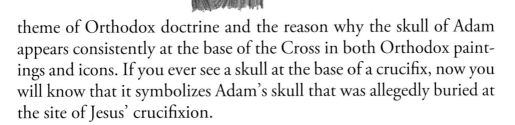

theme of Orthodox doctrine and the reason why the skull of Adam appears consistently at the base of the Cross in both Orthodox paintings and icons. If you ever see a skull at the base of a crucifix, now you will know that it symbolizes Adam's skull that was allegedly buried at the site of Jesus' crucifixion.

These extremely interesting traditions, although unprovable, have retained strong support throughout 2,000 years of Christian history. If it were true, it would be quite amazing that the "Last Adam," Jesus Christ (*see* 1 Corinthians 15:45-47), died for the sins of the world exactly on the spot where the first Adam, the original sinner, was buried. If Jesus' blood ran down the crack in the stone and fell upon Adam's skull, as this early tradition says, it would be very symbolic of Jesus' blood covering sin that originated with Adam's disobedience.

What Do We Definitely Know About the Place of Jesus' Crucifixion?

We definitely know that Jesus was crucified like a criminal by the Roman government just outside the walls of the ancient city of Jerusalem. The question of whether or not He was crucified at the place of Adam's skull is interesting, but not important to our salvation; knowing whether it is true or not has no impact on the redemptive work of the Cross.

Christians may debate exactly where Jesus was crucified, but this question of where this notorious event took place is a good example of the way people get distracted and miss the main point God wants to get across to them. Rather than arguing about which location is correct, we need to rejoice in the truth that *Jesus was crucified for our salvation!*

The apostle Paul wrote, "...Christ died for our sins according to the scriptures; and that he was buried, and that he rose again the third day according to the scriptures" (1 Corinthians 15:3,4). Of this, we can be sure!

What is most important of all is that Jesus' blood was shed to purchase the forgiveness of mankind's sin. Through Adam's disobedience, sin entered the world and death was passed on to all men. But just as sin entered the world through Adam, the gift of God came into the world through the obedience of Jesus Christ. Now the grace of God and the free gift of righteousness abound to all who have called upon Jesus Christ to be the Lord of their lives (*see* Romans 5:12-21).

Jesus Was Crucified

When Jesus arrived at Golgotha to be crucified, the Bible says, "They gave him vinegar to drink mingled with gall..." (Matthew 27:34). According to Jewish law, if a man was about to be executed, he could request a narcotic, mingled together with wine, which would help alleviate the pain of his execution. The word "gall" in this verse refers to this special painkiller.

There was a group of kind women in Jerusalem who made it their good deed to help anesthetize the pain of people who were dying horrific deaths. These women wanted to eliminate as much pain and misery as possible for the scores of people being crucified by the Romans. Therefore, they produced the homemade painkiller that Matthew tells us about in this verse.

Jesus was offered this anesthetic twice — once before His crucifixion and once while He was dying on the Cross, which we read about

160

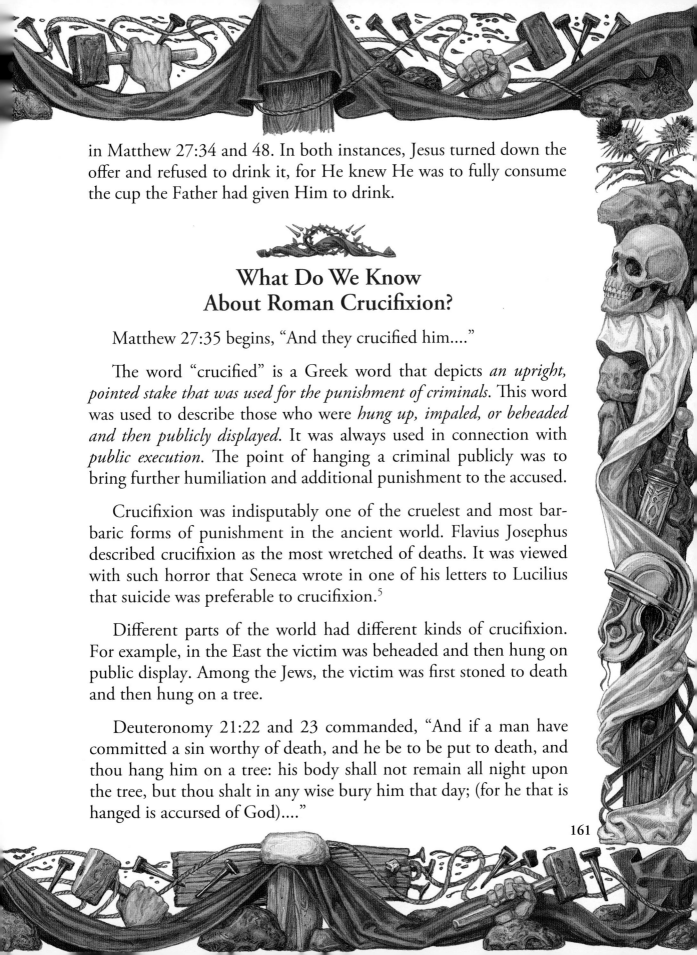

in Matthew 27:34 and 48. In both instances, Jesus turned down the offer and refused to drink it, for He knew He was to fully consume the cup the Father had given Him to drink.

What Do We Know About Roman Crucifixion?

Matthew 27:35 begins, "And they crucified him...."

The word "crucified" is a Greek word that depicts *an upright, pointed stake that was used for the punishment of criminals.* This word was used to describe those who were *hung up, impaled, or beheaded and then publicly displayed.* It was always used in connection with *public execution.* The point of hanging a criminal publicly was to bring further humiliation and additional punishment to the accused.

Crucifixion was indisputably one of the cruelest and most barbaric forms of punishment in the ancient world. Flavius Josephus described crucifixion as the most wretched of deaths. It was viewed with such horror that Seneca wrote in one of his letters to Lucilius that suicide was preferable to crucifixion.[5]

Different parts of the world had different kinds of crucifixion. For example, in the East the victim was beheaded and then hung on public display. Among the Jews, the victim was first stoned to death and then hung on a tree.

Deuteronomy 21:22 and 23 commanded, "And if a man have committed a sin worthy of death, and he be to be put to death, and thou hang him on a tree: his body shall not remain all night upon the tree, but thou shalt in any wise bury him that day; (for he that is hanged is accursed of God)...."

161

But at the time Jesus was crucified, the grueling act of crucifixion was entirely in the hands of the Roman authorities. This punishment was reserved for the most serious offenders, usually for those who had committed some kind of treason or who had participated in or sponsored state terrorism.

Because Israel hated the occupying Roman troops, insurrections frequently arose among the populace. As a deterrent to stop people from participating in revolts, crucifixion was regularly practiced in Jerusalem. By publicly crucifying those who attempted to overthrow the government, the Romans sent a strong signal of fear to those who might be tempted to follow in the others' steps.

The Grueling Process of Crucifixion

Once the convicted criminal had reached the place where the crucifixion was to occur, he was laid on the crossbeam with his arms outstretched. Then a soldier would drive a five-inch (12.7-centimeter) iron nail through each of his wrists into the crossbeam. After being nailed to the crossbeam, the victim was hoisted up by rope, and the crossbeam was dropped into a notch on top of the upright post.

When the crossbeam dropped into the groove, the victim suffered excruciating pain as his hands and wrists were wrenched by the sudden jerking motion. Then the weight of the victim's body caused his arms to be pulled out of their arm sockets. Josephus writes that the Roman soldiers "out of rage and hatred amused themselves by nailing their prisoners in different postures.[6] Crucifixion was truly a vicious ordeal.

Once the victim's wrists were secured in place on the crossbeam, the feet came next. As a rule, a long nail would then be driven between

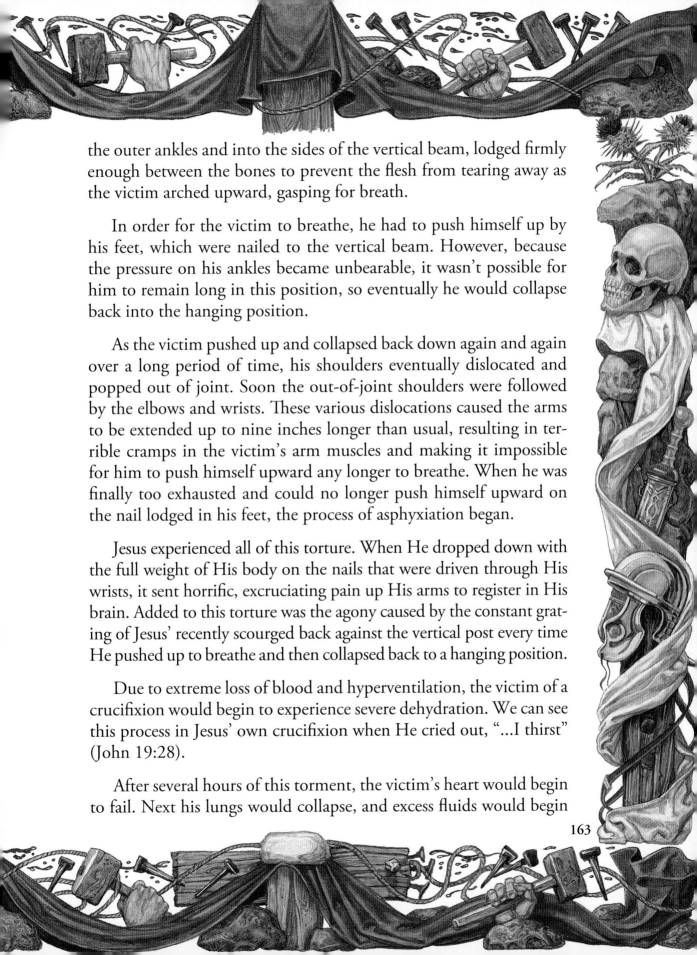

the outer ankles and into the sides of the vertical beam, lodged firmly enough between the bones to prevent the flesh from tearing away as the victim arched upward, gasping for breath.

In order for the victim to breathe, he had to push himself up by his feet, which were nailed to the vertical beam. However, because the pressure on his ankles became unbearable, it wasn't possible for him to remain long in this position, so eventually he would collapse back into the hanging position.

As the victim pushed up and collapsed back down again and again over a long period of time, his shoulders eventually dislocated and popped out of joint. Soon the out-of-joint shoulders were followed by the elbows and wrists. These various dislocations caused the arms to be extended up to nine inches longer than usual, resulting in terrible cramps in the victim's arm muscles and making it impossible for him to push himself upward any longer to breathe. When he was finally too exhausted and could no longer push himself upward on the nail lodged in his feet, the process of asphyxiation began.

Jesus experienced all of this torture. When He dropped down with the full weight of His body on the nails that were driven through His wrists, it sent horrific, excruciating pain up His arms to register in His brain. Added to this torture was the agony caused by the constant grating of Jesus' recently scourged back against the vertical post every time He pushed up to breathe and then collapsed back to a hanging position.

Due to extreme loss of blood and hyperventilation, the victim of a crucifixion would begin to experience severe dehydration. We can see this process in Jesus' own crucifixion when He cried out, "...I thirst" (John 19:28).

After several hours of this torment, the victim's heart would begin to fail. Next his lungs would collapse, and excess fluids would begin

163

filling the lining of his heart and lungs, adding to the slow process of asphyxiation.

Why Was a Spear Thrust Into Jesus' Side?

We are told in John 19:34 that when the Roman soldier came to determine whether Jesus was alive or dead, the soldier thrust a spear into Jesus' side. One expert points out that if Jesus had been alive when the soldier did this, the soldier would have heard a loud sucking sound caused by air being inhaled past the freshly made wound in the chest.

But the Bible tells us that water and blood mixed together came pouring forth from the wound the spear had made — evidence that Jesus' heart and lungs had shut down and were filled with fluid. This was enough to assure the soldier that Jesus was already dead.

It was customary for Roman soldiers to break the lower leg bones of a person being crucified, making it impossible for the victim to push himself upward to breathe and, thus, causing him to asphyxiate at a much quicker rate.

However, because of the blood and water that gushed from Jesus' side, He was already considered dead. Since there was no reason for the soldiers to hasten Jesus' death, His legs were never broken. The apostle John wrote that this was a fulfillment of Old Testament Scripture concerning the Messiah: "For these things were done, that the scripture should be fulfilled, A bone of him shall not be broken" (John 19:36).

But this is a brief taste of Roman crucifixion.

This description of crucifixion is exactly what Jesus experienced on the Cross when He died for you and me. This is why Paul wrote, "And being found in fashion as a man, he humbled himself, and became obedient unto death, *even* the death of the cross" (Philippians 2:8).

In Greek, the emphasis is on the word "even" — which dramatizes the point that Jesus lowered Himself to such an extent that He died *even* the death of a cross — the lowest, most humiliating, debasing, shameful, painful method of death in the ancient world.

The Soldiers Cast Lots for His Garments

Meanwhile, the soldiers near the foot of the Cross "...parted his garments, casting lots..." (Matthew 27:35). They didn't understand the great price of redemption that was being paid at that moment as Jesus hung asphyxiating to death, His lungs filling with fluids so that He couldn't breathe.

According to Roman custom, the soldiers who carried out the crucifixion had a right to the victim's clothes. Jewish law required that the person being crucified would be stripped naked. So Jesus hung there — completely open and naked before the world — while His crucifiers literally distributed His clothes among themselves!

Making this distribution of clothes even cheaper was the fact that the soldiers "cast lots" for His garments. The gospel of John records that "...when they had crucified Jesus, took his garments, and made four parts, to every soldier a part; and also his coat: now the coat was without seam, woven from the top throughout. They said therefore among themselves, Let us not rend it, but cast lots for it..." (John 19:23,24).

This account informs us that four soldiers were present at Jesus' crucifixion. The four parts of His clothing that were distributed among them were His head gear, sandals, girdle, and the *tallith* — the outer garment that had fringes on the bottom.

His "coat," which was "without seam," was a handmade garment that was sewn together from top to bottom. Because it was specially handmade, this coat was a very expensive piece of clothing. This was the reason the soldiers chose to cast lots for it rather than tear it into four parts and spoil it.

When the Bible refers to "casting lots," it indicates a game during which the soldiers wrote their names on pieces of parchment, wood, or stones and then dropped all four pieces with their names written on them into some kind of container.

Because the Roman soldiers who helped crucify Jesus were remotely located, it is probable that one of them pulled off his helmet and held it out to the other soldiers. After the others dropped their names in the helmet, the soldier shook it to mix up the four written names and then randomly withdrew the name of the winner.

It is simply remarkable that all of this was taking place as Jesus was pushing down on that huge nail lodged in His feet so He could gasp for breath before sagging back down into a hanging position. As Jesus' strength continued to drain away and the full consequence of man's sin was being realized in Him, the soldiers at the foot of the Cross played a game to see who would get His finest piece of clothing!

Matthew 27:36 says, "And sitting down they watched him there." The Greek tense for "watched" means *to consistently watch*. It was the responsibility of these soldiers to keep things in order, to keep watch over the crucifixion site, and to make sure no one came to rescue Jesus

166

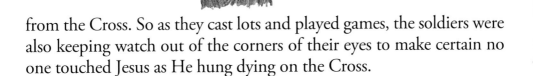

from the Cross. So as they cast lots and played games, the soldiers were also keeping watch out of the corners of their eyes to make certain no one touched Jesus as He hung dying on the Cross.

We Need To Remember What the Cross Was Really Like!

In our world today, the cross has become a fashion item that is decorated with gems, rhinestones, gold, and silver. Beautiful crosses of jewelry adorn women's ears and dangle at the bottom of gold chains and necklaces. Crosses top steeples on churches and adorn altars inside churches. The symbol of the cross is even tattooed on people's flesh.

Certainly there is nothing wrong with adorning ourselves with crosses, but in beautifying the Cross to make it pleasing to look upon, people have unfortunately forgotten that *the* Cross wasn't beautiful or lavishly decorated. The Cross was *shocking* and *appalling*.

Jesus' totally naked body was flaunted in humiliation before a watching world. His flesh was ripped to shreds; His body was bruised from head to toe. He had to heave His body upward for every breath He breathed, and His nervous system sent constant signals of excruciating pain to His brain. Blood drenched Jesus' face and streamed from His hands, His feet, and from the countless cuts and gaping wounds the scourging had left upon His body.

The reality is that the Cross of Jesus Christ was a disgusting, repulsive, nauseating, stomach-turning sight — so entirely different from the attractive crosses people wear today as jewelry or as a part of their attire.

It is good for all of us to remember what the Cross of Jesus Christ was really like, for if we don't choose to meditate on what He went through and the price He paid for our redemption, we will never fully appreciate the price He paid for us. *How tragic it would be if we lost sight of the pain and the price of redemption!*

Blood drenched Jesus' torso, pouring from His head and brow, running like rivers from the deeply torn flesh in His hands and feet. The effect of the scourging that Jesus had received in Pilate's palace began to take its toll as His body swelled up and became horribly discolored. His eyes were matted with the blood that poured from the wounds in His brow — wounds caused by the crown of thorns that bore down into His skull as the soldiers pushed it hard upon His head. The whole scene was foul, repulsive, revolting, sickening, ugly, unsightly, and vile.

When we fail to remember what it cost Jesus to save us, we tend to treat our salvation cheaply and with disregard. That's why Peter wrote, "Forasmuch as ye know that ye were not redeemed with corruptible things, as silver and gold, from your vain conversation received by tradition from your fathers; but with the precious blood of Christ, as of a lamb without blemish and without spot" (1 Peter 1:18,19).

Isaiah's Prophetic Words About the Cross

Approximately 700 years earlier, Isaiah the prophet correctly prophesied Jesus' appearance on the Cross. In Isaiah 52:14, he wrote with a sense of horror, "As many were astonied at thee; his visage was so marred more than any man, and his form more than the sons of men." In Isaiah 53:2, Isaiah continued, "...He hath no form nor comeliness; and when we shall see him, there is no beauty that we should desire him."

Jesus was put through horrendous forms of torture and was atrociously abused and battered. As a result, "...His face and His whole appearance were marred more than any man's, and His form beyond that of the sons of men..." (Isaiah 52:14 *AMPC*). In the *New International Version*, this verse is translated to say, "...His appearance was so disfigured beyond that of any human being and his form marred beyond human likeness...."

In Isaiah 53:3-5, Isaiah wrote, "He is despised and rejected of men; a man of sorrows, and acquainted with grief: and we hid as it were our faces from him; he was despised, and we esteemed him not. Surely he hath borne our griefs, and carried our sorrows: yet we did esteem him stricken, smitten of God, and afflicted. But he was wounded for our transgressions, he was bruised for our iniquities: the chastisement of our peace was upon him; and with his stripes we are healed."

According to these scriptures, when Jesus died on the Cross:

- He bore our griefs.
- He carried our sorrows.
- He was wounded for our transgressions.
- He was bruised for our iniquities.
- He was chastised for our peace.
- He was scourged for our healing.

In this chapter, we have covered much vital information, but in the next chapter, we will discover exactly why Jesus cried out as He was dying, "IT IS FINISHED!" You will be amazed to see what these words mean for you!

QUESTIONS TO PONDER
AND DISCUSS

1. It is interesting that Orthodox tradition has held for 2,000 years that Golgotha is the burial place of Adam's skull. Whether or not that is true is not the point. The point is this: The blood of Jesus cleansed all sin that originated with Adam. God always goes to the root of a matter. To what root issues in your own life do you need to apply the cleansing blood of Jesus Christ?

2. Notice the only "crime" Jesus was convicted of: being the King of the Jews. Are you living your life in such a way — publicly and privately — that the only thing people can accuse and convict you of is fulfilling your divine purpose?

3. Simon of Cyrene was forced to help Jesus carry His actual cross. Jesus has invited you to pick up *your* cross — your own opportunity for obedience to the plan of God — and to follow Him daily. What opportunity for obedience is before you today that will require you to die to your own will and preferences? In what way will you follow Jesus in that situation?

4. What did you learn from this chapter about Jesus' crucifixion that you never knew before? How does this new insight affect your view of the Cross and the price Jesus paid for your redemption?

Jesus' death on the Cross restored to mankind what was lost through Adam's sin (*see* Romans 5:12-19). Jesus did what no other human could ever do and purchased our freedom from sin and the power of darkness forever. If you ever see a skull at the base of a crucifix, it is meant to symbolize Adam's skull that was supposedly buried where Jesus was crucified. This gives new meaning to the phrase "the place of the skull"!

As Jesus breathed His last words on the Cross and declared "IT IS FINISHED!" the very thick veil of the Temple was suddenly torn in two by unseen hands, and the presence of God that used to inhabit the Holy of Holies was now made available to every person who declares Jesus is Lord!

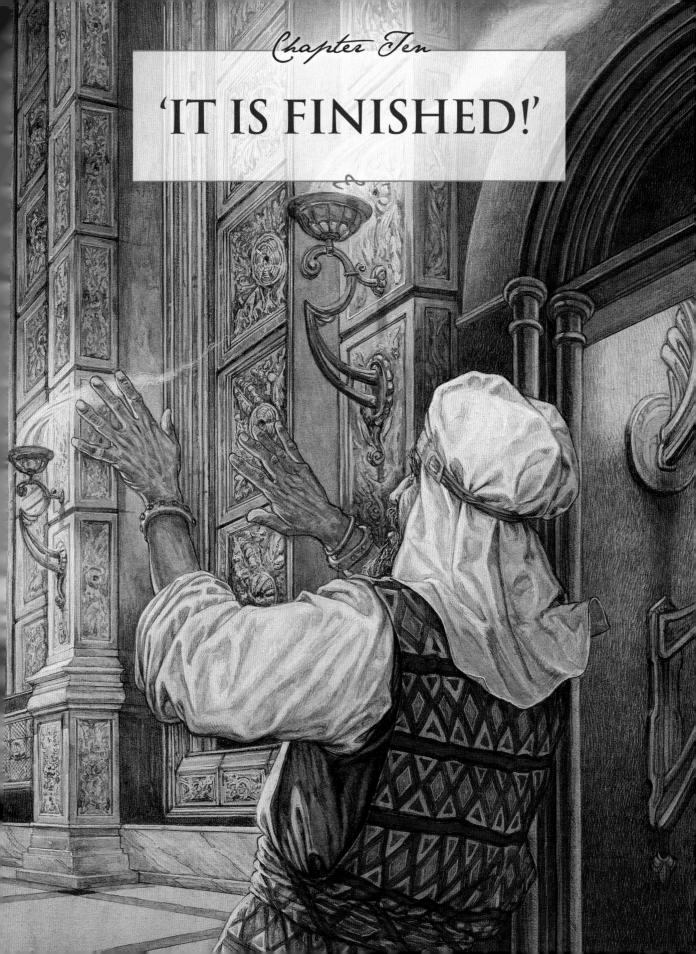

Chapter Ten

'IT IS FINISHED!'

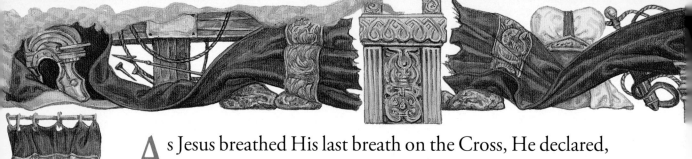

As Jesus breathed His last breath on the Cross, He declared, "IT IS FINISHED!" And Matthew 27:51 tells us that in that very moment, "...Behold, the veil of the temple was rent in twain from the top to the bottom...."

The word "behold" is a very difficult word to translate, for it carries such intense feeling and emotion. The *King James Version* most often translates this word as *behold*, but in our contemporary world, it might be better rendered, *Wow!* This word carries the idea of *shock, amazement, and wonder*. It's almost as if Matthew said, *"Wow! Can you believe it? The veil of the Temple itself rent in twain from top to bottom!"* Matthew wrote about this event many years after the fact, yet he was still so dumbfounded by what happened that day that he exclaimed, in effect, *"Wow! Look what happened next!"*

There were two veils inside the Temple — one at the entrance to the Holy Place and a second at the entrance to the Holy of Holies. Only the high priest was allowed to pass through the second veil once a year during the Festival of Atonement. That second veil was massive and represented a barrier between the sinfulness of man and the presence of God inside the Holy of Holies.

What Happened to That Second Veil When Jesus Took His Last Breath on the Cross?

In his book *The Life and Times of Jesus the Messiah*, Alfred Edersheim wrote about the size and weight of the veil and, also, about the manpower needed to manipulate or move it due to its enormous size. Edersheim wrote:

> **The Veils before the Most Holy Place were 40 cubits (60 feet) long, and 20 (30 feet) wide, of the thickness of the palm of the hand, and wrought in 72 squares, which were joined together; and these Veils were so heavy, that, in the exaggerated language of the time, it needed 3000 [300] priests to manipulate each. If the Veil was at all such as is described in the Talmud, it could not have been rent in twain by a mere earthquake or the fall of the lintel, although its composition in squares fastened together might explain, how the rent might be as described in the Gospel.**[1]

Scholar Maurice Henry Harris writes of the enormity and weight of the veil:

> **Three hundred priests were told off** [or they were designated] **to draw the veil (of the Temple) aside...the thickness of the veil was a handbreadth. It was woven of seventy-two cords, and each cord consisted of twenty-four strands. It was forty cubits long and twenty wide.... When it became soiled, it took three hundred priests to immerse and cleanse it.**[2]

At the very moment Jesus was breathing His last breath on the cross at Golgotha, the high priest was standing at his station in the inner court of the Temple, and in the same instant that Jesus exclaimed, *"It is finished!"* — miles away from Golgotha and deep inside the Temple at Jerusalem — an inexplicable, mystifying supernatural event occurred. The massive, fortified veil that stood before the Holy of Holies was suddenly split in half from the top all the way to the bottom!

The sound of that veil splitting must have been deafening as it ripped and tore, starting from the top and going all the way down to the floor. It was as if invisible, divine hands had reached out to grab it, rip it to shreds, and discard it.

Imagine how shocked the high priest must have been when he heard the ripping sounds inside the Temple and then watched as the veil was torn in half, leaving the two sides of the once-massive curtain lying collapsed to his right and his left. Just think what must have gone through this evil man's mind when he saw that the way to the Holy of Holies was opened — and that God's presence was no longer there. The Spirit of God, through the new birth that Jesus just purchased with the price of His own blood, could now live in the hearts of men, women, and children *everywhere and for all time* who believed in and accepted Jesus as the ultimate Sacrifice — the *only* One who could eternally atone for sin.

You see, when Jesus was lifted up on the Cross, it was no longer necessary for a high priest to continually make sacrifices year after year, for Jesus' blood had now settled the issue forever! For this cause, God Himself reached out to take hold of the veil of the Temple and ripped it in half, declaring that the way to the Holy of Holies was now available to everyone who came to Him through the blood of Jesus. But just before God reached down and took that veil and ripped it from top to bottom, Jesus cried out, *"...It is finished..."* (John 19:30)! And the rest of that verse says, "... And he bowed his head, and gave up the ghost."

The words "it is finished" are a translation of the Greek word *tetelestai*, which is the perfect indicative passive tense of the word *telos*, and it means *to end, to bring to completion, to bring to a conclusion, to complete, to accomplish, to fulfill,* or *to finish.* One scholar notes that anything that has reached this state has arrived at *completion, maturity,* or *perfection.*

176

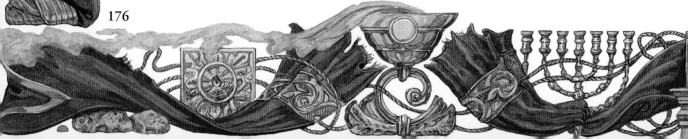

There are many nuances to this word *tetelestai*, but four of them, which I will share with you now, are hugely significant to this defining moment of Christ's holy sacrifice.

1. *Tetelestai* — The Mission Is Accomplished!

First, this was Jesus' exclamation that He had finished the work the Father had sent Him to do. The work having been fully completed, Jesus bowed His head and died.

One writer has noted that when a servant was sent on a mission and then later returned to his master, he would say, *"Tetelestai"*— meaning, *"I have done exactly what you requested"* or, *"The mission is now accomplished."* In that moment when Jesus cried out, He was exclaiming to the entire universe that He had faithfully fulfilled the Father's will and that the mission was now accomplished. No wonder Jesus shouted — for this was the greatest victory in the history of the human race! He had been faithful to His assignment even in the face of unfathomable challenges. But now the fight was over, and Jesus could cry out to the Father, *"I have done exactly what You asked Me to do!"* or, *"The mission is accomplished!"*

2. *Tetelestai* — The Sacrifice Is Complete and Finished

Second, the word *tetelestai* was the equivalent of the Hebrew word spoken by the high priest when he presented a sacrificial lamb without spot or blemish. Annually, the high priest entered the Holy of Holies, where he poured the blood of that sacrificial spotless lamb on the mercy seat of the Ark of the Covenant. The moment that blood touched the mercy seat, atonement was made for the people's sins for one more year — when once again, the high priest would enter beyond the veil of that sacred room to offer blood. This was done year after year to obtain the annual, temporary forgiveness of sin.

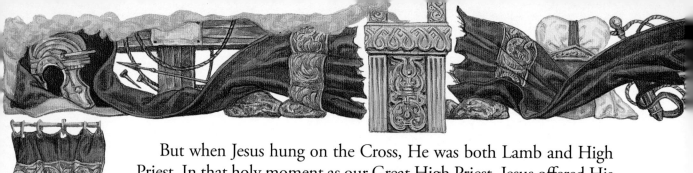

But when Jesus hung on the Cross, He was both Lamb and High Priest. In that holy moment as our Great High Priest, Jesus offered His own blood for the permanent removal of sin. He offered up the perfect sacrifice of which every Mosaic sacrifice was a type and symbol — and in that instant, there remained no more need of offering for sin.

Jesus entered into the Holy Place and offered His own blood — a sacrifice so complete that God never again required the blood of lambs for forgiveness. As Hebrews 9:12 says, "Neither by the blood of goats and calves, but by his own blood he entered in once into the holy place, having obtained eternal redemption for us."

Thus, when Jesus said, "It is finished!" He was declaring the end of sacrifices, because the ultimate Sacrifice had finally been made! Atonement was *completed*, *perfected*, and *fully accomplished*. It was done once and for all — *finished forever*!

3. *Tetelestai* — All Debt Is Paid in Full

Third, in a secular sense, the word *tetelestai* was used in the business world to signify *the full payment of a debt*. When a debt had been fully paid off, the parchment on which the debt was recorded was stamped with *tetelestai*, which meant the debt had been *paid in full*.

This means that once a person calls Jesus the Lord of his life and personally accepts His sacrifice, no debt of sin exists for that person any longer. The debt is wiped out because Jesus paid the price for sin that no sinner could *ever* pay.

When Jesus took our place, He paid the debt of sin we owed. And when we by faith repent and receive Him as Lord, *we are set free!* This is why Paul wrote, "In whom we have redemption through his blood, even the forgiveness of sins" (Colossians 1:14).

When Jesus uttered those words, "It is finished!" it was His declaration that the debt of sin was *fully satisfied*, *fulfilled*, and *complete*. His blood utterly and completely cleansed us forever. It was *far-reaching* and *all-embracing* for all of us who put our faith in Him.

4. *Tetelestai* — The Old Has Ended, the New Has Begun

Fourth, in classical Greek times the word *tetelestai* depicted *a turning point when one period ended and another new period began*. When Jesus exclaimed, "It is finished!" it was indeed a turning point in the entire history of mankind, for at that moment the Old Testament came to an end — finished and closed — and the New Testament began. The Cross was "the Great Divide" in human history. When Jesus cried out, "It is finished!" He was shouting that the Old Covenant had ended and the New Covenant had begun!

In that divine moment when Jesus cried, "It is finished," the Old Testament prophecies about Jesus' earthly ministry were fulfilled. The justice of God had been fully met and satisfied by the Lamb of God. At that moment, the sacrifices of the Old Testament permanently ceased, for the perfect Sacrifice had laid down His life for the salvation of mankind. Jesus' mission was accomplished. Thus, He could cry out that His task was *tetelestai*, or *completed*! Because Jesus was willing to offer His own blood as the full payment of our sinful debt, we are forgiven and utterly debt-free. Now "PAID IN FULL" has been stamped on our past sinful record because Jesus paid the price for our redemption with His own blood!

Isaiah said, "Surely he hath borne our griefs, and carried our sorrows: yet we did esteem him stricken, smitten of God, and afflicted. But he was wounded for our transgressions, he was bruised for our iniquities: the chastisement of our peace was upon him; and with his stripes we are healed" (Isaiah 53:4,5). So remember:

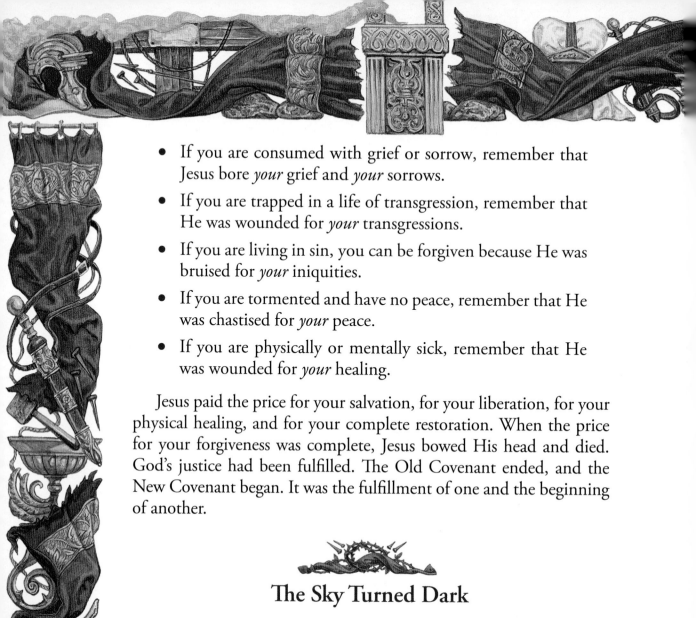

- If you are consumed with grief or sorrow, remember that Jesus bore *your* grief and *your* sorrows.

- If you are trapped in a life of transgression, remember that He was wounded for *your* transgressions.

- If you are living in sin, you can be forgiven because He was bruised for *your* iniquities.

- If you are tormented and have no peace, remember that He was chastised for *your* peace.

- If you are physically or mentally sick, remember that He was wounded for *your* healing.

Jesus paid the price for your salvation, for your liberation, for your physical healing, and for your complete restoration. When the price for your forgiveness was complete, Jesus bowed His head and died. God's justice had been fulfilled. The Old Covenant ended, and the New Covenant began. It was the fulfillment of one and the beginning of another.

The Sky Turned Dark

The day when Jesus was crucified was so paramount that the sky turned dark when Jesus' precious blood fell upon the earth and He cried out, "It is finished!" The historians Phlegon, Thallus, and Julius Africanus all referred to a darkness that covered the earth at the time of Jesus' crucifixion. Critics of the Bible have attempted to explain away this supernatural darkness by alleging that it was due to an eclipse of the sun. This is impossible, however, for the Passover occurred at the time of a full moon.[3]

The Bible informs us that the darkening of the sky started at the sixth hour (*see* Matthew 27:45; Mark 15:33; Luke 23:44).

This is very significant, for the sixth hour (noontime, or halfway between sunrise and sunset) was the very moment that the high priest Caiaphas, arrayed in his full priestly garments, began the procession in which he would enter the temple courts to slaughter a pure, spotless Passover lamb. A great number of unblemished lambs were slaughtered in the temple courts during those hours — one lamb slaughtered for every household in Israel (unless, of course, the household was too small).

This supernatural darkness that covered the land lasted until the ninth hour — about the time when the sacrifices of the Passover lambs would be coming to an end. It was at this moment that Jesus cried out, *"It is finished!"* (*see* John 19:30).

As He heaved upward to breathe for the last time, Jesus gathered enough air to speak forth a victory shout. His assignment was complete! And after proclaiming those words with His last ounce of strength, Matthew 27:50 tells us that He "...yielded up the ghost."

And what came next is simply amazing! As noted earlier, the massive, fortified veil that stood before the Holy of Holies was rent from top to bottom. God Himself ripped the veil of the Temple in half, declaring that the way to the Holy of Holies was now available to everyone who came to Him through the blood of Jesus!

This is why the apostle Paul wrote that Jesus "...hath broken down the middle wall of partition between us" (Ephesians 2:14), and Matthew 27:51 records that the massive veil which hung inside the Temple in front of the Holy of Holies was shockingly ripped from the very top all the way to the very bottom.

181

The Earth Trembled

Jesus' death was such a dramatic event that even the earth reacted to it. Matthew 27:51 says, "...The earth did quake, and the rocks rent." The word "earth" describes *the whole earth*. The word "quake" means *to shake*, *to agitate*, or *to create a commotion*. It is where we get the word for a *seismograph*, the apparatus that registers the intensity of an earthquake. It is interesting to note that Origen, the early Christian leader, recorded that there were "great earthquakes" at the time of Jesus' crucifixion.[4]

It is amazing that Israel rejected Jesus and the Roman authorities crucified Him, but creation *always* recognized Him. During His life on this earth:

- Wind and waves obeyed Him.
- Water turned to wine at His command.
- Fishes and bread multiplied at His touch.
- Atoms in water solidified so He could walk across them.

Hence, it should come as no surprise that Jesus' death was a traumatic event for creation. The earth shook, trembled, and shuddered at the death of its Creator, for it instantly felt its loss. The earth shuddered so violently at the moment Jesus died that even "...the *rocks* rent...." The word "rocks" refers to *large rocks*. Matthew used this word to tell us that *huge rocks* were "rent" by the shaking of the earth. The word "rent" means *to rend*, *to tear*, *to violently tear asunder*, or *to terribly fracture*. This was a *serious* earthquake! It makes me realize all over again the incredible significance of the death of Jesus Christ.

The Way to the Holy of Holies Was Opened

When Jesus' blood was accepted at the Cross as final payment for man's sin, the need to habitually offer sacrifices year after year was eliminated, and the Holy of Holies, a place limited only to the high priest once a year, was opened and became accessible to all of us! Now as "believer-priests," we each can enjoy the presence of God every day.

This is why Hebrews 10:19-22 says, "Having therefore, brethren, boldness to enter into the holiest by the blood of Jesus.... Let us draw near with a true heart in full assurance of faith, having our hearts sprinkled from an evil conscience...."

The way into the Holy of Holies has been thrown wide open to us because of Jesus' sacrifice. Now it's up to us to take a few minutes each day to enter into the presence of God to worship Him and to make our requests known. Jesus died for us so we could "...come boldly unto the throne of grace, that we may obtain mercy, and find grace to help in time of need" (Hebrews 4:16). Jesus has done His part. Now it's up to us to come with boldness before the throne of grace to receive the divine help God has already provided for us.

In the next chapter, we will irrefutably rebuff any skeptic who has ever alleged that perhaps Jesus did not really die on the Cross and was not really resurrected. Some claim that He simply recovered from His experience, but in the next chapter, you will see indisputably that Jesus' corpse was handled by numerous people, it was completely examined multiple times, and the process that was used by Romans proved beyond a doubt that Jesus was factually dead — and God really raised Him from the dead on the third day!

QUESTIONS TO PONDER AND DISCUSS

1. The cross symbolizes one of the most barbaric forms of execution in history, and when we beautify it, we tend to minimize the appalling reality of all it represents. How long has it been since you've taken time to reflect upon the horrific death Jesus willingly experienced for you?

2. As Jesus died, He forgave even those who played a part in His death. If Jesus could go through that degree of suffering because of your sins against the Father and then forgive you, how can you justify refusing to release in forgiveness those who have sinned against you?

3. If every debt and credit-card bill you owed was suddenly paid off, how would you act? Jesus paid in full your debt to sin. How should that truth influence what you say and do on a daily basis?

4. The earth and its elements have always recognized and responded to the voice and the presence of the One who created them. How readily do you respond to the voice and the presence of the Holy Spirit who resides within you? God personally removed all barriers that once blocked man from His holy presence. Are you tolerating any unnecessary hindrances in your life that prevent you from coming boldly before the throne of God? What can you do to remove them from your life?

When the Roman soldier thrust a spear into Jesus' side, it confirmed His death had already taken place and there was no need to break His legs. The apostle John later wrote that this was a fulfillment of Old Testament Scripture concerning the Messiah — "For these things were done, that the scripture should be fulfilled, A bone of him shall not be broken" (John 19:36).

Mark 15:43 tells us Joseph of Arimathea boldly went before Pilate and "craved the body of Jesus." Then he and another secret follower of Jesus prepared Jesus' body for burial, as is illustrated here. Our Savior gave His very life to set us free, and His devoted followers risked everything to honor Him in His death.

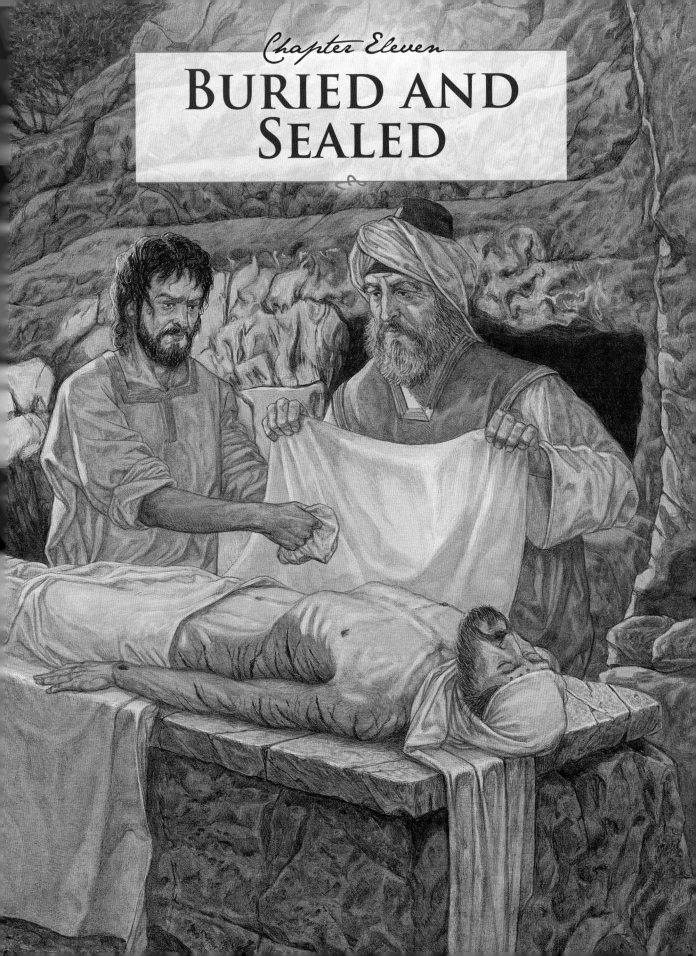

Chapter Eleven

BURIED AND SEALED

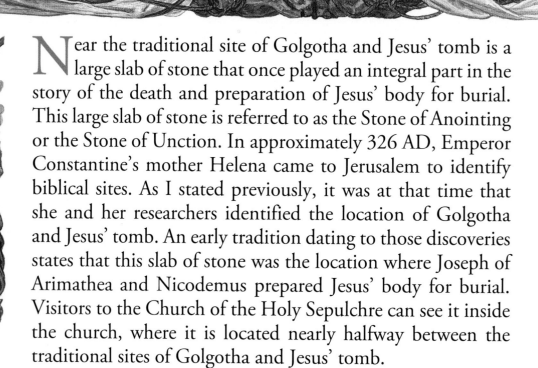

Near the traditional site of Golgotha and Jesus' tomb is a large slab of stone that once played an integral part in the story of the death and preparation of Jesus' body for burial. This large slab of stone is referred to as the Stone of Anointing or the Stone of Unction. In approximately 326 AD, Emperor Constantine's mother Helena came to Jerusalem to identify biblical sites. As I stated previously, it was at that time that she and her researchers identified the location of Golgotha and Jesus' tomb. An early tradition dating to those discoveries states that this slab of stone was the location where Joseph of Arimathea and Nicodemus prepared Jesus' body for burial. Visitors to the Church of the Holy Sepulchre can see it inside the church, where it is located nearly halfway between the traditional sites of Golgotha and Jesus' tomb.

But during the Middle Ages, the slab of stone was damaged, and some allege that in the Twelfth Century it was replaced with a new one. This replacement led to serious disputes among Christian denominations. Eventually a historical church agreement called *Status Quo* emerged as a guarantee that this historical site, and others, would remain unchanged. Because the Church of the Holy Sepulchre is one of the most important religious sites within Christianity, it was agreed that the church would be shared by several denominations with each having its own designated area within the complex.

Today five Christian communities are allowed to use various spaces in the Church of the Holy Sepulchre, including Copts, Syrians, and Ethiopians, but the site is officially held under the shared custody of the Greek Orthodox, Roman Catholic, and Armenian Apostolic

Churches, all three of which share control and management of the church's sacred spaces.

But if we peer back to the time of Jesus' death, we read that Pilate received a surprise visit from a high-ranking member of the Sanhedrin, who was a secret follower of Jesus, as the time approached for Jesus' body to be brought down from the Cross (*see* Mark 15:42,43). That high-ranking member of the Sanhedrin's name was Joseph, and he was from the city of Arimathea; therefore, we know this man as *Joseph of Arimathea*. But another high-ranking member of the Sanhedrin accompanied Joseph — he was also a secret disciple of Jesus whose relationship with Him began with a visit in the middle of the night, which is recorded in John 3:1-21. The second admirer's name was *Nicodemus*.

Joseph of Arimathea

Let's begin with Joseph of Arimathea to see what we know of him. To obtain an accurate picture of this man, we must turn to Mark 15:42 and 43, which says, "And now when the even was come, because it was the preparation, that is, the day before the sabbath, Joseph of Arimathaea, an honourable counsellor, which also waited for the kingdom of God, came, and went in boldly unto Pilate, and craved the body of Jesus."

This verse tells us that Joseph of Arimathea was an "honorable counselor." The Greek word for "honorable" refers to *people who have a good reputation, people who have a good standing in society,* or *people who are prominent, influential, and wealthy.* The word "counselor" is the word to depict *a member of the Sanhedrin.* By using this word,

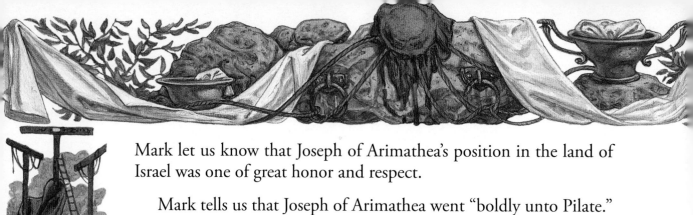

Mark let us know that Joseph of Arimathea's position in the land of Israel was one of great honor and respect.

Mark tells us that Joseph of Arimathea went "boldly unto Pilate." John 19:38 informs us that this Joseph had never publicly announced he was a follower of Jesus "for fear of the Jews."

As a member of the Sanhedrin, he was well aware of the exultation the supreme council members felt over Jesus' death. If it became known that Joseph was the one who took the body and buried it, it could place him in considerable jeopardy. Therefore, going to Pilate to request that he might remove the body of Jesus before the Sabbath began was an act of bravery on Joseph's part.

But Joseph's desire to take the body of Jesus and prepare it for burial was so powerful that Mark 15:43 says he "*craved* the body of Jesus."

The word "craved" is a Greek word that means *to be adamant in requesting and demanding something*. In the New Testament, this particular word is used to portray *a person addressing a superior*, as in this case when Joseph of Arimathea appealed to Pilate. It carries the idea that the person may *insist* or *demand* that a need be met, but he approaches and speaks to his superior with *respect*.

Therefore, although Joseph showed respect toward Pilate's position, he also presented a strong demand to the governor, adamantly insisting that Jesus' body be released to him.

The word "body" in the original text refers to *a dead body* and was often translated as "corpse" which informs us that Joseph of Arimathea knew Jesus' body was already dead. Roman custom was to leave the body hanging on the cross until it rotted or until the vultures had picked away

190

at it. Then afterward, they would discard the corpse in the wilderness, where it would be eaten by wild dogs.

The Jews, however, held the human body in great honor because it was made in the image of God. Even those who were executed by the Jews were respected in the way they were handled after death. Thus, it was not permitted for a Jew's body to hang on a cross after sunset or to be left to rot or for the birds to devour.

Mark 15:44,45 tells us, "And Pilate marvelled if he were already dead: and calling unto him the centurion, he asked him whether he had been any while dead. And when he knew it of the centurion, he gave the body to Joseph."

Nicodemus, Who Came to Jesus by Night

It was at this point that *Nicodemus* entered the picture. The third chapter of John gives the greatest insight into who Nicodemus was. It says, "There was a man of the Pharisees, named Nicodemus, a ruler of the Jews: the same came to Jesus by night, and said unto him, Rabbi, we know that thou art a teacher come from God: for no man can do these miracles that thou doest, except God be with him" (John 3:1,2).

John 3:1 tells us that Nicodemus was a "Pharisee." During the time Jesus lived, the Pharisees were the most respected and esteemed religious leaders in Israel. The Pharisees believed in the supernatural and earnestly waited for the arrival of the Messiah, contrary to the Sadducees who did *not* believe in the supernatural and did *not* wait for the Messiah's coming. The Pharisees held strictly to the Law, whereas the Sadducees took a more liberal approach to the Law that the Pharisees found unacceptable.

Verse 1 goes on to tell us that Nicodemus was "a ruler of the Jews." The word "ruler" means *chief one*, *ruler*, or *prince*. This word was used to denote *the rulers of local synagogues and members of the Sanhedrin* who were the *highest authorities* in the land. Due to this high-ranking position, Nicodemus, like Joseph of Arimathea, was *prominent*, *influential*, and *wealthy*.

Nicodemus' notoriety among the Jews in Jerusalem was the reason he visited Jesus by night and not during the daytime. His fame most likely created a stir every time he passed through the city. Therefore, Nicodemus wanted to avoid visiting Jesus by day, as it would draw attention to the fact that he was spending time with a teacher the Sanhedrin viewed to be a "maverick" and out of their control. Consequently, he came to Jesus by night when his visit would not be observable.

What he told Jesus during this visit reveals much about the spiritual hunger that Nicodemus possessed. First, he called Jesus "Rabbi." The word itself means *great*, but it was used as a title of respect only in reference to the great teachers of the Law.

The Pharisees loved to be called "Rabbi," for they viewed themselves as the chief keepers of the Law. So for Nicodemus to call Jesus "Rabbi" was remarkable indeed. The Jewish leader would never have used that title unless he had already heard Jesus interpret the Law and thereby judged His ability to do so. The fact that Nicodemus called Jesus by this privileged title, given only to those who were viewed as the greatest theologians in Israel, tells us that he was very impressed with Jesus' knowledge of the Scriptures.

This means that Nicodemus, like Joseph of Arimathea, was open-minded enough to receive from people who were "outside the circle" of what most religious people viewed as acceptable. In fact, Nicodemus

192

was so hungry to find a touch from God that it appears he himself had seen some of Jesus' meetings that had just been conducted in the city of Jerusalem prior to their secret meeting.

John 2:23 says, "Now when he [Jesus] was in Jerusalem at the passover, in the feast day, many believed in his name, when they saw the miracles which he did."

When Nicodemus visited with Jesus, he referred to these miracles, saying in John 3:2, "...Rabbi, we know that thou art a teacher come from God: for no man can do these miracles that thou doest, except God be with him."

It seems Nicodemus had come close enough to these miracle meetings to personally view the miracles. It must have been on these occasions when he heard Jesus teach and began to deem Him worthy of the title "Rabbi."

As a Pharisee, Nicodemus believed in the supernatural, so he was moved by the miracles and was convinced of their legitimacy, causing him to want to personally meet Jesus and ask Him questions.

In the conversation that followed, Jesus told Nicodemus, "...Verily, verily, I say unto thee, Except a man be born again, he cannot see the kingdom of God" (John 3:3).

Where Your Treasure Is, There Is Your Heart Also

After hearing Joseph of Arimathea's request to remove Jesus' body from the Cross, Pilate gave him permission, so Joseph took the body to begin preparations for burial. John 19:39 tells us what happened next: "And there came also Nicodemus, which at the first came to Jesus by

night, and brought a mixture of myrrh and aloes, about an hundred pound weight."

This verse tells us Nicodemus "...brought a mixture of myrrh and aloes, about an hundred pound weight...." "Myrrh" was an expensive yellowish-brown, sweet-smelling gum resin that was obtained from a tree and had a bitter taste. It was chiefly used as a chemical for embalming the dead. "Aloes" was a sweet-smelling fragrance derived from the juice pressed from the leaves of a tree found in the Middle East. It was used to ceremonially cleanse, to purify, and to counter-act the terrible smell of a corpse as it decomposed. Like myrrh, this substance was also very expensive and rare — yet the Bible tells us that Nicodemus "brought a mixture" of both substances — about a hundred pounds' worth.

Nicodemus' cost for this offering of love must have been out of sight. Only a rich man could have purchased such a massive combination of these costly, uncommon substances. Nicodemus obviously intended to fully cover the body of Jesus, so he spared no cost in preparing the body for burial, demonstrating his love for Jesus even after His death.

John goes on to tell us, "Then took they the body of Jesus, and wound it in linen clothes with the spices, as the manner of the Jews is to bury" (v. 40).

The word for "linen" is a word that describes *a cloth made of very fine and extremely expensive materials* that was fabricated primarily in Egypt. Nobles in that day were known to pay very high prices to have robes made for their wives from this material.

When we read the early story of the moment when Lazarus came forth from the tomb after being resurrected by Jesus, we are told that he was "...bound hand and foot with graveclothes: and his face was bound about with a napkin..." (John 11:44). This shows that Lazarus was bound with bandages made of strips of material.

However, the word "linen" used to describe the cloth Jesus was buried in suggests that Jesus was carefully laid in a large linen sheet of fine weave. Specially prepared spices were then mingled between the folds of this high-priced garment in which Jesus' dead body was wrapped.

This is an amazing story of two men who dearly loved Jesus. Although Joseph and Nicodemus lived in circumstances that made it difficult for them to publicly follow Jesus, they chose to follow Him to their fullest capability. When Jesus died, they continued to demonstrate their deep love for Him, treating His dead body with tender care and using their personal wealth to bury Him with honor. As far as they understood at the time, this was their last opportunity to show Jesus how much they loved Him, and they were going to take full advantage of it.

Jesus taught, "For where your treasure is, there will your heart be also" (Matthew 6:21). When these two men used their wealth to bury Jesus, they illustrated that their hearts were with Jesus. He was their highest priority, so they invested their assets in showing their love for Him. They literally sowed their money into the ground when they bathed Jesus in 100 pounds of those rare substances, wrapped Him in an expensive cloth, and then buried Him in a rich man's tomb.

But by the time Jesus' body was prepared for burial, perhaps at the site inside the Church of the Holy Sepulchre — on a stone that today is referred to as the Stone of Anointing or the Stone of Unction — His dead body had been handled many hours by those who prepared it for placement in the tomb. If there was a pulse to be felt

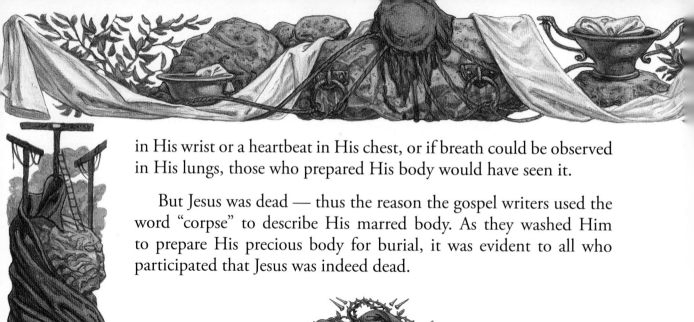

in His wrist or a heartbeat in His chest, or if breath could be observed in His lungs, those who prepared His body would have seen it.

But Jesus was dead — thus the reason the gospel writers used the word "corpse" to describe His marred body. As they washed Him to prepare His precious body for burial, it was evident to all who participated that Jesus was indeed dead.

The Tomb Where Jesus Was Buried

The Church of the Holy Sepulchre is so-called because it also is the site of the enshrined tomb where earliest Christian records state Jesus was buried. According to the earliest historical records, Christ's corpse was indeed buried in a tomb, and that tomb was officially sealed by Pilate's men.[1]

What else do we know from Scripture about Christ's tomb? All four gospels tell us the tomb where Jesus was buried was very near where Jesus was crucified.

John 19:41 and 42 says, "Now in the place where he was crucified there was a garden; and in the garden a new sepulchre…. There laid they Jesus therefore because of the Jews' preparation day; for the sepulchre was *nigh* at hand." The word "nigh" is the Greek word *eggus*, meaning *nearby*.

But let's look in this passage at the word "sepulchre," which is another word for "tomb." In particular, notice the phrase "new sepulchre."

John 19:41 tells us that in the garden was "…a *new sepulchre*, wherein was never man yet laid." The word "new" is a form of the Greek word *kainos*, meaning *fresh* or *unused*. This doesn't necessarily mean that the tomb had recently been made, but that it was a tomb that had never been used — thus, the reason John wrote, "…Wherein was never man yet laid."

Matthew, Mark, and Luke all record that this tomb belonged to Joseph of Arimathea, suggesting that it was the tomb he had prepared for his own burial. The fact that it was a tomb "hewn out in the rock" (Matthew 27:60; Mark 15:46; Luke 23:53) confirms the personal wealth of Joseph of Arimathea. Only royalty or wealthy individuals could afford to have their tombs carved out of a wall of stone or in the side of a mountain. Poorer men were buried in simple graves.

The word "hewn" in Matthew, Mark, and Luke comes from a Greek word meaning *to cut out* or *to polish*, and it implies that it was *a special, highly developed, refined tomb* or *a tomb that was splendid and expensive*.

Isaiah 53:9 prophesied that the Messiah would be buried in a rich man's tomb, and this word for Christ's tomb in the gospels confirms this was indeed the expensive tomb of a rich man.

Jesus' Dead Body Was Carefully Inspected Again

What else do the gospels tell us about Jesus' burial? John 19:42 goes on to say, "There laid they Jesus.…"

The word "laid" comes from the word *tithemi*, which means *to set, to lay, to place, to deposit*, or *to set in place*. As used here, it portrays the careful and thoughtful placing of Jesus' body in its resting place inside the tomb.

Luke 23:55 tells us that after Jesus' body was placed in the tomb, the women who came with Him from Galilee "...beheld the sepulchre, and how his body was laid." The word "beheld" in Greek is a form of the word *theaomai*, which is where we get the word *theater*. The word *theaomai* means *to gaze upon*, *to fully see*, or *to look at intently*. This is very important, for it proves the women *inspected* the tomb, *gazing upon* the dead body of Jesus *to see* that it had been honorably laid in place.

Mark 15:47 identifies these women as Mary Magdalene and Mary the mother of Joses and says that these women "...beheld where he [Jesus] was laid" in the tomb. The imperfect tense is used in Mark's account, alerting us to the fact that these women took their time to make sure Jesus was properly laid there. It could be translated, *"They carefully contemplated where he was laid."*

If Jesus had still been alive, those who buried Him would have known it, for they spent substantial time preparing His body for burial. Then after His dead body was deposited into the tomb, they lingered there, checking once again to see that the body was treated with the greatest love, care, and attention.

A Great Stone Door Sealed the Tomb

Once the group responsible for Jesus' burial were certain everything was done properly, Joseph of Arimathea "...rolled a great stone to the door of the sepulchre, and departed" (Matthew 27:60). It was rare to find a stone entrance to a Jewish tomb in biblical times; most Jewish tombs had doors with certain types of hinges. A large stone rolled before the tomb would be much more difficult to move, making the burial site more permanent.

However, the chief priests and Pharisees weren't so sure the site was secure. Fearing that Jesus' disciples would come to steal the body and claim by His absence that Jesus had been resurrected, the Jewish leaders went to Pilate and said, "...Sir, we remember that that deceiver said, while he was yet alive, After three days I will rise again. Command therefore that the sepulchre be made sure until the third day, lest his disciples come by night, and steal him away, and say unto the people, He is risen from the dead: so the last error shall be worse than the first" (Matthew 27:63,64).

In response, Pilate said, "...Ye have a watch: go your way, make it as sure as ye can" (Matthew 27:65). Verse 66 says, "So they went, and made the sepulchre sure, sealing the stone, and setting a watch."

Wasting no time, the chief priests and elders hastened to the tomb with their government-assigned soldiers and the special officers assigned to inspect the tomb before placing Pilate's seal upon it.

The Official Seal of Pilate Was Placed on the Tomb

The chief priests and Pharisees had asked that "...the sepulchre be *made sure...*" (v. 64). The Greek word used for "made sure" describes *a legal seal* that was placed on documents, letters, possessions — or, in this case, a tomb. Its purpose was *to authenticate that the sealed item had been properly inspected before sealing and that all the contents were*

199

in order. As long as the seal remained unbroken, *it guaranteed that the contents inside were safe and sound.*

In this case, the word *sphragidzo* is used to signify *the sealing of the tomb.* In all probability, it was a string that was stretched across the stone at the entrance of the tomb, which was then sealed on both sides by Pilate's legal authorities.

Before sealing the tomb, however, these authorities were first required to inspect the inside of the tomb to see that the body of Jesus was in its place. After guaranteeing that the corpse was where it was supposed to be, they rolled the stone back in place and then *sealed* it with the official seal of the governor of Rome.

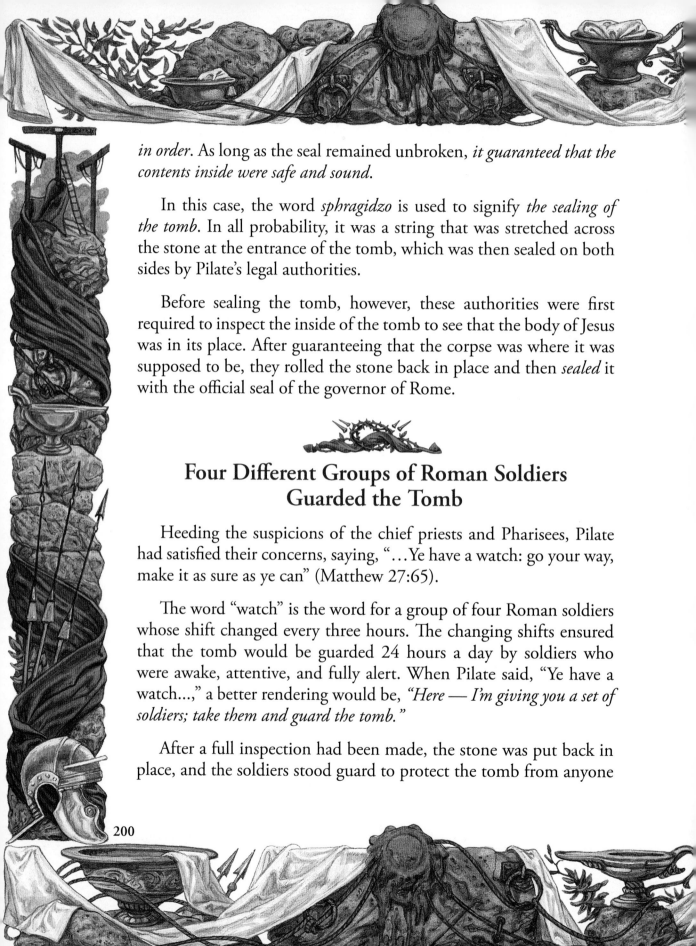

Four Different Groups of Roman Soldiers Guarded the Tomb

Heeding the suspicions of the chief priests and Pharisees, Pilate had satisfied their concerns, saying, "…Ye have a watch: go your way, make it as sure as ye can" (Matthew 27:65).

The word "watch" is the word for a group of four Roman soldiers whose shift changed every three hours. The changing shifts ensured that the tomb would be guarded 24 hours a day by soldiers who were awake, attentive, and fully alert. When Pilate said, "Ye have a watch…," a better rendering would be, *"Here — I'm giving you a set of soldiers; take them and guard the tomb."*

After a full inspection had been made, the stone was put back in place, and the soldiers stood guard to protect the tomb from anyone who would attempt to touch it or remove its contents. Every three hours, new guards arrived to replace the old ones. These armed soldiers guarded the entrance to Jesus' tomb so firmly that *no one* would have been able to come near it.

The purpose of the seal was to authenticate that Jesus was dead; therefore, we can know that His body was thoroughly inspected again for proof of death. There is no doubt that Jesus was dead, for He was examined again and again, even as He lay in the tomb.

Some critics have claimed that only Jesus' own disciples inspected His body and that they could have lied about His being dead. However, an officer from Pilate's court also examined the body of Jesus. We can also be fairly certain that the chief priests and elders who accompanied the soldiers to the burial site demanded the right to view His dead body as well so they could verify that He was truly dead.

When Jesus came out of that grave several days later, it was no hoax or fabricated story. In addition to all the people who saw Him die on the Cross, the individuals and groups listed in the next section verified that His dead body was in the tomb before the stone was permanently sealed by an officer from the Roman court of law.

Multiple Witnesses Verified Jesus Was Dead

In review, there were many who saw and handled Jesus' dead body before it was sealed and buried.

- Joseph of Arimathea carefully laid Him inside the tomb.

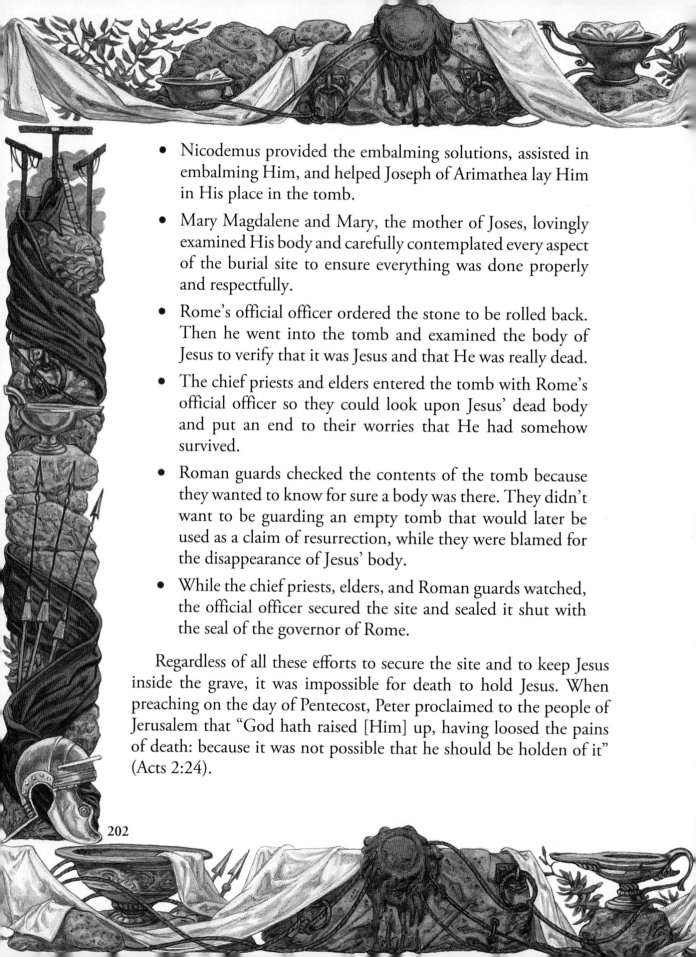

- Nicodemus provided the embalming solutions, assisted in embalming Him, and helped Joseph of Arimathea lay Him in His place in the tomb.

- Mary Magdalene and Mary, the mother of Joses, lovingly examined His body and carefully contemplated every aspect of the burial site to ensure everything was done properly and respectfully.

- Rome's official officer ordered the stone to be rolled back. Then he went into the tomb and examined the body of Jesus to verify that it was Jesus and that He was really dead.

- The chief priests and elders entered the tomb with Rome's official officer so they could look upon Jesus' dead body and put an end to their worries that He had somehow survived.

- Roman guards checked the contents of the tomb because they wanted to know for sure a body was there. They didn't want to be guarding an empty tomb that would later be used as a claim of resurrection, while they were blamed for the disappearance of Jesus' body.

- While the chief priests, elders, and Roman guards watched, the official officer secured the site and sealed it shut with the seal of the governor of Rome.

Regardless of all these efforts to secure the site and to keep Jesus inside the grave, it was impossible for death to hold Jesus. When preaching on the day of Pentecost, Peter proclaimed to the people of Jerusalem that "God hath raised [Him] up, having loosed the pains of death: because it was not possible that he should be holden of it" (Acts 2:24).

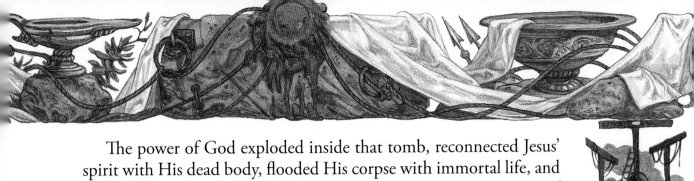

The power of God exploded inside that tomb, reconnected Jesus' spirit with His dead body, flooded His corpse with immortal life, and He arose! So much power was released behind the sealed entrance of His tomb that the earth itself reverberated and shuddered from the explosion. Then an angel rolled the stone from the entrance, and *Jesus physically walked through the door of that tomb alive!* Today the tomb in Jerusalem is empty because Jesus arose on the third day!

In the next chapter, we will examine what the Bible tells us about Jesus' resurrection. And as we proceed, remember that Romans 8:11 declares the same power that raised Christ from the dead dwells inside every believer. If you release it, that divine power will flow in your life and take you into a whole new realm of victory and the miraculous.

But now, let's see what we can learn about Jesus' resurrection as we read further.

QUESTIONS TO PONDER
AND DISCUSS

1. Joseph of Arimathea displayed great love for Jesus as he boldly and insistently requested that Pilate hand over to him the body of Jesus. Joseph risked his reputation and acceptance among the Jews when he identified himself as a follower of Jesus. Has your identification with Jesus ever cost you anything of value?

2. The purpose of the seal on Jesus' tomb was to authenticate that He was indeed dead and His dead body was securely sealed there. Due to their own ignorance and arrogance, Pilate's soldiers and the religious leaders really believed they could control and contain the body of the Son of God. Are there any areas of your life that you have kept sealed in an attempt to prevent God from stirring or affecting change in you?

3. When Jesus died and was then buried, creation was shocked and His disciples were devastated. But God raised Jesus to new life. What seemed to be the end was only the beginning. How has making Jesus the Lord of your life given you a new beginning?

4. If you flip through the pages of your own life's story, what promise from God to you seems incapable of coming to pass? What hope or dream in your life have you buried? Have you spent time remembering that the power of the One who raised Jesus from the dead can cause His promise to you to come to pass too?

Pictured here is the tomb where Jesus was buried. A great stone was rolled in front of the entrance and then it was sealed with the official seal of the governor. When Jesus' body was finally laid in the tomb, there was no doubt He was really dead. The contents of the tomb had been examined again and again, ensuring that this was no hoax — Jesus really did die for you

On the third day, Jesus Christ, the Son of God, was brought back to life and burst out of the grave. This is no legend or fairy tale. *This is the foundation of our faith!* In this an awe-inspiring, earth-shaking, glorious moment, the King of kings stepped into His resurrected body to reconvene on the earth.

Chapter Twelve

'BEHOLD, HE IS RISEN!'

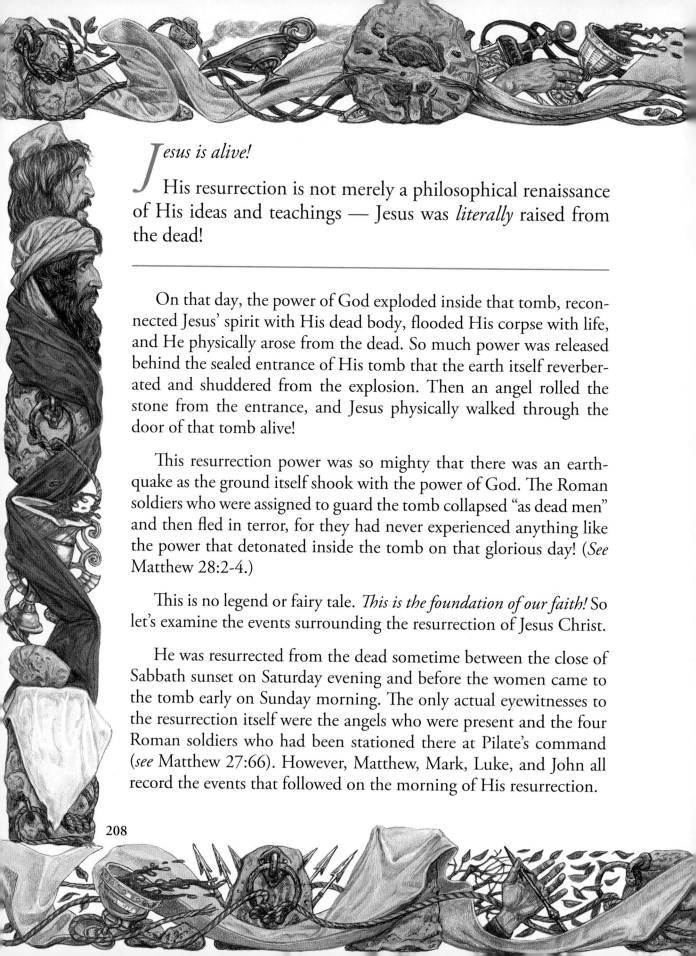

*J*esus is alive!

His resurrection is not merely a philosophical renaissance of His ideas and teachings — Jesus was *literally* raised from the dead!

On that day, the power of God exploded inside that tomb, reconnected Jesus' spirit with His dead body, flooded His corpse with life, and He physically arose from the dead. So much power was released behind the sealed entrance of His tomb that the earth itself reverberated and shuddered from the explosion. Then an angel rolled the stone from the entrance, and Jesus physically walked through the door of that tomb alive!

This resurrection power was so mighty that there was an earthquake as the ground itself shook with the power of God. The Roman soldiers who were assigned to guard the tomb collapsed "as dead men" and then fled in terror, for they had never experienced anything like the power that detonated inside the tomb on that glorious day! (*See* Matthew 28:2-4.)

This is no legend or fairy tale. *This is the foundation of our faith!* So let's examine the events surrounding the resurrection of Jesus Christ.

He was resurrected from the dead sometime between the close of Sabbath sunset on Saturday evening and before the women came to the tomb early on Sunday morning. The only actual eyewitnesses to the resurrection itself were the angels who were present and the four Roman soldiers who had been stationed there at Pilate's command (*see* Matthew 27:66). However, Matthew, Mark, Luke, and John all record the events that followed on the morning of His resurrection.

In the next several pages, we'll look at the sequence of those events:

- A great earthquake occurred.
- The stone was rolled away.
- The women saw angels at the site.
- Women became the first to preach Christ's resurrection.
- Peter and John ran to the tomb.

A Great Earthquake Occurred

What happened at the moment of Christ's resurrection? Matthew 28:2 says, "And, *behold*, there was a great earthquake...."

When describing the magnitude of the earthquake, Matthew used the word "behold." The *King James Version* translates this Greek word as *behold*, but it might be better translated, *Wow!* This word carries the idea of *shock*, *amazement*, and *wonder*.

So when Matthew said, "And, behold, there was a great earthquake...," he literally meant, *"Wow! Can you believe it?"*

This word could also carry this idea: *"Whew! Listen to the amazing thing that happened next...."* Although Matthew wrote his gospel many years after the fact, he still experienced *amazement* when he thought of this miraculous event!

Matthew told us that there was "a *great* earthquake." The word "great" is a Greek word that leaves no room for doubt as to the magnitude of this event. The word suggests something *huge*, *massive*, or *enormous*. The word "earthquake" is the word for *a literal earthquake*.

Just as creation shook when its Creator died on the Cross, now the earth exploded with exultation at the resurrection of Jesus!

The Stone Was Rolled Away

Mark 16:4 tells us that when certain women arrived at the tomb, they found "...the stone was rolled away: for it was *very* great." The word "very" is a word meaning *very, exceedingly,* or *extremely.* The word "great" again pictures something that is *huge, massive,* or *enormous.* In other words, this was no normal stone. The authorities placed *an extremely, exceedingly massive stone* in front of the entrance to Jesus' tomb. Yet when the women arrived, it had been removed!

Matthew tells us *how* the stone was removed. It says, "...The angel of the Lord descended from heaven, and came and rolled back the stone from the door, and sat upon it" (Matthew 28:2). The word "sat" is a form of the Greek word *kathemai,* which means *to sit down.* Some have suggested that the ability of the angel to sit on top of such a huge stone may also indicate his immense size.

In other words, he could have been so huge that he could sit on top of the enormous stone as if it were a chair. One can imagine that the removal of the stone by an angel would have been a simple feat. Matthew also informs us that not only was the angel strong, but that "his countenance was like lightning, and his raiment white as snow" (v. 3).

The intense shuddering and shaking of the earth beneath their feet and the immense power and brilliance of this angel explains why the Roman guards collapsed and then fled the scene. Matthew 28:4 tells us, "And for fear of him the keepers did shake, and became as dead men." The word "fear" in the original text means *to fear*. In this case, it was such a *panic-stricken fear* that it caused the guards to "shake."

This word "shake" is derived from the identical root word for *earthquake*. The mighty, fierce, and feared Roman soldiers trembled and quaked at the sight of the angel. In fact, they "...became as dead men." The words "dead men" are translated from the Greek word for *a corpse*. The soldiers were so terrified at the appearance of the angel that they fell to the ground, violently trembling and so paralyzed with fear that they were unable to move. When they were finally able to move again, these guards fled the scene to report to the chief priests all that they had witnessed! (*See* Matthew 28:11.)

The Women Saw Angels at the Site

In Luke's account, the women who were a part of the group that had laid the deceased body of Jesus in a new tomb returned after the Sabbath to finish anointing Christ's body. Luke 24:1 and 2 tells us they brought the burial spices to the site and found the stone had been rolled away from the tomb. Verse 3 says, "And they entered in, and found not the body of the Lord Jesus."

But what did they find inside the tomb besides the vacant spot where Jesus had been placed? Verse 4 says, "…As they were much perplexed thereabout, behold, two men stood by them in shining garments."

As these women stood in the empty tomb, "...they were much *perplexed* thereabout...." This Greek word for "perplexed" means *to lose one's way*. It is the picture of someone who is so confused that he can't figure out where he is, what he's doing, or what is happening around him. This person is completely *bewildered* by surrounding events.

211

Of course these women were perplexed! They came expecting to see the stone in front of the tomb, but it was *removed*. Sitting on top of the massive stone was *a dazzling angel* (*see* Matthew 28:2,5-7). And inside the tomb, they discovered there was *no dead body*.

Then Luke 24:4 tells us that all of a sudden "...two men stood by them in shining garments." The words "stood by" are from a Greek word which means *to come upon suddenly*; *to take one by surprise*; *to burst upon the scene*; *to suddenly step up*; or *to unexpectedly appear*.

In other words, while the women were trying to figure out what they were seeing, suddenly, to the women's amazement, *two angels* were standing inside the tomb in "shining garments"! The word "shining" depicts something that *shines* or *flashes like lightning*. The words "shining garments" no doubt referred to the angels' shining appearance.

These women didn't expect to encounter *any* of these unusual events that morning. It would have been *perfectly* normal for their heads to be whirling with questions!

In the pages that follow, I'll explain in detail some of the variations among the gospel writers concerning the number of angels and their whereabouts in relation to Jesus' empty tomb. But for now, let's continue the sequence of events surrounding Jesus' resurrection from the dead.

'Why Seek Ye the Living Among the Dead?'

Luke 24:5-7 tells us that when the women saw the angels inside the tomb, "...They were afraid, and bowed down their faces to the earth, they [the angels] said unto them, Why seek ye the living among the dead? He is not here, but is risen: remember how he spake unto you when he was yet in Galilee, saying, The Son of man must be delivered into the hands of sinful men, and be crucified, and the third day rise again."

When the angels rehearsed to the women Christ's own words about what would occur concerning His crucifixion and resurrection, the women suddenly "...remembered his words" (v. 8).

Women Were the First To Preach Christ's Resurrection

Mark records that after the two angels proclaimed the joyful news of Jesus' resurrection, they instructed the women, "...Go your way, tell his disciples and Peter that he [Jesus] goeth before you into Galilee: there shall ye see him, as he said unto you" (Mark 16:7). *And that's exactly what these women did.*

- Matthew 28:8 says they "...did run to bring his disciples word."

- Mark 16:8 says, "And they went out quickly, and fled from the sepulchre...."

- Luke 24:9,10 says the women returned and "...told these things unto the apostles."

Can you imagine how flustered these women must have been as they tried to tell the apostles what they had seen and heard that morning? Luke 24:11 says, "And their words seemed to them as idle tales, and they believed them not." The words "idle tales" are from a Greek word that means *nonsense*, *idle talk*, *babble*, or *delirium*. In other words, the women's presentation of the Gospel probably wasn't extremely clear or refined, but it stirred enough interest in Peter and John to cause them to get up and go find out for themselves about Jesus!

When we've had a supernatural encounter with the Lord, it isn't always easy to put that experience into words. This is a frustration all of us who know the Lord have felt at one time or another. However, we can't let that keep us from spreading the Good News of what Jesus Christ has done in our lives. We should never forget that although these women seemed to be babbling and speaking nonsense, their words were all that was needed to spark an interest in those men and compel them to get up and go find out about Jesus for themselves.

As you share Jesus Christ with your family and friends, it is your job to "give it your best shot." Tell the good news of the Gospel the best way you know how! But don't overlook the fact that the Holy Spirit is also speaking to their hearts at the same time you are speaking to their ears. The Spirit of God will use you and your witness to stir hunger deep in their hearts. Long after you are finished talking, God will still be dealing with them. And when they come to Jesus, they won't remember if you sounded confusing the day you presented the Gospel to them. They will simply be thankful that you loved them enough to care for their souls! So get up, get going, and start telling the Good News that Jesus Christ is alive and well!

But by the time the women reached the apostles, they must have sounded very *confused*. On one hand, the women reported that the angels said Jesus was alive — *raised from the dead!* But on the other hand, they sounded confused as they exclaimed, "…They have taken away the Lord out of the sepulchre, and we know not where they have laid him" (John 20:2).

214

Fear always produces confusion, and these women were so confused that at first, the apostles didn't take what they said seriously. As we have seen, Luke 24:11 says, "…Their words seemed to them as idle tales, and they believed them not." Again, the words "idle tales" are from a Greek word meaning *nonsense, idle talk, babble*, or *delirium*. Who did these women think removed Jesus from the tomb? Which story was true? Was He resurrected and alive as the women first told the apostles, or was He stolen away?

Peter and John Ran to the Tomb

John 20:3 and 4 says, "Peter therefore *went forth*, and that other disciple, and came to the sepulchre. So they ran both together: and the other disciple [John] did outrun Peter, and came first to the sepulchre." When the Bible says Peter and John "went forth," the Greek tense indicates that their feet were moving before the conversation with the women concluded. When they heard that something had happened at the tomb, both men were on the move to get there as quickly as possible. We also know from John 20:11 that Mary Magdalene soon followed Peter and John back to the tomb, for she was present at the site and remained there after Peter and John returned to the apostles.

It is interesting that when Peter and John raced to the tomb to see whatever it was that the women were trying to communicate to them, none of the other apostles joined them. The others apparently just sat and watched Peter and John start running, but they didn't join the two men. Instead, the rest of the apostles probably stayed behind to discuss what they had heard and to debate or consider what it meant.

Because Peter and John ran to the garden, they experienced something the other apostles missed by staying home. *It is simply a fact that if you want to experience Jesus Christ and His power, you must get up from where you are and start moving in His direction.*

John Outran Peter to the Tomb

But John outran Peter to the garden where the tomb was located. As soon as John arrived, John 20:5 tells us, "And he stooping down, and looking in, saw the linen clothes lying; yet went he not in." The Greek word for "stooping down" means *to peer into*, *to peep into*, *to bend low to take a closer look*, or *to stoop down to see something better*.

John bent down so he could take a closer peek into the tomb, and he "...saw the linen clothes lying...." The word "saw" means *to see*. It was just enough of a *glance* to see the linen clothes lying there.

The words "linen clothes" are translated from the same exact word used in John 19:40 when referring to the expensive Egyptian-made garment in which Joseph of Arimathea and Nicodemus had buried Jesus. If Jesus had been stolen, whoever took Him would have taken this expensive garment as well, but John saw that these linen clothes had been left lying in the tomb.

Graves were a place of respect for the Jews, which may explain the reason John was hesitant to enter the tomb. It is also quite possible that he observed the broken seals and realized that it looked like an unlawful entry had occurred. Perhaps he was thinking twice before he found himself connected to an alleged potential crime scene.

Regardless of why John hesitated, the Bible tells us that Peter did *not* hesitate, but promptly barged right into the tomb to check it out

216

for himself: "Then cometh Simon Peter following him, and went into the sepulchre, and seeth the linen clothes lie, and the napkin, that was about his head, not lying with the linen clothes, but wrapped together in a place by itself" (John 20:6,7).

John only glanced into the interior of the tomb, but verse 6 says Peter went into the sepulchre and "...*seeth* the linen clothes lie." The word "seeth" is from the same Greek word where we get our word *theater*. It means *to fully see* or *fully observe*, like a patron who carefully watches every act of a play at the theater.

Peter Inspected the Interior of the Tomb

When Peter entered that tomb, he surveyed it like a professional surveyor. He looked over every nook and cranny, paying special attention to the linen clothes and the way they were left there.

John 20:7 tells us he saw "...the napkin, that was about his head, not lying with the linen clothes, but wrapped together in a place by itself."

The word "napkin" refers to *a napkin that could be used for wiping perspiration from one's face*. This word was also used in connection with *a burial cloth that was gently placed upon the face of the dead at burial*. Apparently, Jesus' entire body was wrapped in a large white linen sheet, but His face was covered with such a napkin in traditional Jewish burial style.

The most fascinating fact about this facial cloth was that it was "...wrapped together in a place by itself." The word "wrapped" is a Greek word that means *to neatly fold*, *to nicely arrange*, or *to arrange in an orderly fashion*.

217

The reason this word is so interesting is that it indicates to us that Jesus was calm and completely in control of His faculties when He was raised from the dead. He removed the expensive burial cloth from His body, sat upright, and then removed the burial napkin from His face.

Likely sitting in that upright position, Jesus neatly folded the burial cloth and gently laid it down to one side, separate from the linen clothes that He probably laid down on His other side.

As Peter gazed at the scene inside the tomb, he could see the empty spot where Jesus had sat between these two pieces of burial clothing after He was raised from the dead. Imagine the thoughts flying through Peter's mind in that gloriously surreal moment!

John Joined Peter Inside the Tomb

John 20:8 says, "Then went in also that other disciple, which came first to the sepulchre, and he saw, and believed."

This verse tells us that when John saw the empty stone slab where Jesus' body had previously lain and the burial clothes lying to the right and to the left, surrounding the likely empty spot where Jesus sat after He was resurrected, John then "believed."

It is amazing that even though Peter had spent a longer time than John inside the tomb, he was still uncertain as to the meaning of it all.

Luke 24:12 says that Peter "...departed, wondering in himself at that which was come to pass." John, on the other hand, left the tomb believing Jesus was alive.

218

Concerning the Angels Present at the Tomb of Jesus — Which Is the Correct Version of the Story?

When you first read all four accounts of what happened that morning as it was discovered Jesus was no longer in the tomb where His body had been laid, it may appear that a contradiction exists between the details told in the various gospels. But when they are chronologically aligned, the picture becomes clear and the impression of contradiction is wiped away. Various gospel writers recorded the events of Jesus' life and ministry on Earth, including His death and resurrection, in various degrees of detail.

For example, in Mark's and Luke's recordings of Jesus casting the legion of demons out of "the madman of Gadara," they talked about one man with an unclean spirit (Mark 5:2; Luke 8:27). But Matthew writes that as they exited that ship on the other side of the sea of Galilee, *two* men "possessed with devils" met Jesus (Matthew 8:28). We can surmise that one man was either more oppressed or received greater ministry, but all three writers were uniquely retelling the same event in various, differing degrees of detail.

Let me give you an example of what appears to be a contradiction surrounding the angels at Jesus' tomb but is not a contradiction at all.

- The gospel of Matthew says there was *one angel outside the tomb*.

- The gospel of Mark says there was *one angel inside the tomb*.

- The gospel of Luke says there were *two angels inside the tomb*.

219

The gospel of John says *nothing* about angels in this scene, but does say that when Mary returned later, she saw *two angels inside the tomb*, who were positioned at the head and foot of the place where the body of Jesus had been laid — this was likely just *seconds* before Jesus Himself stood before her in His resurrected state!

- So how many angels *were* there? *Some believe there were two, and some say there were three angels present at this event.*
- And who is telling the correct version of the event? *They all were.*

As I said, in order to see the entire scenario that transpired that day, we have to put the events in all four gospels in proper, chronological sequence. To help simplify this question of the events of Christ's resurrection and how many angels were witnessed at the tomb in connection with that momentous event, the following are the passages in each of the four gospels in which these activities are recorded:

- Matthew 28:1-7
- Mark 16:1-7
- Luke 24:1-7
- John 20:1-13 (especially vv. 11-13)

Who Were the Women at the Tomb That Day?

Matthew 28:1 says, "In the end of the sabbath, as it began to dawn toward the first day of the week, came Mary Magdalene and the other Mary to see the sepulchre." In addition to Mary Magdalene and the other Mary, who was the mother of James, Luke 24:10 tells us that "Joanna" and "other women" also came to the tomb.

Luke 8:3 tells us that this "Joanna" was the wife of Herod's steward — evidently a wealthy woman who was a financial supporter of Jesus' ministry. According to Luke 23:55 and 56, many of these women were present when Jesus was placed inside the tomb and then returned home to prepare "spices and ointments" so they could anoint His body for burial when they returned after the Sabbath.

These women had no way of knowing that the chief priests and elders had gone to Pilate the day after Jesus was buried to request a watch of four Roman soldiers to guard the tomb and an official from the Roman court to "seal" the tomb. *How would these women have known this?* They were at home, preparing spices and ointments. Yet while these women were preparing to return to anoint Jesus' dead body, the tomb was being officially sealed shut and Roman soldiers had been ordered to guard the tomb 24 hours a day.

Had the women known that the tomb was being legally sealed and could not therefore be opened, they wouldn't have returned to the tomb to anoint the body of Jesus with the burial spices, for it would have been legally impossible at that time to request the stone to be removed.

As they drew near to the garden where the tomb was located, they wondered among themselves who would remove the stone for them (*see* Mark 16:3). But to their surprise, when they reached the tomb, they saw that the stone was already gone.

How Many Angels?

First, we know from Matthew 28:2 that certain women saw an angel sitting on top of the stone at the entrance of the tomb. In

221

Matthew 28:1-7, the one angel rolled away the stone, sat upon it, and caused such fear in the "keepers"— or guards — that they collapsed "as dead men." Then he said to Mary Magdelene and "the other Mary": "...Fear not ye: for I know that ye seek Jesus, which was crucified. He is not here: for he is risen, as he said. Come, see the place where the Lord [did] lay" (vv. 5-7). Then the angel apparently escorted the women inside the tomb so they could see for themselves — and instructed them to go tell the others that Christ had indeed risen.

Now, from Mark's account we know that the women saw another angel inside the tomb whose appearance was like a young man (*see* Mark 16:5). The words "young man" are from a Greek word that refers to *a young man who is filled with vigor and energy and who is in the prime of his life*. This illustrates the *vitality*, *strength*, and *ever-youthful appearance* of angels.

The Bible also tells us that this angel was "...clothed in a long white garment..." (v. 5). The word "clothed" pictures *a garment draped about his shoulders*, as a mighty warrior or ruler would be dressed. The word "garment" is from a word that represents *the long, flowing robe that adorned royalty, commanders, kings, priests, and other people of high distinction*.

Then in Luke's account, as we've already seen, when the women saw the stone rolled away and entered the sepulchre to investigate, they saw inside that tomb *"two men,"* who stood by them "in shining garments" (*see* Luke 24:4).

Did the angel sitting atop the stone (*see* Matthew 28:2) suddenly come down from his spot to escort the women inside and join the other *one* angel, as Mark described (Mark 16:5), who was present inside the tomb?

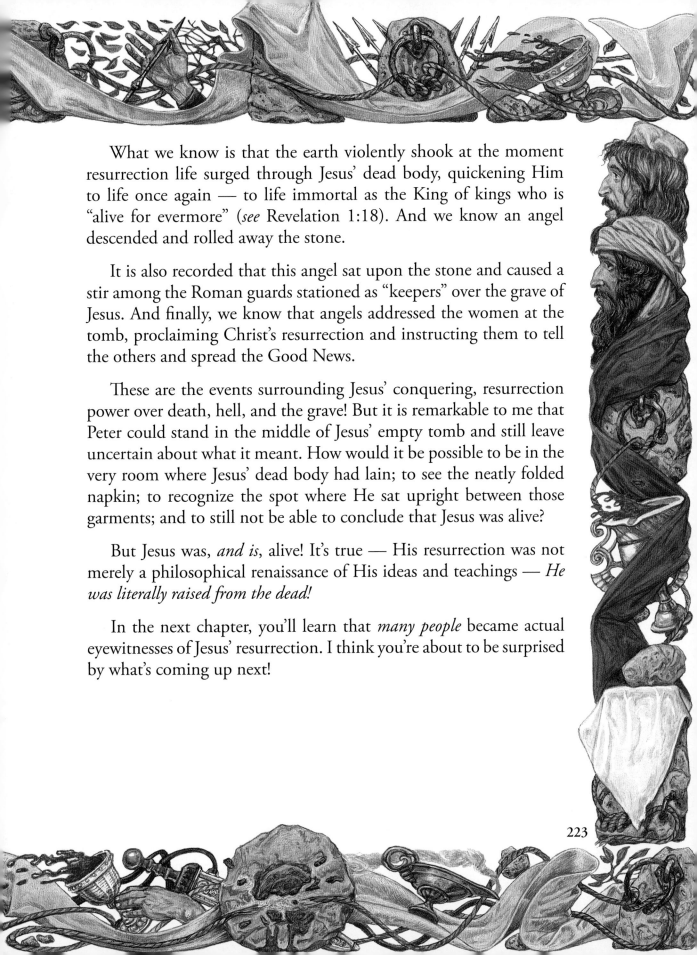

What we know is that the earth violently shook at the moment resurrection life surged through Jesus' dead body, quickening Him to life once again — to life immortal as the King of kings who is "alive for evermore" (*see* Revelation 1:18). And we know an angel descended and rolled away the stone.

It is also recorded that this angel sat upon the stone and caused a stir among the Roman guards stationed as "keepers" over the grave of Jesus. And finally, we know that angels addressed the women at the tomb, proclaiming Christ's resurrection and instructing them to tell the others and spread the Good News.

These are the events surrounding Jesus' conquering, resurrection power over death, hell, and the grave! But it is remarkable to me that Peter could stand in the middle of Jesus' empty tomb and still leave uncertain about what it meant. How would it be possible to be in the very room where Jesus' dead body had lain; to see the neatly folded napkin; to recognize the spot where He sat upright between those garments; and to still not be able to conclude that Jesus was alive?

But Jesus was, *and is*, alive! It's true — His resurrection was not merely a philosophical renaissance of His ideas and teachings — *He was literally raised from the dead!*

In the next chapter, you'll learn that *many people* became actual eyewitnesses of Jesus' resurrection. I think you're about to be surprised by what's coming up next!

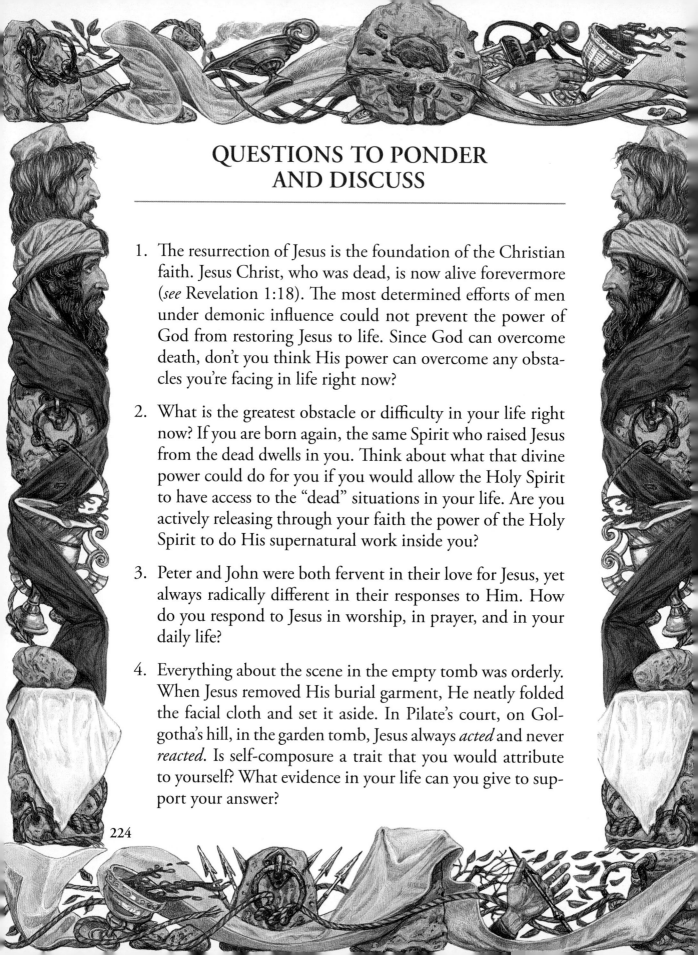

QUESTIONS TO PONDER
AND DISCUSS

1. The resurrection of Jesus is the foundation of the Christian faith. Jesus Christ, who was dead, is now alive forevermore (*see* Revelation 1:18). The most determined efforts of men under demonic influence could not prevent the power of God from restoring Jesus to life. Since God can overcome death, don't you think His power can overcome any obstacles you're facing in life right now?

2. What is the greatest obstacle or difficulty in your life right now? If you are born again, the same Spirit who raised Jesus from the dead dwells in you. Think about what that divine power could do for you if you would allow the Holy Spirit to have access to the "dead" situations in your life. Are you actively releasing through your faith the power of the Holy Spirit to do His supernatural work inside you?

3. Peter and John were both fervent in their love for Jesus, yet always radically different in their responses to Him. How do you respond to Jesus in worship, in prayer, and in your daily life?

4. Everything about the scene in the empty tomb was orderly. When Jesus removed His burial garment, He neatly folded the facial cloth and set it aside. In Pilate's court, on Golgotha's hill, in the garden tomb, Jesus always *acted* and never *reacted*. Is self-composure a trait that you would attribute to yourself? What evidence in your life can you give to support your answer?

Jesus' followers were shocked to find His tomb empty and His graveclothes lying there. After mourning the death of the Lord, they couldn't understand where He had gone. But Jesus is alive, and He went about assuring His disciples this was, and is, true.

Illustrated here is Mary Magdalene when she surprisingly encountered two angels inside Jesus' tomb. Perplexed by these unexpected visitors, Mary left the tomb weeping until Jesus found her. Mary was one of the first to whom Jesus revealed Himself, confirming again that He truly was raised from the dead.

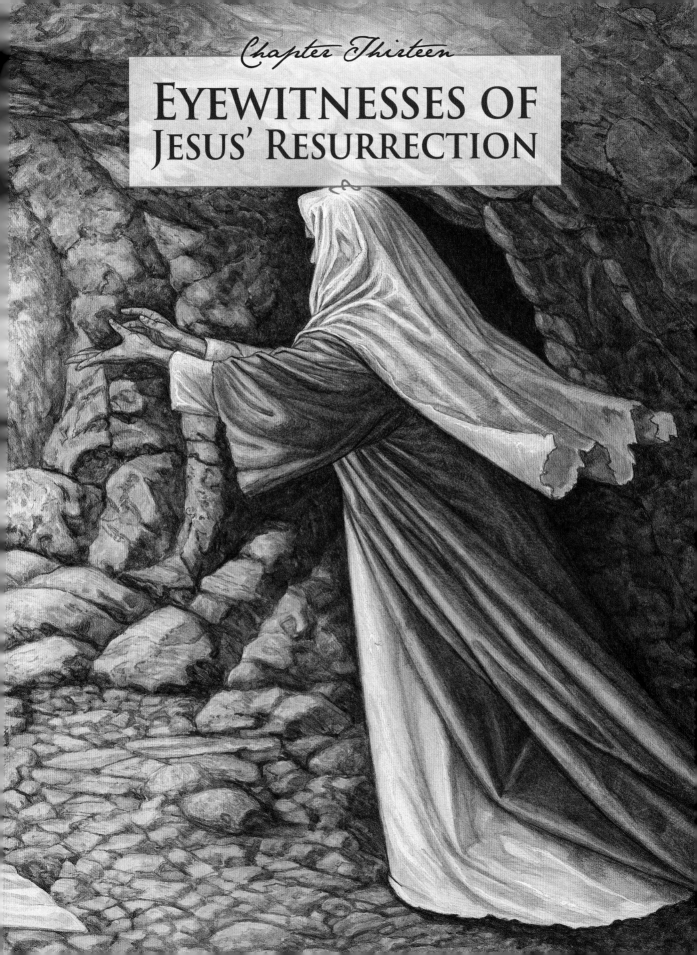

Chapter Thirteen
EYEWITNESSES OF JESUS' RESURRECTION

When Peter and John left the garden, where Jesus had been entombed and then resurrected, the Bible tells us that Mary Magdalene remained behind (*see* John 20:11). She had followed the two men to the tomb, possibly hoping to obtain a clearer understanding of what she was experiencing. At that point, she only knew that Jesus was no longer in the tomb where they had placed Him and prepared His body for burial.

Mary started that day with a desire to go to the tomb to anoint the body of Jesus, but when she arrived, the stone had been rolled away, and an angel was sitting on top of that great stone (*see* Matthew 28:2). Then Mark's gospel records that when she entered the tomb, she discovered another angel (*see* Mark 16:5). Luke writes that she then suddenly found herself in the presence of *two* angels inside the tomb (*see* Luke 24:4). And the angels told Mary, "He is not here, but is risen..." (Luke 24:6).

But if Jesus was risen as the angels had said, where was He? How could she find Him?

Mary Magdalene Inspected the Interior of the Tomb

In this same passage in John 20, the Bible tells us that after Peter and John left the garden, Mary stood outside the tomb weeping. The Greek tense means she was *continually weeping*, highlighting the fact

she was extremely perplexed about the inexplicable events that were taking place. Foremost on her mind was Jesus' whereabouts — she wanted to know what had happened to her Lord.

John wrote, "...As she wept, she *stooped down*, and looked into the sepulchre..." (John 20:11). The word "stooped down" is the same word used in verse 5 to portray John taking *a peek into* the tomb. Now it was Mary's turn to bend low and peer into the empty sepulchre — but when she looked inside, she saw something she didn't expect!

Mary Magdalene Saw Two Angels in White

John tells us, "...She stooped down, and looked into the sepulchre, and *seeth* two angels in white sitting, the one at the head, and the other at the feet, where the body of Jesus had lain" (John 20:11,12).

The word "seeth" is a Greek word which tells us assuredly that Mary *fixed her eyes* on the angels and *determined to look them over and to take in the whole experience*.

First, Mary saw that the two angels were "in white." This agrees with all the other experiences involving angels on that eventful day. All of them had been dressed in shining white with a lightning-bright appearance. All the angels seen that day also wore the same type of robe — like the long, flowing regal robes worn by warriors, kings, priests, or any other person of great power and authority. Mary *visibly studied* every single detail of the angels she saw there in the tomb.

John went on to inform us that Mary saw these angels "...sitting, the one at the head, and the other at the feet, where the body of Jesus

229

had lain." This statement is in perfect agreement with the interior of a rock-hewn tomb during biblical times.

Past the entrance of such a tomb, a smaller, separate room with a table-shaped pedestal, also carved from stone was usually located to one side. On this rock slab, the corpse was laid to rest after being dressed in burial clothes and perfumed by loved ones.

The head would be slightly elevated, causing the trunk of the corpse to lie in a sloping downward position with the feet resting against a small ledge or in a groove, either of which was designed to keep the body from slipping from the slab.[1]

When Mary saw the angels, she noted that one was seated at the top of the burial slab and the other was seated at the foot. In between these angels, she could see the empty place where she had personally viewed Jesus days earlier.

Luke 23:55 tells us that after Jesus' body was placed in the tomb, Mary Magdalene and other women who came from Galilee "...*beheld* the sepulchre, and how his body was laid."

The word "beheld" means *to gaze upon*, *to fully see*, or *to look at intently*. These women *inspected* the tomb, *gazing upon* the dead body of Jesus *to see* that it had been honorably laid in place. And because Mark 15:47 — in Mark's record of events — uses the imperfect tense to tell us how the women looked upon Jesus' dead body, it means these women took plenty of time to make certain He was properly laid to rest there.

Now Mary was seeing the same spot where she had so carefully labored days before, but the dead body of the Lord that she cherished was no longer there.

Mary Recognized Him When He Called Her By Name

As Mary beheld the now empty slab and wept, the angels asked her, "...Woman, why weepest thou?..." (John 20:13). She answered them, "...Because they have taken away my Lord, and I know not where they have laid him." Then verse 14 goes on to say, "And when she had thus said, she turned herself back, and saw Jesus standing, and knew not that it was Jesus."

Mary withdrew from the tomb just in time to see a Man standing nearby. Due to Jesus' resurrected, changed appearance, she was unable to recognize Him. Verse 15 tells us what happened next: "Jesus saith unto her, Woman, why weepest thou? whom seekest thou? She, supposing him to be the gardener, saith unto him, Sir, if thou have borne him hence, tell me where thou hast laid him, and I will take him away."

At that very moment, Jesus tenderly said, "Mary." Upon hearing that voice and recognizing the old familiar way in which He called her name, "...she turned herself, and saith unto him, Rabboni; which is to say, Master" (v. 16). Although Jesus' appearance was different now, Mary knew Him by His voice, in particular, by the way He called to her personally. This reminds me of John 10:27, when Jesus told His disciples, "My sheep hear my voice...." Mary knew His voice and recognized that it was her Shepherd who stood before her.

It appears that Mary reached out to cling to Jesus with her hands, but Jesus forbade her, saying, "...Touch me not; for I am not yet ascended to my Father: but go to my brethren, and say unto them, I

ascend unto my Father, and your Father; and to my God, and your God" (John 20:17).

With this one statement, Jesus let it be known that everything had changed because of the Cross. *Now a new relationship with God was available to the apostles and to all who would call upon the name of Jesus Christ!*

But John 20:18 goes on to say, "Mary Magdalene came and told the disciples that she had seen the Lord, and that he had spoken these things unto her." In telling the disciples about her experience with the risen Lord, Mary became the first woman preacher of the Gospel!

Other Eyewitness Accounts That Jesus Rose From the Dead

On Resurrection Day itself, Jesus appeared to the disciples at various times and places. It was simply a physical impossibility for Him to be at so many different places in one day, and these appearances therefore revealed that Jesus' glorified body didn't have the same limitations His earthly body possessed before His resurrection and glorification. The Bible makes it plain that in His glorified condition, He was able to appear, to disappear, to travel great distances, and to even supernaturally pass through a wall or the locked door of a house (*see* John 20:26).

Matthew, Mark, Luke, and John all recorded these eyewitness events. In the following paragraphs, I refer to passages from the gospels of Matthew, Luke, and John to discuss the activities of Jesus after His resurrection.

Jesus Appeared to Two Disciples on the Road to Emmaus

On the same day Jesus was raised from the dead, He not only appeared to Mary Magdalene outside the garden tomb (*see* John 20:14-17), but also to two disciples as they walked from Jerusalem to the city of Emmaus (Luke 24:13-31).

When the three men sat down to eat together, Jesus blessed the food. After hearing the way He blessed the food, the two disciples instantly recognized it was the Lord — just as He suddenly "...vanished out of their sight" (v. 31).

Jesus Appeared to the Eleven Disciples Behind Closed Doors

Soon Jesus supernaturally walked right through the walls of a room where the 11 disciples were gathered, and He miraculously appeared right in front of them. John 20:19 tells us about this amazing event: "Then the same day at evening, being the first day of the week, when *the doors were shut* where the disciples were assembled for fear of the Jews, came Jesus and stood in the midst...."

This verse says that when the disciples gathered for dinner, they made certain "the doors were shut." The word "door" lets us know this was a door that was *large* and *solid*. But as if this were not enough, the verse tells us that these doors "were shut."

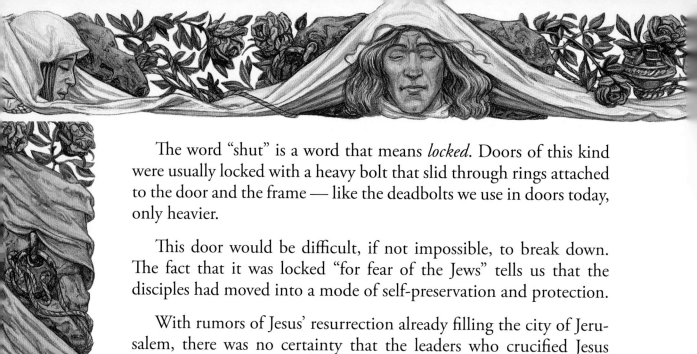

The word "shut" is a word that means *locked*. Doors of this kind were usually locked with a heavy bolt that slid through rings attached to the door and the frame — like the deadbolts we use in doors today, only heavier.

This door would be difficult, if not impossible, to break down. The fact that it was locked "for fear of the Jews" tells us that the disciples had moved into a mode of self-preservation and protection.

With rumors of Jesus' resurrection already filling the city of Jerusalem, there was no certainty that the leaders who crucified Jesus wouldn't try to take into custody the rest of the apostles and do the same to them as they had done to Jesus.

The Roman Guards Saw Jesus Resurrected

The Bible tells us that the Roman guards who fled the resurrection site "...shewed unto the chief priests all the things that were done" (Matthew 28:11). They were there and witnessed the resurrection and knew that Jesus was raised from the dead!

But to prevent the people of Israel from knowing the truth of Jesus' resurrection, the chief priests and elders bribed the soldiers to keep their mouths shut about what they had seen. Verse 12 tells us, "And when they were assembled with the elders, and had taken counsel, they gave large money unto the soldiers."

The chief priests and elders fabricated a story and told the soldiers what to say when people asked them what happened: "...Say ye, His disciples came by night, and stole him away while we slept" (v. 13).

234

The soldiers' admission that they had slept on the job would deem them worthy of punishment in Pilate's sight, so the religious leaders further assured them, "And if this come to the governor's ears, we will persuade him, and secure you" (v. 14). The soldiers listened to the religious leaders' plan and were satisfied with the amount of money being offered to them to keep silent.

Verse 15 then says, "So they took the money, and did as they were taught...."

Once the chief priests and elders had cleverly paid for the false testimony of the Roman guards, they were positioned to make some serious arrests.

First, we know that they were already asserting that the disciples had stolen the body of Jesus. But to steal the body, they would have had to either overpower the Roman guards or creep past them as they slept. Either way, this would be deemed a terrible dishonor to the guards' reputation. And if the disciples were caught, they'd potentially be put to death for this action.

To open the tomb, the governor's seal also had to be broken. Breaking that seal was an offense that required the death penalty, for this was a breach of the empire's power. And no doubt the same angry mobs that cheered while Jesus carried His crossbeam to Golgotha were still in the city, and the city itself was already in turmoil due to such strange happenings — the sky turning dark in the middle of the day with no natural explanation; the veil of the Temple rent in half; the various earthquakes shaking the entire surrounding territory.

It wouldn't take too much to put the whole city on edge and turn them against the disciples. This is why the disciples were locked behind closed doors that evening.

Jesus Told the Disciples To Touch His Resurrected Body

Although the doors where the disciples were hiding were sealed tightly shut, Jesus supernaturally passed right through the solid matter and appeared in the midst of them. John 20:19 says Jesus came "...and stood in the midst, and saith unto them, Peace be unto you."

No doubt this sudden appearance must have terrified the disciples. Luke 24:37 tells us that "...they were terrified and affrighted, and supposed that they had seen a spirit." This is why Jesus told them, "...Why are ye troubled? and why do thoughts arise in your hearts? Behold my hands and my feet, that it is I myself: *handle* me, and see; for a spirit hath not flesh and bones, as ye see me have" (vv. 38,39).

Notice Jesus said, "Handle me." The word "handle" means *to touch, to squeeze,* or *to feel.* Jesus gave the disciples permission to examine His resurrected body to see that it was a real body and not a spirit.

As the disciples were pondering Jesus' words, He asked them, "...Have ye here any meat?" The following verses say, "And they gave him a piece of a broiled fish, and of an honeycomb. And he took it, and did eat before them" (Luke 24:42,43).

After eating the fish and honeycomb, Jesus began to speak to them from the Scriptures, pointing out key Old Testament prophecies having to do with Him. Luke 24:45 says, "Then opened he their understanding, that they might understand the scriptures."

Jesus explained to the disciples that repentance would have to be preached in His name among all the nations, but that it was to begin

in Jerusalem. This is when He told them, "...As my Father hath sent me, even so send I you" (John 20:21).

The disciple Thomas had not been present in the room that night when Jesus passed through solid matter and entered into the room. But later that evening Thomas joined the disciples and heard the news, and by that time Jesus was already gone.

Thomas scoffed at the other disciples and said, "...Except I shall see in his hands the print of the nails, and put my finger into the print of the nails, and thrust my hand into his side, I will not believe" (John 20:25).

Jesus Appeared to the Disciples Again — and Also to Thomas

Days later, the disciples were behind locked doors again, but this time Thomas was present. John 20:26 and 27 says, "...Then came Jesus, the doors being shut, and stood in the midst, and said, Peace be unto you. Then saith he to Thomas, Reach hither thy finger, and behold my hands; and reach hither thy hand, and thrust it into my side: and be not faithless, but believing." Of course, after this event, Thomas believed!

Jesus Appeared to the Disciples at the Sea of Tiberias

Jesus appeared to His disciples again, this time at the Sea of Tiberias. Peter, Thomas Didymus, Nathanael, the sons of Zebedee, and

two other disciples followed Peter to the seacoast to go fishing. But after fishing all night, the disciples had caught nothing.

The Bible tells us that in the morning Jesus stood on the shore and called to the disciples to cast their nets on the other side of the boat. Although they weren't sure who was instructing them, the men obeyed anyway — and caught so many fish that they weren't even able to pull their nets into the boat! That's when they recognized that the Man who had instructed them was the Lord (*see* John 21:2-7).

Before the evening was finished, Jesus sat around a campfire with them, ate fish with them, and spent time fellowshipping with them. John 21:14 says, "This is now the third time that Jesus shewed himself to his disciples, after that he was risen from the dead."

Jesus Appeared to the Disciples in Galilee

Then finally, the disciples gathered on the same mountain in Galilee where Jesus had first ordained them. He appeared to them there and gave them the Great Commission, which is our commission today as the Body of Christ.

Jesus told them, "...All power is given unto me in heaven and in earth. Go ye therefore, and teach all nations, baptizing them in the name of the Father, and of the Son, and of the Holy Ghost: teaching them to observe all things whatsoever I have commanded you: and, lo, I am with you alway, even unto the end of the world. Amen" (Matthew 28:18-20).

After all those days and hours apart, Jesus' disciples were with the great Teacher and Master again to learn what He desired them to do for the rest of their lives.

238

Jesus Appeared to More Than 500 People at One Time

In addition to these appearances recorded in the gospels, First Corinthians 15:5-7 says, "And that he was seen of Cephas, then of the twelve: after that, he was seen of above five hundred brethren at once; of whom the greater part remain unto this present, but some are fallen asleep. After that, he was seen of James; then of all the apostles."

Acts 1:3 also says, "...He shewed himself alive after his passion by many infallible proofs, being seen of them forty days, and speaking of the things pertaining to the kingdom of God."

From what you just read in this chapter, it is clear that Jesus was "in the midst" of His disciples after His resurrection. They ate with Him, talked to Him, fellowshipped with Him, and Jesus even helped them catch fish!

The resurrected Jesus drew near to His disciples — but let me ask you: Do you draw near to Him as you go about the activities of your daily life? Do you experience Jesus Christ in your daily routine, or is Jesus just relegated to church services and Sunday school?

The Holy Spirit is the Great Revealer of Jesus Christ, so ask the Holy Spirit to show you Jesus, and He will be faithful to make Jesus more real to you than your natural mind can imagine.

In the next chapter, we will look to the Scriptures to see exactly what Jesus has been doing for the last 2,000 years. What you are about to discover will make you want to stand up and shout, for it is the best news you've ever heard in your life!

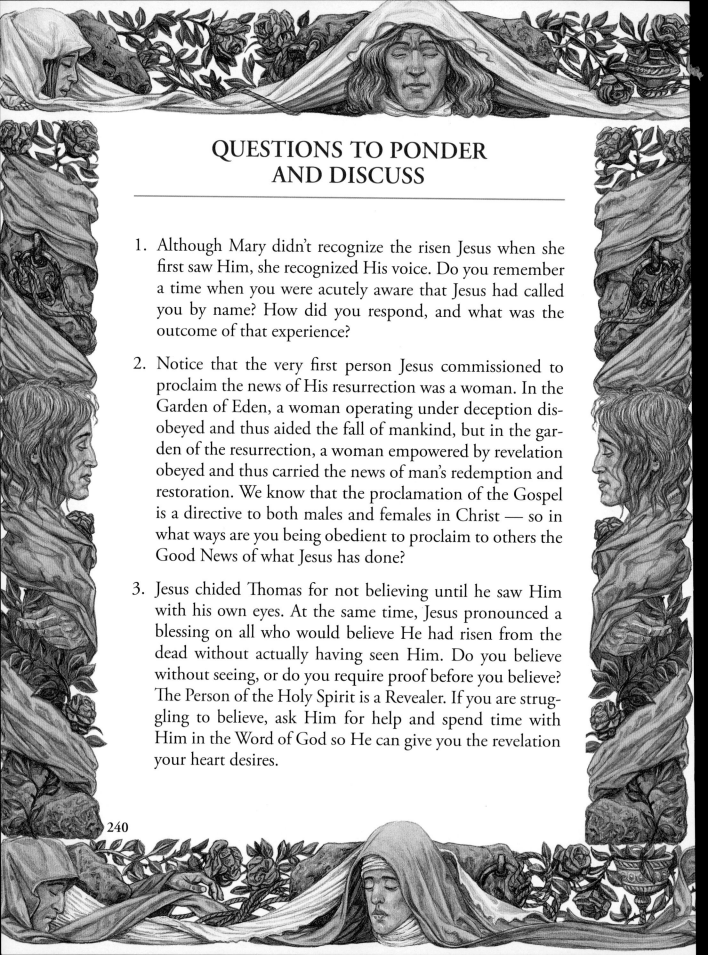

QUESTIONS TO PONDER
AND DISCUSS

1. Although Mary didn't recognize the risen Jesus when she first saw Him, she recognized His voice. Do you remember a time when you were acutely aware that Jesus had called you by name? How did you respond, and what was the outcome of that experience?

2. Notice that the very first person Jesus commissioned to proclaim the news of His resurrection was a woman. In the Garden of Eden, a woman operating under deception disobeyed and thus aided the fall of mankind, but in the garden of the resurrection, a woman empowered by revelation obeyed and thus carried the news of man's redemption and restoration. We know that the proclamation of the Gospel is a directive to both males and females in Christ — so in what ways are you being obedient to proclaim to others the Good News of what Jesus has done?

3. Jesus chided Thomas for not believing until he saw Him with his own eyes. At the same time, Jesus pronounced a blessing on all who would believe He had risen from the dead without actually having seen Him. Do you believe without seeing, or do you require proof before you believe? The Person of the Holy Spirit is a Revealer. If you are struggling to believe, ask Him for help and spend time with Him in the Word of God so He can give you the revelation your heart desires.

This illustration captures the moment Jesus revealed Himself to more than 500 people at once, declaring the miraculous news of His resurrection. He walked on the earth in His resurrected body for 40 days teaching and fellowshipping with His disciples before ascending to Heaven where He now sits enthroned at the right hand of the Father. This really is good news, and we have the honor of sharing it with everyone we meet!

Illustrated here is the wonderous moment Jesus ascended into Heaven in a cloud of glory. It was also the last time Jesus was ever seen on Earth in His physical human form. But the Bible tells us *He will return*, and when He does, it will be in exactly the same way He ascended nearly 2,000 years ago. Except this time Jesus will not come as a humble servant — He will return as the King of kings and Lord of lords!

Chapter Fourteen
WHAT HAS JESUS BEEN DOING FOR THE LAST 2,000 YEARS?

When Luke wrote Acts chapter 1, he chronicled events in the final days of Jesus' appearance on earth, and he said that Jesus "...shewed himself alive after his passion by many infallible proofs, being seen of them forty days, and speaking of the things pertaining to the kingdom of God" (v. 3).

In Acts 1:9, Luke went on to tell us that at the end of those 40 days after Jesus had spoken to His followers one final time, "...he was taken up; and a cloud received him out of their sight."

Then Luke continued, "And while they [the apostles] looked stedfastly toward heaven as he went up, behold, two men stood by them in white apparel; which also said, Ye men of Galilee, why stand ye gazing up into heaven? this same Jesus, which is taken up from you into heaven, shall so come in like manner as ye have seen him go into heaven" (Acts 1:10,11). On that day, the angels declared Jesus would return in the same manner He left nearly 2,000 years ago.

Days later when Peter preached his first message on the Day of Pentecost, he declared that Jesus would remain in Heaven until the fulfillment of all Scripture at the end of the age (*see* Acts 3:21). Only when every prophecy that is yet unfulfilled has finally been fulfilled, and every soul that will be saved has been saved, will Jesus return — and when He does return, He will return in exactly the same way He ascended nearly 2,000 years ago. However, in His Second Coming (which is subsequent to the rapture of the Church), Jesus will not return as a humble Servant. The Bible declares He will return as the King of kings and the Lord of lords! (*See* Revelation 19:16.)

When the disciples watched Jesus ascend into a cloud of glory that received Him into Heaven, it was the last time Jesus was ever seen on the earth in His physical human form. Of course, since that time, people have experienced supernatural moments when they've seen Jesus in the Spirit, whether in visions or in dreams. And we also know that Jesus is touching people's lives today through His Church, which Scripture even refers to as the *Body* of Christ.

But Jesus Himself — in His actual physical form — left the earth 2,000 years ago, and He has been absent ever since. And He will remain absent until every scripture related to the last days has been fulfilled and until the last soul to be saved has been saved. Although we may be able to recognize the season of the Rapture and then Jesus' Second Coming, Matthew 24:36 tells us that only the Father knows the exact day and hour when Jesus will come for the Church and then visibly return in His Second Coming at the end of the age.

When Peter preached to his audience in Jerusalem after Jesus ascended to Heaven, he told them that Jesus sat down at the Father's right hand, and that once seated in His new permanent position at the Father's right hand, His first order of business was to pour out the gift of the Holy Spirit upon the Church (*see* Acts 2:33). And that is *exactly* what happened on the Day of Pentecost.

Where Is Jesus Now and What Is He Doing?

We know Jesus ascended into Heaven to sit at the Father's right hand as the King of kings and Lord of lords who is "alive for evermore" (*see* Revelation 1:18). But exactly what has He been doing for the last 2,000 years?

When Jesus' feet lifted from Earth and He was received into Heaven, He started the next phase of His ministry — a phase so wonderful that the Bible calls it "...*a more excellent ministry*, by how much also he is the mediator of a better covenant, which was established upon better promises" (Hebrews 8:6).

The Greek word for "excellent" means *incomparable, unparalleled, unsurpassed, unmatched, finest, greatest*, or *most excellent*. This means Jesus' present-day ministry is *not even to be compared* to His previous earthly ministry. In fact, Hebrews 8:6 emphatically lets us know that Jesus' ministry in this Dispensation of the Holy Spirit is His *finest, greatest*, and *most excellent* ministry.

- Why is this phase of Jesus' ministry so excellent?
- What is He doing right now that is so mighty?

Jesus Is Our Great High Priest

The moment Jesus sat down at the Father's right hand, His ministry was initiated as the Great High Priest to everyone who calls upon His name.

Under the Old Covenant, there were many priests, but each of them eventually died due to their human condition. However, Hebrews 7:24 and 25 declares, "But this man [Jesus], because he continueth ever, hath an unchangeable priesthood. Wherefore he is able also to save them to the uttermost that come unto God by him, seeing he ever liveth to make intercession for them."

Hebrews 4:15,16 describes the power of Jesus' present-day ministry: "For we have not an high priest which cannot be touched with the feeling of our infirmities; but was in all points tempted like as we are, yet without sin. Let us therefore come boldly unto the throne of grace, that we may obtain mercy, and find grace to help in time of need."

Think about it. Jesus has become your Great High Priest — your personal Representative who sits at the right hand of the Father in Heaven. His ministry today is to represent *you* to the Father. And because Jesus lived on the earth as a Man, He understands every problem or temptation that will ever come your way.

Jesus has faced every temptation that any human being has ever encountered in life. This means He has experienced every temptation *you* face. Anything you talk to Jesus about is something that He was personally tempted with when He walked the earth and that He personally understands. But the Bible declares that although He was tempted in all ways just as we are, Jesus was without sin. Therefore, He is qualified today to sit at the Father's right hand and intercede on our behalf.

The Throne of Grace
We Can Approach for Help

Hebrews 4:16 goes on to tell us, "Let us therefore come *boldly* unto the throne of grace, that we may obtain mercy, and find grace to help in time of need."

The word "boldly" comes from the often-used Greek word which refers to *freedom of speech*. It presents the picture of a person who *speaks his mind* and who does it *straightforwardly* and with great *confidence*.

Frequently in the First Century, this word "boldly" depicted a *frankness* that was so *bold*, it could be met with resistance, hostility, and opposition. Many thought it just wasn't acceptable to speak so candidly. Therefore, when someone spoke his mind and his thoughts this freely, his outspokenness could be met with rebuke.

But in Hebrews 4:16, we are commanded to come "boldly" before God's throne of grace. This means that not only does Jesus beckon us to come to Him, but He also invites us to be *straight-to-the-point* when we talk to Him!

You need never fear that you are *too frank, too bold, too forthright, too honest, too outspoken,* or *too blunt* when you open your heart to God about your needs and struggles or when you request His help. Of course, you should never be irreverent — but neither do you need to be afraid to speak exactly what is on your heart. The Greek word used in Hebrews 4:16 for "boldly" emphatically tells you and me that Jesus will never be turned off, offended, or insulted when you freely speak your heart and mind to Him.

Jesus *wants* to hear what you and I have to say to Him!

Jesus Has Mercy Waiting for You

Hebrews 4:16 goes on to tell us to "...come boldly unto the throne of grace, that we may *obtain* mercy, and find grace to help in time of need."

The word "obtain" is from a word that means *to seize* or *to lay hold of something in order to make it your very own.* It is the picture of reaching out *to grab, to capture,* or *to take possession* of something. Depending on the context in which it is used, it can either mean *to violently lay hold of something to seize and take it as one's very own,* or it can depict a person who *gently and graciously receives something that is freely and easily given.*

Jesus is always there, waiting mercifully to help anyone who comes to Him by faith. But your own personal circumstances or inward struggles could affect the ease with which you receive His help.

If your struggle is intense, if your mind is tortured, if your flesh resists you, or if it seems like the world is pressing against you, you may find it difficult to freely receive from the Lord. So in those moments, you have to press through each barrier and reach out to *forcibly lay hold* of the help God offers you.

Jesus is ready and willing to give you exactly what you need. All you have to do is open your heart and by faith *receive* it. So shove those negative circumstances and emotions out of the way, and reach out by faith to *lay hold of* the grace and mercy that Jesus so freely offers.

It's time for you to *receive* the mercy Jesus wants to give. But don't stop with mercy!

Grace To Help in Time of Need

If you'll keep pressing forward by faith, Hebrews 4:16 promises that you will "...find grace to help in time of need."

The word "find" denotes *a discovery made by searching*. It usually denotes *a discovery made as a result of an intense investigation, scientific study*, or *scholarly research*. Imagine a researcher who, after working long hours and searching for a long time, suddenly finds what he has been seeking! In that unforgettable moment of joyful euphoria, he shrieks, "EUREKA!" — which means, "I FOUND IT!" In fact, the word *eureka* is derived from this same Greek word in Hebrews 4:16 that is translated "find." It lets us know the kind of intense joy that you can experience when you find the help you have sought for so long.

Praise God for special times when a believer "happens" upon the help of God. I'm especially talking about times when someone is young in the Lord or when a person is too inexperienced to know what he's doing or even how to properly pray. Or perhaps a believer is innocently making all kinds of mistakes. Then somehow God's mercy and grace overrides all his blunders, and that precious believer is divinely and supernaturally plugged into help that causes him to rise above his circumstances and overcome every obstacle. That believer can't even explain what happened or how he received that divine assistance. All he knows is that suddenly he was *empowered*. In that moment, he "found" the help he needed to overcome what he was facing in life.

However, "help" doesn't usually come by happenstance; rather, it comes when a person diligently seeks the help he needs. When that diligent seeker lays hold of his answer from Heaven, such euphoria floods his heart that he exclaims, "I'VE FOUND IT!" or, "I'VE RECEIVED IT!" At long last, the seeker is holding in his hand the answer he needed from God!

But I must point out one more very important thing about the word "find" in Hebrews 4:16. The original Greek word can also be used to picture *someone who diligently seeks and therefore acquires something for someone else*. This has *powerful* connotations, and I want to tell you why. It means you can go to Jesus, the Great High Priest, to obtain mercy and find help for others about whom you are burdened. You can obtain help:

- For those who need healing for their bodies.
- For those who are bound and need deliverance.

- For those who are tormented and need peace.

- For marriages and families that are in trouble.

- For provision to be given to those who need a financial breakthrough.

- For those who are in need in any area of their lives.

So not only can you take your own needs to Jesus, but you can also take *others'* needs to Jesus and obtain the help *they* so desperately need.

Divine Help for Anyone in Need

But now let's look at the phrase "help in time of need" — which is a translation of a word that primarily has military connotations. It can simply be translated to *help* meet someone's needs, but when you understand the military implications of this word, it becomes truly powerful.

This particular word was first and foremost used to describe that moment when a soldier got into trouble. When his fellow soldiers were alerted to his dangerous situation, they were completely dedicated to the goal of going into battle to defend their co-fighter and contending for his well-being, safety, and security. Just hearing that a fellow soldier was in need was enough to beckon the other soldiers into battle and motivate them to spare no effort to rescue him and bring him back to a place of safety and protection.

Because this is the word used in this text, we know that when we get into trouble and Jesus is alerted about it, He comes to our defense! He will go to *battle* for us in our time of need. If we will go to Jesus, our Great High Priest, and present our case to Him, He will intercede for us — and that means He will rise up like a Mighty Warrior who is ready to go into battle to fight for us until we are delivered, freed, and brought to a place of safety! That is the kind of "help" we will find if we present our needs to Jesus!

But the word "help" used in Hebrews 4:16 has other meanings in the original Greek text that are important in this verse. It also pictures *protection*, *a rescue*, or *a remedy* to whatever ails a person. That means Jesus supplies protection to those who call out to Him in faith; He provides rescue to those who are in trouble and who call out for help in faith; and He brings a remedy to whatever problem is ailing any person if he will boldly come to Him in faith and ask for His assistance!

Think about it: Why would we ever try to fight our battles alone when the Greatest Warrior in the universe — the One who possesses ultimate power — is willing to fight for us?

So What Has Jesus Been Doing for the Past 2,000 Years?

After Jesus' work on the Cross was finished and He was raised from the dead, He ascended on High where He sat down at the Father's right hand and poured out the gift of the Holy Spirit upon the Church.

Today — and that means *right now* — Jesus is making intercession for you and for anyone who comes to Him by faith. He fights for every believer who comes boldly and honestly and who earnestly seeks His assistance. This ministry has kept Jesus very busy for the past 2,000 years!

Why would Jesus come to earth, humble Himself to the point of dying on the Cross, be raised from the dead, and pour out the gift of the Holy Spirit to empower you — only to reject or resist you when you come to Him with your needs? He wouldn't! From His highly exalted position, He still has His eyes fixed on *you*.

Nearly 2,000 years ago, Jesus died for you, but today — at this very moment — He lives to intercede for you and fight for your every need. Push past your own inner struggles to go before Him boldly and ask Him for help. Jesus will swing into action to lead you, guide you, and fight for you! By the strength of His Spirit, He will enable you to do whatever the will of God is for your life!

QUESTIONS TO PONDER
AND DISCUSS

1. You have a personal Representative in Heaven who completely identifies with your human condition. No matter what situation you may be facing, Jesus is for you; He is *not* against you. Are you coming boldly to Him for the help you need right now?

2. People may feel challenged by direct, confident communication, but God likes straight talk. He wants you to be honest when you pour out your heart to Him. But you can't be honest with God or confident in His presence until you're willing to be honest with yourself. Have you honestly expressed your heart to Him about what you are going through, about your concerns for others, or for whatever is on your heart?

3. The ministry of the Holy Spirit is to help you do the will of God, just as He empowered Jesus to do during His earthly ministry. Are there specific areas in your life in which you need to ask for or yield to the help of the Holy Spirit?

4. Jesus conquered death, hell, and the grave, and now He lives forever to make intercession for you! Have you let the truth of this reality sink in? Jesus paid the penalty for every sin you would ever commit, and now He is seated beside the Father in Heaven, speaking on your behalf, because He wants to help you and be near to you. How does this truth shape your perception of Jesus and His care for the details of your life?

Jesus is now gloriously seated in Heaven at the right hand of the Father. For 2,000 years, He has been sitting in this place of honor, interceding for His people as Great High Priest. Jesus' life, death, and resurrection opened the way for us to come directly into His presence so we can boldly ask for what we need. Jesus is for you! And He is waiting mercifully to help you as soon as you come to Him in faith.

Jesus is our great Master and Teacher, and we need to learn from Him how to live. Just like a student learning to write, we must study the Word of God and examine how Jesus responded in every circumstance so we can replicate His response in our own life. With the heart of a student who endeavors to copy every stroke of his teacher's pen, commit to model your life after Jesus no matter what obstacles you face.

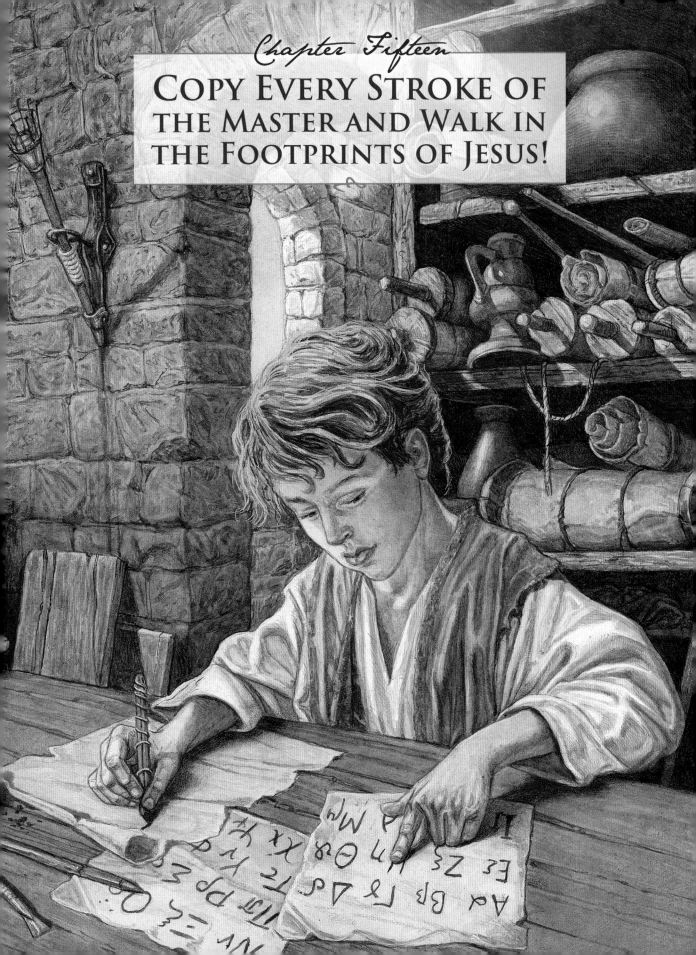

Chapter Fifteen

COPY EVERY STROKE OF THE MASTER AND WALK IN THE FOOTPRINTS OF JESUS!

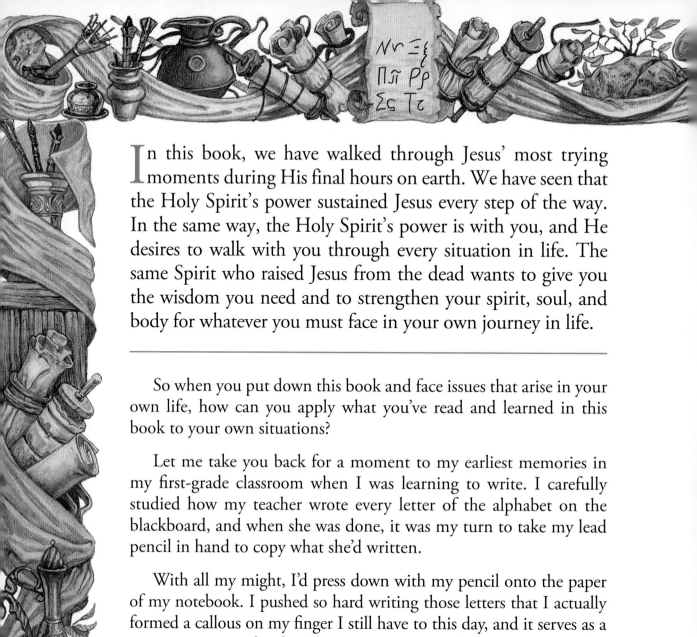

In this book, we have walked through Jesus' most trying moments during His final hours on earth. We have seen that the Holy Spirit's power sustained Jesus every step of the way. In the same way, the Holy Spirit's power is with you, and He desires to walk with you through every situation in life. The same Spirit who raised Jesus from the dead wants to give you the wisdom you need and to strengthen your spirit, soul, and body for whatever you must face in your own journey in life.

So when you put down this book and face issues that arise in your own life, how can you apply what you've read and learned in this book to your own situations?

Let me take you back for a moment to my earliest memories in my first-grade classroom when I was learning to write. I carefully studied how my teacher wrote every letter of the alphabet on the blackboard, and when she was done, it was my turn to take my lead pencil in hand to copy what she'd written.

With all my might, I'd press down with my pencil onto the paper of my notebook. I pushed so hard writing those letters that I actually formed a callous on my finger I still have to this day, and it serves as a permanent reminder that I gave 100 percent of my concentration to exactly duplicating every letter my teacher had written on that blackboard. Day after day, I'd write those letters over and over on my Big Chief® writing tablet with its newspaper-type paper and widely spaced lines. I'd fill *pages* with writing until I finally mastered each letter of the alphabet. It took concentration and commitment, but in time, I learned to write those letters exactly as my teacher had shown me.

Can you remember when you first learned to write? Interestingly, that image of a student diligently following the instruction of a teacher is precisely the picture that Peter had in mind when he told early believers, "For even hereunto were ye called: because Christ also *suffered* for us, leaving us an example, that ye should follow his steps" (1 Peter 2:21).

At the time Peter wrote these words, early believers were suffering for their faith at the hands of the Roman government, and for them, there was no legal recourse to take. They were suffering unjustly, and there was nothing they could do legally to defend themselves. Because these believers were suffering, Peter reminded them that Jesus' example would show them step by step what to do.

Christ's Example in Suffering

The word "suffered" in this verse comes from a Greek word meaning *to suffer*, and it's the word used to describe the *passion* or *suffering* that Jesus experienced when He died on the Cross. Now that you've read this book, I hope you have a deeper understanding of all that Jesus endured in His final hours. But there are many other examples of the word "suffered" in the New Testament, and they all carry the idea of *suffering, undergoing hardship, being ill-treated,* or *experiencing adversity.*

The truth is, Jesus experienced a brunt of harsh experiences throughout His entire life on this earth. When He was a child, His family suffered as they fled from the murderous plots of King Herod. Later Jesus suffered at the hands of religious leaders who hated Him and continually leveled false accusations against Him. Jesus had to constantly put up with the immature behavior of His disciples as He loved them, taught them, and set an example for them.

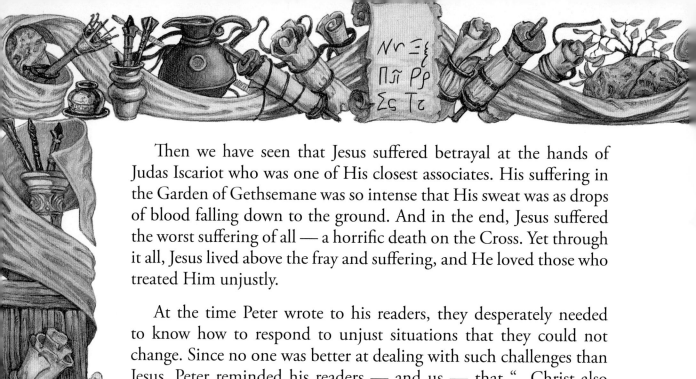

Then we have seen that Jesus suffered betrayal at the hands of Judas Iscariot who was one of His closest associates. His suffering in the Garden of Gethsemane was so intense that His sweat was as drops of blood falling down to the ground. And in the end, Jesus suffered the worst suffering of all — a horrific death on the Cross. Yet through it all, Jesus lived above the fray and suffering, and He loved those who treated Him unjustly.

At the time Peter wrote to his readers, they desperately needed to know how to respond to unjust situations that they could not change. Since no one was better at dealing with such challenges than Jesus, Peter reminded his readers — and us — that "...Christ also suffered for us, leaving us an *example*...."

Now we must return to the image of a child learning to write the letters of the alphabet. You see, when Peter chose to use the word "example" in this verse, he literally reached into the world of early childhood education to borrow a word that paints a picture of a school child who carefully watches his teacher write the letters of the alphabet and then painstakingly copies each letter, matching it as closely as possible to the original letters written by his teacher.

If you remember your childhood as well as I remember mine, it probably isn't too hard for you to remember straining to see exactly how the teacher wrote each letter and then trying to copy every stroke.

This is exactly what Peter had in mind when he told his readers — and you and me — that when we are in a hard situation, we need to follow the "example" of Jesus. Since Jesus is our Teacher and Master, we must focus on the spiritual blackboard — which is the Word of God — to learn from Jesus' example and then replicate His example in our own lives.

260

We must learn:

- *How Jesus* dealt with unfair criticism so we can respond like Him when we are unfairly criticized.

- *How Jesus* responded to attacks that were waged against Him so we can know how to respond in His strength to attacks that come against us.

- *How Jesus* responded to people when they failed or betrayed Him so we can respond the same way when people disappoint or hurt us.

- *How Jesus* carried Himself with grace and dignity even in the midst of unspeakable abuse so we can draw on His strength to walk through difficult situations with the same grace and dignity.

- *How Jesus* forgave His accusers every step of the way so we can similarly forgive those who mistreat or malign us.

We can't avoid the fact that sometimes we face unpleasant situations in which we may feel mistreated, abused, or discriminated against. As long as we live in a world where the devil operates and unsaved people, or those operating in the flesh, have their way, evil and injustice will touch our lives from time to time. So when we find ourselves subjected to a situation that seems unfair and unjust, we must learn to ask, *How did Jesus respond in a similar situation, and how does God expect me to respond?*

Of course, we should each pray for God to change whatever difficult situation we face. Prayer can make a huge difference in any circumstance. But what if the situation doesn't change as quickly as you wished? Then how should you respond?

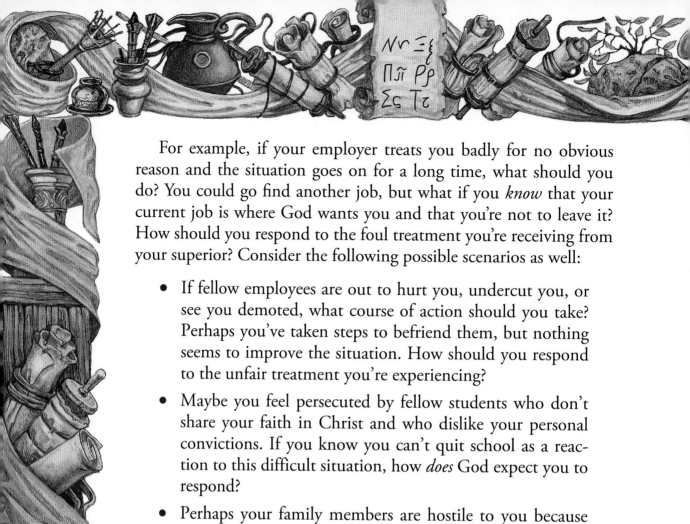

For example, if your employer treats you badly for no obvious reason and the situation goes on for a long time, what should you do? You could go find another job, but what if you *know* that your current job is where God wants you and that you're not to leave it? How should you respond to the foul treatment you're receiving from your superior? Consider the following possible scenarios as well:

- If fellow employees are out to hurt you, undercut you, or see you demoted, what course of action should you take? Perhaps you've taken steps to befriend them, but nothing seems to improve the situation. How should you respond to the unfair treatment you're experiencing?

- Maybe you feel persecuted by fellow students who don't share your faith in Christ and who dislike your personal convictions. If you know you can't quit school as a reaction to this difficult situation, how *does* God expect you to respond?

- Perhaps your family members are hostile to you because they don't understand your faith or they don't agree with the direction you're taking in life. How should you respond to your loved ones? It's so very important that you know how to respond when your family doesn't agree or support what you are doing — especially when you know the Holy Spirit is the One leading you to take that course or direction.

Certainly we must do everything possible to resolve conflicts with friends and family and to protect ourselves and our reputation spiritually and legally. Yet sometimes things happen that are beyond our control, that are not so easily resolved, and for which there is no easy recourse. Whenever you are feeling maligned and mistreated,

it's a prime opportunity for the devil to tempt you to become bitter, angry, hardhearted, and resentful toward those who have treated you unjustly. But if you yield to that temptation, your wrong response won't do anything to improve your situation; it *will*, instead, produce negative consequences in your own life. That's why you must absolutely refuse to allow the devil to sow into your heart those negative emotions that bear only bad fruit. Harboring such emotions is *never* the answer, no matter what situation you might be facing in life.

My prayer is that by reading this book, you've gained new insight into the journey of pain, betrayal, and disappointment Jesus experienced in His final hours. I encourage you to take some time to deeply contemplate the great love He has for you and the power He has made available to you by laying down His own life. Perhaps in a deeper way than you've ever done before, invite Jesus to walk with you through your own journey, guiding you by His Spirit through each difficulty and challenge that arises along the way.

It's very important that you know *exactly* how God expects you to respond when you find yourself in a difficult predicament you have no ability to change — and there's no better example to emulate than Jesus. So go to the gospels and begin to read those pages with the heart of a student who studies and endeavors to copy every stroke of his teacher's pen. Seek to extract truth and specific answers for your life and the situations you're facing right now. Observe how Jesus conducted Himself in similar circumstances. Then like a child learning to write, make your best effort to copy each stroke of the Master!

You probably won't get it exactly right the first time, but like a student who is learning to write, you must commit to try and try again until you have finally mastered each stroke and have learned to successfully respond to difficult situations as Jesus did when He walked the earth.

We Are Called To Follow Jesus' Steps

There is something else really important in First Peter 2:21 that you need to understand. In addition to copying each stroke of the Master, Peter then added that we should "follow his [Jesus'] steps."

The original Greek word for "steps" in this verse means *footprints*. It reminds me of when Denise and I would take our sons to the beach when they were very young. I would walk before them and leave my footprints in the sand, and they would do their best to exactly follow me by stepping in each of my footprints. I would wander this way, then that way, and form a path for them to follow.

And now, when Denise and I and our sons find that we are in a difficult spot, we know it is time for us to look to the example of Jesus. Just as I led my sons on the beach and they followed in my footprints, Jesus has gone before us, leaving His footprints to show us what we must do in each situation. Rather than figure it out by ourselves, we must focus on Jesus and step exactly where He stepped. This means He has given us a pattern to follow — and if we will walk in His steps, we will do what is right in each circumstance.

Perhaps you've been praying for guidance, trying to understand how to deal with the conflicts you've encountered. The answers you need are found in the life of Jesus. He is your Chief Example, your Teacher, your Master — the One you are called to copy and to follow. So in addition to praying for wisdom and guidance, you must open your Bible to read from all four gospels and see what Jesus did in the same type of situations you are facing. Learn from the Master and walk through your situation in the same manner that Jesus did as He walked through His own challenges in this world.

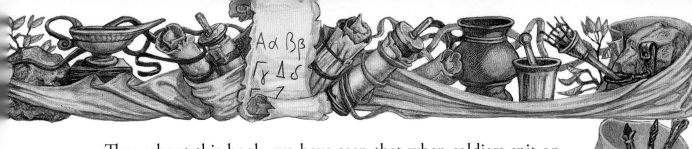

Throughout this book, we have seen that when soldiers spit on Jesus, when Pilate ordered Him to be scourged, when religious leaders laughed at Him, and even when He was betrayed by one of His own disciples — Jesus continued to walk in love, forgiving them all. He is our Example, showing us how we should respond when we face injustice, when someone offends or hurts us, or when we find ourselves in difficult circumstances beyond our control.

Are you facing difficult times right now? Are you being accused of things you didn't do or blamed for things for which you have no knowledge? Are you being mistreated or discriminated against?

If you answered "yes" to any of these questions, this is the moment for you to turn your eyes to the blackboard — God's Word — to study each stroke of the Master. Once you see what Jesus did and how He responded in situations similar to yours, it is then your assignment to copy Him to the best of your ability.

If you'll take this approach to the challenges you're facing right now that seem so distressing, the Holy Spirit will empower you and you'll be able to respond to every situation more like Jesus. So make it your earnest goal to apply to your own life the principles of Jesus' life — especially the truths and principles revealed in what He experienced in His final days on earth — and endeavor to pen each stroke of your life to reflect each stroke of the Master.

What a blessing that you don't have to figure it all out by yourself. Just study the strokes of the Master, follow in His footprints, and press forward by faith to copy His actions and to walk as He did with every challenge that arises. By yourself, you can't do it, but Jesus didn't leave you to face the challenges of life alone and without help. He sent the Holy Spirit as your Teacher and Guide to empower you so you can walk as Jesus walked through every situation you will ever face.

265

QUESTIONS TO PONDER
AND DISCUSS

1. Do you remember when you first learned to write? Think about what it was like and what attitude you had as you held the pencil steady and moved it across the page. What similarities and differences do you see between this example and in the way you follow Jesus in your daily life? Does this motivate you to change anything about how you relate to Jesus as your Teacher and having Him show you step by step what to do?

2. Jesus suffered many unpleasant experiences throughout His entire life on this earth, especially in the final hours before His death. How does what you've learned by reading this book impact the way you see the areas of your own life in which you are either facing difficulty or are suffering? In what ways do you think Jesus wants to encourage you and help you?

3. Have you ever been in an unjust situation in which you were treated unfairly and the circumstances were out of your control? Jesus was certainly put in situations like this by the religious leaders as well as by one of His closest friends. How has seeing Jesus' response to those who put Him in these unjust predicaments changed the way you want to respond to similar types of people in your own life?

4. We are told in First Peter 2:21 to follow in Jesus' exact footsteps. Do you find it easy or difficult to follow Jesus and imitate His example? Why or why not?

With every challenge that arises in your life, turn your eyes to your spiritual blackboard — God's Word — to study each stroke of the Master. Once you see what Jesus did and how He responded in situations similar to yours, copy Him to the best of your ability. Make it your earnest goal to apply the principles of Jesus' life to your own — especially the truths and principles revealed in what He experienced in His final days on Earth. Follow in His footprints, press forward by faith, and lean in to the help of the Holy Spirit so you can copy His actions and walk as He did.

Chapter Sixteen

A FINAL WORD

On the opposite facing page is an illustration of the alleged original stairs from Pilate's palace in Jerusalem that were transported from there to Rome in the Fourth Century by Helene, the mother of the Emperor Constantine the Great. In the Middle Ages, they were known as *Scala Pilati*, or the *Stairs of Pilate*, but today they are called *Scala Sancta*. According to tradition, the Holy Stairs were the steps leading up to the praetorium of Pontius Pilate in Jerusalem and on which Jesus Christ stepped on His way to His trial before Pilate. The 28 steps of stairs were first located in St. John Lateran Church, but in 1589, Pope Sixtus V ordered the Holy Stairs be moved to their present location at the Pontifical Sanctuary of the Holy Stairs. Since ancient times, people have come to Rome from around the world to see these stairs and to ascend them on their knees as a sign of penitence until they reach a fresco at the top that shows Christ on the Cross.

But from Gethsemane's garden to Golgotha's hill, Jesus Christ experienced the full spectrum of emotional and physical anguish — more than any other human would ever endure. Such suffering was the penalty of sin, and Jesus accepted it by choice. The holiness and justice of God required sin's penalty to be paid, but God's love and devotion for every living person prompted Him to mercifully provide a substitute that could adequately satisfy the claims of justice.

Initially, God allowed the blood of animals to provide a temporary *covering* for sin. But only a Man with sinless blood could provide cleansing for sin, paying the ultimate price by offering His life as payment in full for the judgment against mankind. Thus, Jesus Christ — God in the form of a perfect Man — came to take away the sins of the world. Jesus died to pay the ultimate price once and for all and to break the power of sin. Then He rose triumphant over death, hell, and the grave to provide enduring freedom from sin and its destructive consequences.

Jesus was wounded for *your* transgressions and bruised for *your* iniquities. The chastisement that was needed to obtain *your* peace of mind was laid on Him. And by the stripes that wounded Jesus, *you* were healed. From this moment forward, your life can be different than it has ever been before because your debt of sin has been *paid in full* by Jesus Christ.

PRAYER OF SALVATION

When Jesus Christ comes into your life, you are immediately emancipated — totally set free from the bondage of sin! If you have never received Jesus as your personal Savior, it is time to experience this new life for yourself! The first step to freedom is simple.

Just pray this prayer from your heart:

Lord, I can never adequately thank You for all You did for me on the Cross. Jesus, You came and gave Your life for me, and right now I repent and turn from my sin and receive You as my Savior. I ask You to wash away my sin by Your precious blood. I thank You from my heart for doing what no one else could do for me. Had it not been for Your willingness to lay down Your life for me, I would be eternally lost.

Jesus, I am thankful that You bore my sin, my sickness, my pain, my lack of peace, and my suffering on the Cross. Your blood has cleansed me from my sin, washed me whiter than snow, and has given me rightstanding with the Father. Because I surrender my life to Your lordship, I am a new creature — old things have passed away, and all things have become new (2 Corinthians 5:17).

Jesus, because of You, I am forgiven, filled with peace, and a joint heir with You! Satan no longer has a right to lay any claim on me. With a grateful heart, I will faithfully serve You the rest of my days!

If you prayed this prayer (and really meant it), then you just became a child of God. Evil that once exacted every ounce of your being and required your all-inclusive servitude no longer possesses the authorization to control you or to dictate your destiny. As a result of your decision to turn your life over to Jesus Christ, your eternal home has been decided forever, and Heaven will be your permanent eternal address.

As a result of this faith-expressed prayer, God's Spirit just moved into your heart and now lives inside you. Jesus is now your Lord and Master, and from this moment forward, the Spirit of God will work in you and will energize you to fulfill all the wonderful plans that God has designed for your life.

PRAYER OF FORGIVENESS

No one is spared opportunities for offense in this life. Not one person escapes times of dealing with disappointment and hurt as the result of other people's words or actions. But how one *responds* to hurt, betrayal, or offense makes all the difference in the outcome — in the lives of both the offender and the one offended.

In this matter of forgiveness, you are called to follow the example of Jesus, for the Bible declares that "…as He is, so are we in this world" (1 John 4:17). Jesus walked the path of forgiveness in the face of unspeakable horrors committed against Him during His final hours on this earth. In light of His example, can you do any less than release in forgiveness those who have hurt or offended you?

Take the time to pray this prayer from your heart:

Dear Heavenly Father,

I thank You for the great love You expressed when You sent Jesus to be my Savior, my Substitute, and my Example. As I look at Jesus' life and His responses to all that He experienced, I see Your heart and mind revealed. Thank You, Father, for loving me so completely and for forgiving me so fully.

Right now, Father, I come before You as humbly and as sincerely as I know how to honor You for the great sacrifice of Your Son. I honor You by acknowledging and receiving the power of the blood that Jesus so willingly shed for the forgiveness and removal of my sins. And just as I require and receive the power of that precious blood in my life, I release its cleansing power in forgiveness toward those who have hurt or wronged me in the past.

Father, as an act of my will, I choose to believe and act upon Your Word that tells me to forgive. I know You said that great peace belongs to those who love Your law and that nothing shall offend them (Psalm 119:165). I feel the sting of betrayal, but I'm not ignorant of the enemy's devices. The purpose of betrayal is to produce a root of bitterness in me, and I refuse to yield to that sin. Father, I forgive — and I ask You to forgive those who have hurt me, too, for they don't know what they're doing. They don't realize that what has been said and done against me has been said and done against You. Forgive them, Father.

Holy Spirit, I ask You to help me yield to the love of God that has already been shed abroad in my heart by Your presence within me. As You strengthened Jesus, please strengthen me. Help me walk in the love, the Word, and the will of God toward those who have wronged me. Help me respond just as Jesus responded when He was spitefully treated and wrongfully accused. I take comfort and find strength in Jesus' example before me and in Your mighty presence within me, Holy Spirit. Help me lean upon You without reservation and to respond to You without hesitation. And help those I have forgiven to turn their hearts toward You. May we both embrace Your wisdom and Your ways so that Your purpose may be fulfilled in each of our lives.

Thank You, Father, for the Blood that has the power to cleanse sin and to remove barriers. I ask that You intervene in our hearts and in this situation to turn all that the enemy meant for evil toward our good and Your glory. I receive this as done in Jesus' name. Amen.

PRAYER FOR HEALING

Jesus purchased complete redemption for you. Through the sacrifice of His life and the spilling of His blood, He paid the full price for your freedom from sin *and* sickness.

With every stroke of the vicious Roman whip He suffered, Jesus bore the penalty of your physical pains, sicknesses, and diseases. Today Heaven declares that "…by whose [Jesus'] stripes, you *were* healed" (1 Peter 2:24). The price has been paid in full for you to receive the gift of divine health though Jesus Christ. Receive by faith complete healing for your body as you pray this prayer.

Dear Heavenly Father,

Jesus endured the horrors of the Roman scourge to pay the penalty for my sin. Before Jesus ever stood in that place, You declared through Isaiah that His suffering secured my deliverance and by the stripes that wounded Him, I was healed (Isaiah 53:5).

Jesus, the Lamb of God, justified many — and through the sacrifice of Himself, my debt was paid in full. Therefore, I come boldly before Your throne of grace to receive the help and healing I need.

I thank You, Father, that it pleased You to lay my sickness, infirmity, and disease upon Jesus so that I might receive health and healing in exchange. Right now I behold the Lamb, who was slain to set me free. And I receive freedom — the freedom He died and rose again to purchase for me — from sin, sickness, and disease. With every torturous lash of the whip and every mutilating gash it produced, Jesus purchased my healing with His own blood.

Today, Father, I come before You to receive the healing Jesus purchased for me. Just as my salvation is based on Jesus and His completed work, so is my healing. I don't have to beg You for it. I simply receive. And as I receive Your great gift of healing, I honor Your Son's great sacrifice that opened the door for me to receive Your life-giving power to meet my every need. For this and for all You've done for me, I thank You, Father, in Jesus' name. Amen.

ENDNOTES

Chapter 1

[1] "THE WARS OF THE JEWS, The History Of The Destruction Of Jerusalem, Book VI, Chapters I-X, Flavius Josephus, 75 C.E.," Translated from the Greek by William Whiston, Early Accounts of the Temple of Jerusalem – Sources, https://avande1.sites.luc.edu/jerusalem/sources/wars6.htm#:~:text=A%20history%20written%20in%2075,city%2C%20and%20a%20holy%20people. Accessed October 13, 2024.

[2] "Gethsemane," seetheholyland.net, https://www.seetheholyland.net/gethsemane/. Accessed October 13, 2024.

[3] "Church of All Nations," seetheholyland.net, https://www.seetheholyland.net/church-of-all-nations/. Accessed October 13, 2024.

[4] "Grotto of Gethsemane – Where the Disciples Fell Asleep," DannytheDigger.com, https://dannythedigger.com/grotto-of-gethsemane/. Accessed October 13, 2024.

[5] Inês Rossio, Ana Gonçalves, "HAEMATIDROSIS: THE RARE PHENOMENON OF SWEATING BLOOD," EJCRIM 2014, https://www.ejcrim.com/index.php/EJCRIM/article/download/144/183?inline=1. Accessed October 13, 2024.

Chapter 2

[1] The Editors of the Madain Project, "Antonia Fortress According to Josephus," Madain PROJECT, https://madainproject.com/antonia_fortress_according_to_josephus. Accessed October 13, 2024.

Chapter 5

[1] Antiquities of the Jews – Book XX, CHAPTER 9.1, www.penelope.uchicago.edu, https://penelope.uchicago.edu/josephus/ant-20.html. Accessed October 16, 2024.

[2] Mike Nappa, "Who Were the Sadducees in the Bible? What Were Their Beliefs?," Christianity.com, September 6, 2019, https://www.christianity.com/wiki/people/who-were-the-sadducees-in-the-bible-what-were-their-beliefs.html. Accessed October 16, 2024.

Chapter 6

[1] MD Harris Institute, "Tensions Between Rome and the Jews During the Early 1st Century AD," MD Harris Institute, January 28, 2012, https://mdharrismd.com/2012/01/28/tensions-between-rome-and-the-jews-during-the-early-1st-century-ad/. Accessed October 16, 2024.

[2] Antiquities of the Jews – Book XVIII, CHAPTER 4.2, www.penelope.uchicago.edu, https://penelope.uchicago.edu/josephus/ant-18.html. Accessed October 16, 2024.

[3] "Book II, CHAPTER 7," Translated by Arthur Cushman McGiffert, The Church History of Eusebius, Christian Classics Ethereal Library, https://ccel.org/ccel/schaff/npnf201/npnf201.iii.vii.viii.html. Accessed October 25, 2024.

Chapter 7

[1] Kenneth Berding, "How Many Herods Are There in the Bible?," The Good Book Blog, Talbot School of Theology Faculty Blog, BIOLA UNIVERSITY, March 3, 2014, https://www.biola.edu/blogs/good-book-blog/2014/how-many-herods-are-there-in-the-bible#:~:text=Herod%20the%20Great:%20Christmas%20story,Trial%20of%20Paul%20in%20Caesarea. Accessed October 17, 2024.

[2] Antiquities of the Jews – Book XVIII, CHAPTER 4.6, www.penelope.uchicago.edu, https://penelope.uchicago.edu/josephus/ant-18.html. Accessed October 17, 2024.

Chapter 8

[1] Duncan Heaster, "The Death of the Cross," aletheiacollege.net, https://www.aletheiacollege.net/cross/1-1-4-1flogging__scourging.htm. Accessed October 17, 2024.

[2] "Church History (Book IV), Chapter 15. Under Verus, Polycarp with Others suffered Martyrdom at Smyrna.," Translated by Arthur Cushman McGiffert, NewAdvent.org, https://www.newadvent.org/fathers/250104.htm. Accessed October 17, 2024.

Chapter 9

[1] "The Garden Tomb's Story," THE GARDEN TOMB: Witness & Worship in Jerusalem, https://gardentomb.com/about/. Accessed October 17, 2024.

[2] "Church of the Holy Sepulchre," https://churchoftheholysepulchre.net/. Accessed October 17, 2024.

[3] "THE ENTHRALLING HISTORY OF DI SIMONE'S CAMPOSANTO OF PISA," The Italian Tribune, https://italiantribune.com/camposanto-of-pisa-the-other-monument/. Accessed October 17, 2024.

[4] "Letter 46," Translated by W.H. Fremantle, G. Lewis and W.G. Martley, NewAdvent.org, https://www.newadvent.org/fathers/3001046.htm. Accessed October 18, 2024.

[5] "SENECA, LETTERS TO LUCILIUS: 101," Aikaterini Laskaridis Foundation TOPOS TEXT, https://topostext.org/work/736. Accessed October 18, 2024.

[6] Of the War – Book V, CHAPTER 11, www.penelope.uchicago.edu, https://penelope.uchicago.edu/josephus/war-5.html. Accessed October 18, 2024.

Chapter 10

[1] "CHAPTER XV. 'CRUCIFIED, DEAD, AND BURIED.'," Christian Classics Ethereal Library, Life and Times of Jesus, https://ccel.org/ccel/edersheim/lifetimes/lifetimes.x.xv.html. Accessed October 18, 2024.

[2] "Hebraic Literature: Translations from THE TALMUD, MIDRASHIM and KABBALA" [Note: reference section 196 in the left margin], The Project Gutenburg eBook, Hebraic Literature; Translations from the Talmud, Midrashim and Kabbala, by Various, et al, Edited by Maurice Henry Harris, https://www.gutenberg.org/files/14368/14368-h/14368-h.htm. Accessed October 18, 2024.

[3] Joshua Arnold, "The Miraculous Darkness at Jesus's Crucifixion," The Washington Stand, April 9, 2024, https://washingtonstand.com/commentary/the-miraculous-darkness-at-jesuss-crucifixion. Accessed October 18, 2024.

[4] "Contra Celsum, Book II," Translated by Frederick Crombie, NewAdvent.org, https://www.newadvent.org/fathers/04162.htm. Accessed October 21, 2024.

Endnotes

Chapter 11

[1] Wayne Jackson, "The Burial of Christ's Body," Christian Courier, https://christiancourier.com/articles/the-burial-of-christs-body. Accessed October 21, 2024.

Chapter 13

[1] "Jesus' Tomb," IsraelJerusalem.com, https://www.israeljerusalem.com/jesus-tomb.htm. Accessed October 21, 2024.

ABOUT THE AUTHOR

Rick Renner (**renner.org**) holds an earned ThD (Doctor of Theology) from a prominent Russian university and is a respected Bible teacher and leader in the international Christian community. He is the author of an extensive list of books, including bestsellers *Sparkling Gems From the Greek 1* and *2*, and his accumulated titles have sold millions of copies worldwide. Rick's understanding of the Greek language and biblical history opens up the Scriptures in a unique way that enables his audience to gain wisdom and insight while learning something brand new from the Word of God.

Today Rick is the overseer of the Good News Association of Churches, founder of the Moscow Good News Church, pastor of the Internet Good News Church, founder of Media Mir, and president of the Good News Channel — the largest Russian-speaking Christian satellite network in the world, which broadcasts the Gospel 24/7 to countless viewers in more than 83 nations. He is also founder of TBV, a national channel that broadcasts to all of Russia.

Rick is the founder of RENNER Ministries in Broken Arrow, Oklahoma, and host to his TV program, also seen around the world in multiple languages via television, Internet, and satellite. He leads this amazing work with Denise, his wife and lifelong ministry partner, along with their sons and committed leadership team.

CONTACT RENNER MINISTRIES

For further information
about RENNER Ministries,
please contact the office nearest you,
or visit the ministry website at:
www.renner.org

**ALL USA
CORRESPONDENCE:**
RENNER Ministries
1814 W. Tacoma St.
Broken Arrow, OK 74012
(918) 496-3213
Or 1-800-RICK-593
Email: renner@renner.org
Website: www.renner.org

MOSCOW OFFICE:
RENNER Ministries
P. O. Box 789
101000, Moscow, Russia
+7 (495) 727-1467
Email: blagayavestonline@ignc.org
Website: www.ignc.org

OXFORD OFFICE:
RENNER Ministries
Box 7, 266 Banbury Road
Oxford OX2 7DL, United Kingdom
+44 1865 521024
Email: europe@renner.org

RIGA OFFICE:
RENNER Ministries
Unijas 99
Riga LV-1084, Latvia
+371 67802150
Email: church@goodnews.lv
Website: www.goodnews.lv

WITH US!

facebook.com/rickrenner • facebook.com/rennerdenise
youtube.com/rennerministries • youtube.com/deniserenner
instagram.com/rickrrenner • instagram.com/rennerministries_
instagram.com/rennerdenise

BOOKS BY RICK RENNER

Apostles and Prophets
Build Your Foundation*
Chosen by God*
Christmas — The Rest of the Story
Dream Thieves*
Dressed To Kill*
Fallen Angels, Giants, Monsters, and the World Before the Flood
The Holy Spirit and You*
How To Keep Your Head on Straight in a World Gone Crazy*
How To Receive Answers From Heaven!*
Igniting a Powerful Prayer Life
Insights on Successful Leadership*
Last-Days Survival Guide*
A Life Ablaze*
Life in the Combat Zone*
A Light in Darkness, Volume One,
      Seven Messages to the Seven Churches series
The Love Test*
My Peace-Filled Day
My Spirit-Empowered Day
No Room for Compromise, Volume Two,
      Seven Messages to the Seven Churches series
Paid in Full*
The Point of No Return*
Renner A to Z
    Comments and Quotes by Rick Renner on 400 Bible Topics A to Z!
Renner Interpretive Version (RIV) of James and Jude
Repentance*
Signs You'll See Just Before Jesus Comes*
Sparkling Gems From the Greek Daily Devotional 1*
Sparkling Gems From the Greek Daily Devotional 2*
Spiritual Weapons To Defeat the Enemy*
Ten Guidelines To Help You Achieve Your Long-Awaited Promotion!*
Testing the Supernatural
365 Days of Increase
365 Days of Power
Turn Your God-Given Dreams Into Reality*
Unlikely — Our Faith-Filled Journey to the Ends of the Earth*
Why We Need the Gifts of the Holy Spirit*
The Will of God — The Key to Your Success*
You Can Get Over It*

*Digital version available for Kindle, Nook, and iBook.
Note: Books by Rick Renner are available for purchase at:
www.renner.org

CHRISTMAS
THE REST OF THE STORY

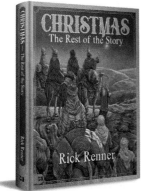

304 pages
(Hardback)

In this storybook of biblical history, Rick takes you on the "magical" journey of Christ's coming to earth in a way you've probably never heard it before. Featuring full-color, original illustrations, *Christmas — The Rest of the Story* gives the spellbinding account of God's masterful plan to redeem mankind, and vividly portrays the wonder of the Savior's birth and His "ordinary" life marked by God's *extraordinary* plan.

If you want to be taken back in your imagination to this earth-shaking course of events that changed the history of the whole world, this book is a *must-have* not just for the Christmas season, but for all time. *Topics include:*

- Why God chose Mary and Joseph.

- The significance of the *manger* and *swaddling clothes*.

- Why angels viewed *God in the flesh* with such wonderment.

- Why King Herod was so troubled by this historical birth.

- How we can prepare for Christ's *next* coming.

Christmas — The Rest of the Story is sure to be a favorite in your family for generations to come! Jesus' birth is truly *the greatest story on earth* — perhaps never more uniquely told than in the pages of this book.

To order, visit us online at: **www.renner.org**

Book Resellers: Contact Harrison House at 800-722-6774
or visit **www.HarrisonHouse.com** for quantity discounts.

SPARKLING GEMS FROM THE GREEK 1

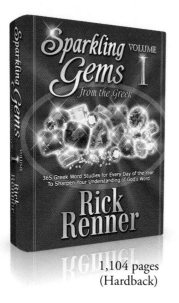

Rick Renner's *Sparkling Gems From the Greek 1* has gained widespread recognition for its unique illumination of the New Testament through more than 1,000 Greek word studies in a 365-day devotional format. *Sparkling Gems 1* remains a beloved resource that has spiritually strengthened believers worldwide. As many have testified, the wealth of truths within its pages never grows old. Year after year, *Sparkling Gems 1* continues to deepen readers' understanding of the Bible.

To order, visit us online at: **www.renner.org**

1,104 pages
(Hardback)

SPARKLING GEMS FROM THE GREEK 2

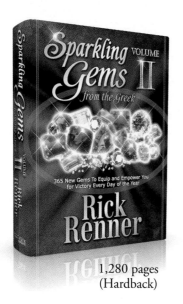

Rick infuses into *Sparkling Gems From the Greek 2* the added strength and richness of many more years of his own personal study and growth in God — expanding this devotional series to impact the reader's heart on a deeper level than ever before. This remarkable study tool helps unlock new hidden treasures from God's Word that will draw readers into an ever more passionate pursuit of Him.

To order, visit us online at: **www.renner.org**

1,280 pages
(Hardback)

DRESSED TO KILL
A BIBLICAL APPROACH
TO SPIRITUAL WARFARE AND ARMOR

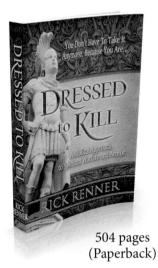

504 pages
(Paperback)

Rick Renner's book *Dressed To Kill* is considered by many to be a true classic on the subject of spiritual warfare. The original version, which sold more than 400,000 copies, is a curriculum staple in Bible schools worldwide. In this beautiful volume, you will find:

- 504 pages of reedited text in paperback

- 16 pages of full-color illustrations

- Questions at the end of each chapter to guide you into deeper study

In *Dressed To Kill,* Rick explains with exacting detail the purpose and function of each piece of Roman armor. In the process, he describes the significance of our *spiritual* armor not only to withstand the onslaughts of the enemy, but also to overturn the tendencies of the carnal mind. Furthermore, Rick delivers a clear, scriptural presentation on the biblical definition of spiritual warfare — what it is and what it is not.

When you walk with God in deliberate, continual fellowship, He will enrobe you with Himself. Armed with the knowledge of who you are in Him, you will be dressed and dangerous to the works of darkness, unflinching in the face of conflict, and fully equipped to take the offensive and gain mastery over any opposition from your spiritual foe. You don't have to accept defeat anymore once you are *dressed to kill*!

To order, visit us online at: **www.renner.org**

Book Resellers: Contact Harrison House at 800-722-6774 or visit **www.HarrisonHouse.com** for quantity discounts.

THE RENNER INTERPRETIVE VERSION (RIV) OF JAMES AND JUDE

A PARALLEL STUDY BIBLE FOR PEOPLE OF FAITH

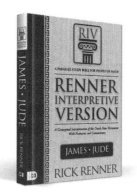

288 pages
(Hardcover)

Do you long for deeper insight into your personal study of the Word of God? If so, the *RIV* is for you!

Equipped with footnotes and commentary, the *RIV* will open up the world of the New Testament in a whole new way. While it is not a word-for-word translation — the *RIV* is a conceptual interpretation that draws upon concepts in the Greek language and expresses them in a way that supplies a broader comprehension of Scripture. By bringing out imagery presented in the Greek language and conveying it to readers using contemporary speech, Rick helps draw lovers of the Bible into a deeper study of God's message to people for all time.

This first installment of the *RIV* is taken from the books written by James and Jude. James and Jude were Jesus' half-brothers, younger sons of Joseph and Mary, and in this representation, their Spirit-inspired words will thrill your heart, challenge your thinking, and open the eyes of your spirit in greater ways to see the unchanging nature of God — His wisdom, goodness, power, and love.

FALLEN ANGELS, GIANTS, MONSTERS, AND THE WORLD BEFORE THE FLOOD

HOW THE EVENTS OF NOAH'S ARK AND THE FLOOD ARE RELEVANT TO THE END OF THE AGE

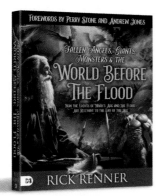

480 pages
(Paperback)

In his book *Fallen Angels, Giants, Monsters, and the World Before the Flood — How the Events of Noah's Ark and the Flood Are Relevant to the End of the Age* — which includes more than 300 photos and illustrations — Rick Renner answers long-held questions about the fascinating story of Noah's Ark.

Presenting Scripture as well as the recordings of early writers, such as Irenaeus, Josephus, Origen, Tertullian, and many others, Rick explains such details as the population explosion on the earth just before the Flood; the likely reason the writings of Enoch survived the Flood; who "the sons of God" and "the daughters of men" in Genesis were; why God ultimately saved only Noah and his family of eight; what happened when they finally exited the Ark; Jesus' own prophecy that certain elements of Noah's day would happen again; *and much, much more!*

Using findings from his own expedition of the remains of Noah's Ark in the Ararat mountains — along with other empirical evidence of the Ark's present location — Rick fascinates readers in this book and helps the Bible *come alive* concerning this favorite childhood story from the Bible!

God has had a plan from the beginning concerning Jesus as "the Seed born of a woman" who would destroy the works Satan wrought in the Fall of man. And just as God has faithfully executed that plan in the past, He will continue to carry it out until Christ's rapture of His Church *and beyond.*

To order, visit us online at: **www.renner.org**

Book resellers: Contact Harrison House at 800-722-6774
or visit **www.HarrisonHouse.com** for quantity discounts.

RENNER A TO Z
COMMENTS AND QUOTES BY RICK RENNER
ON 400 BIBLE TOPICS A TO Z!

592 pages
(Paperback)

Has your mind ever buzzed with questions about the Bible that you couldn't find answers for? Have you wished you had a resource to turn to for quick answers to life's perplexing problems?

With more than 45 years of ministry experience, prolific author Rick Renner shares hundreds of his own comments and quotes on hundreds of topics to bring you helpful advice on how to answer life's questions with God's wisdom and to live a committed life in Christ.

In this book, *Renner A to Z — Comments and Quotes by Rick Renner on 400 Bible Topics A to Z!*, you will find 1,780 alphabetically arranged comments and quotes packed full of practical, Spirit-filled counsel you can meditate on and apply to your life.

This comprehensive resource is sure to answer long-held questions and bring insight to a wide variety of topics. Whether you're looking to deepen your personal study of the Bible or you're interested in what Scripture has to say on a particular subject, this book is fun and easy to use and is sure to be an invaluable addition to your Christian library.

JESUS IS YOUR HEALER
THE POWER OF HIS SACRIFICE BOTH TO SAVE AND TO HEAL

By Denise Renner

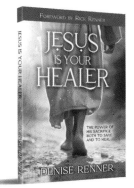

224 pages
(Paperback)

There is *nothing* in the heart of the will of God that wants you to stay sick or in pain. *He doesn't use sickness or infirmity as a means to teach you a single thing!* In fact, God sent his Son to bear the punishment for every sickness and disease known and unknown to man so that you could live strong and disease-free all the days of your life.

This is what author Denise Renner wants you to *know* with the same certainty that you know you are a child of God. She states, "I wrote this book so that through the power of the Holy Spirit, God can use the words contained in these pages to paint this eternal truth on the canvas of your mind and heart: *Jesus is your Healer!* When all that happens and you claim that spiritual reality as your very own, you will receive all the magnificent power that is extended to you through the horrible beating and crucifixion Jesus endured for you."

Chapter titles include:

- The Delivering Voice of God

- Hope Pushes Through to the Miracle

- The Power of Forgiveness

- The Power of Controlling Your Emotions

- God Has a Miracle for You!

The Father's compassions of healing and wholeness have already been poured out. They are yours for the taking! The simple but profound truths found in *Jesus Is Your Healer* will equip you to believe for and walk in the divine health that is already yours in Christ!

To order, visit us online at: **www.renner.org**

Book Resellers: Contact Harrison House at 800-722-6774 or visit **www.HarrisonHouse.com** for quantity discounts.

MY SPIRIT-EMPOWERED DAY
A SPARKLING GEMS FROM THE GREEK
GUIDED DEVOTIONAL JOURNAL

240 pages
(Paperback)

When faced with life's difficulties, do you long for a personal coach to guide you? Do you feel inadequate, even powerless, to achieve what God has asked you to do?

You can experience the same inseparable union with the Holy Spirit that empowered Jesus during His earthly ministry! With the Holy Spirit's help, *you* can participate for yourself with His mission to be your ultimate Comforter, Advocate, Counselor, and Friend.

In *My Spirit-Empowered Day: A Sparkling Gems From the Greek Guided Devotional Journal*, Rick Renner shows you how to escape a powerless Christian life. This interactive journal includes thought-provoking questions that will engage your heart and mind to go deeper with the Holy Spirit.

Through 31 insightful devotional entries, Rick unveils from the Greek text the purpose of the Holy Spirit in a Christian's life. Rick's teaching will help you understand the workings of the Holy Spirit, discover how to receive divine guidance, and exercise spiritual power and authority.

Experience a life of close fellowship with the Holy Spirit and see your life flourish under His favor!

To order, visit us online at: **www.renner.org**

Book resellers: Contact Harrison House at 800-722-6774
or visit **www.HarrisonHouse.com** for quantity discounts.

IGNITING A POWERFUL PRAYER LIFE

A Sparkling Gems From the Greek
Guided Devotional Journal

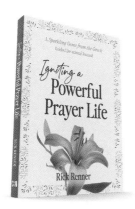

256 pages
(Paperback)

Igniting a Powerful Prayer Life: A Sparkling Gems From the Greek Guided Devotional Journal can take you from feeling overwhelmed by the signs of the times to enjoying a serene sense of wholeness and well-being as you walk and live in God's presence.

You are not impotent against the struggles of broken families and relationships, decaying morality, rumors of wars, and unstable economies! The Father longs for you to release His power in your sphere through prayer. You only need to know how.

In *Igniting a Powerful Prayer Life*, Rick Renner uses scriptural principles and spiritual wisdom that can set ablaze in your heart a passion for potent prayer. Each lesson in this 31-day journal also includes a prayer and a confession to put the Word in your mouth and stimulate a fervent, effectual prayer life.

Topics and word studies include:

- Unleashing new prayer dimensions.

- Praying with boldness and confidence.

- Moving from fear to faith and from defeat to victory.

- Experiencing Jesus as our personal Intercessor.

Don't stand by and let the enemy oppress or destroy you *or* your family. Use this guided journal to ignite your prayer life and set your world *on fire* with the power of God!

To order, visit us online at: **www.renner.org**

Book Resellers: Contact Harrison House at 800-722-6774 or visit **www.HarrisonHouse.com** for quantity discounts.

MY PEACE-FILLED DAY
A SPARKLING GEMS FROM THE GREEK
GUIDED DEVOTIONAL JOURNAL

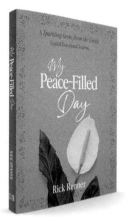

256 pages
(Paperback)

Do you feel like you're on a merry-go-round of stress and anxiety that just won't stop? Do you feel like the circumstances around you are shouting *loudly* as you search for peace and calm?

Help is here! You *can* live in peace — fearless and free!

In *My Peace-Filled Day: A Sparkling Gems From the Greek Guided Devotional Journal*, Rick Renner shares 31 teachings, expounding from his thorough knowledge of the Greek language, to help you take hold of the God-given peace that belongs to you. As you devote yourself to the scriptural truths in each devotional — and journal your answers to thought-provoking questions — the power of God will melt away the fears, anxieties, and cares of this world until His peace takes centerstage in your life.

Don't let the turmoil of this world swirl you into an emotional frenzy. As you encounter God on every page of this devotional journal, you will find yourself living the peace-filled life your loving Heavenly Father wants for you!

To order, visit us online at: **www.renner.org**

Book Resellers: Contact Harrison House at 800-722-6774
or visit **www.HarrisonHouse.com** for quantity discounts.

BUILD YOUR FOUNDATION

Six Must-Have Beliefs for Constructing an Unshakable Christian Life

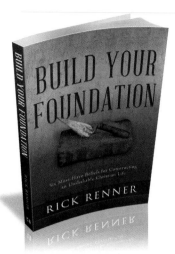

248 pages
(Paperback)

A building contractor has a top priority every time he begins a construction project: *to get the foundation right.* He knows that's the key to the stability of the structure he is building. If the foundation is laid incorrectly, the rest of the building might look good — but it will always have problems and will possibly never fulfill its purpose for being constructed in the first place.

That same principle is true as you build your life in Christ. You will never last long in your quest to fulfill what God has put you on the earth to accomplish *unless* you first focus on laying your spiritual foundation *"rock-solid"* on the truths of His Word.

In this book, author Rick Renner provides the scriptural "mortar and brick" that defines the six fundamental doctrines listed in Hebrews 6:1 and 2 — the exact ingredients you need to lay a solid foundation for the structure called your life in Christ.

Topics include:

- An Honest Look at the Modern Church
- Let's Qualify To *'Go On'*
- Remorse vs. Repentance
- The Laying on of Hands
- Three Baptisms and Three Resurrections
- The Great White Throne Judgment
- The Judgment Seat of Christ
- *And many more!*

To order, visit us online at: **www.renner.org**

Book Resellers: Contact Harrison House at 800-722-6774 or visit **www.HarrisonHouse.com** for quantity discounts.

Equipping Believers to Walk in the Abundant Life

John 10:10b

Connect with us for fresh content and news about forthcoming books from your favorite authors...

Facebook @ HarrisonHousePublishers

Instagram @ HarrisonHousePublishing

www.harrisonhouse.com